To See the
Saw Movies

To See the *Saw* Movies

Essays on Torture Porn and Post-9/11 Horror

Edited by
JAMES ASTON *and*
JOHN WALLISS

McFarland & Company, Inc., Publishers
Jefferson, North Carolina, and London

LIBRARY OF CONGRESS CATALOGUING-IN-PUBLICATION DATA

To see the Saw movies : essays on torture porn and post–9/11 horror / edited by James Aston and John Walliss.
    page cm
  Includes bibliographical references and index.

  ISBN 978-0-7864-7089-1
  softcover : acid free paper ∞

  1. Saw films—History and criticism. 2. Horror films—History and criticism. I. Aston, James, 1973– II. Walliss, John, 1974–
  PN1995.9.S246T6   2013
  791.43'6164—dc23   2013016087

BRITISH LIBRARY CATALOGUING DATA ARE AVAILABLE

© 2013 James Aston and John Walliss. All rights reserved

No part of this book may be reproduced or transmitted in any form or by any means, electronic or mechanical, including photocopying or recording, or by any information storage and retrieval system, without permission in writing from the publisher.

On the cover: Tobin Bell as Jigsaw in *Saw III*, 2006 (Lions Gate Films/Photofest); blood splatter image (Zoonar/Thinstock)

Manufactured in the United States of America

McFarland & Company, Inc., Publishers
  Box 611, Jefferson, North Carolina 28640
  www.mcfarlandpub.com

Contents

Introduction
    James Aston and John Walliss 1

"I've never murdered anyone in my life. The decisions are up to them": Ethical Guidance and the Turn Toward Cultural Pessimism
    James Aston and John Walliss 13

Body Horror
    Ben McCann 30

The Spectacle of Correction: Video Games, Movies and Control
    Evangelos Tziallas 45

From Jigsaw to Phibes: God, Free Will and Foreknowledge in Conflict
    Fernando G. Pagnoni Berns and Amy M. Davis 73

A Voice and Something More: Jigsaw as Acousmêtre and Existential Guru
    Brian H. Collins 86

Twisted Pictures: Morality, Nihilism and Symbolic Suicide
    Steve Jones 105

The Jigsaw Assemblage
    Jacob Huntley 123

Work Is Hell: Life in the Mannequin Factory
    Dean Lockwood 139

Monstrous Bodies and Gendered Abjection
    Madeleine Smith 157

Hearing the Game: Sound Design
    Jeffrey Bullins 176

About the Contributors 195
Index 197

Introduction

James Aston and *John Walliss*

> *The Horror film has consistently been one of the most popular and, at the same time, the most disreputable of Hollywood genres.... They are dismissed with contempt by the majority of reviewer-critics, or simply ignored.* — Wood, 1979:13

Robin Wood's comment on the complex characteristic of horror cinema is never truer than in today's horror saturated cinematic landscape. Horror dominates the American popular imagination from the real and authentic horror of *The Blair Witch Project* (Myrick & Sánchez, 1999) to *Cloverfield* (Reeves, 2008), the return of 1970s "pure" horror from remakes as diverse as *The Thing* (van Heijningen) to *Straw Dogs* (Lurie, both 2011) and atmospheric ghost stories of which *The Others* (Amenábar, 2001) and *Paranormal Activity* (Peli, 2007) serve as successful commercial examples.

However, it is the *Saw* franchise, a collection of seven movies produced between 2004 and 2010, that has emerged as the most successful horror franchise of all time, grossing $872 million worldwide and $416 million at the U.S. box office (BoxOfficeMojo). Yet, and in keeping with Wood's comment on the reception of horror films, the overwhelming majority of the film critic community has rejected wholesale any positive value the franchise may provide. For example, Benjamin Strong of *The Village Voice* casually dismissed *Saw II* as a "cursory dud" (2005) while Nathan Lee of the *New York Times* simply stated that *Saw V* was "boring" and that its overly convoluted narrative provided viewers (and critics) with characters in peril where the ultimate reaction was to be, "Who cares?" (2008); Andrew O'Hehir of *Salon* complained that *Saw 3-D* contained nothing of note, instead providing a "muddy mediocrity" whereby, as it represented the climactic film of the series, he would "never have to see any more of these ever again" (2010). These comments were indicative of the general consensus within mainstream publications and can perhaps best be summarized by Mike Hale of the *New York Times* who, not content with criticizing the lack of appeal for an individual *Saw* film, instead rejected the entire collection of films, denouncing the franchise as "meretricious garbage" (2010).

The tendency to dismiss the *Saw* films for producing a standard of filmmaking that withholds any significant artistic value was mainly predicated on the sadistic qualities of the series. Even the original *Saw* was rebuked for its excessive brutality, despite being the most positively received film of the series and, ironically, the entry that was most restrained when it came to representations of violence. Roger Ebert of the *Chicago Sun* commented that although the film produced some efficient moments it nonetheless contained enough "sadistic horrors" to ultimately "make [it] not quite worth the ordeal it puts us through" (2004). Further developing Ebert's position, but more explicit in his condemnation of the series's resort to bloodshed, was David Edelstein of the *New York Times* who, in describing *Saw* along with *The Devil's Rejects* (Zombie, 2005), *The Passion of the Christ* (Gibson, 2004) and *Wolf Creek* (McLean, 2005), came up with the term "torture porn" and sees such films as offering a "titillating and shocking" spectacle that pushes audiences to the margins of depravity in order for them to "feel something" (2006). Edelstein's term "torture porn" has since become a synecdoche for the entire franchise and critics have predictably latched onto and exploited this provocative though reductive term to disparage and dismiss the films. Thus, Mark Savlov of the *Austin Chronicle* described *Saw IV* in terms of how sadistic violence has become some kind of pornographic spectacle by saying, "torture, you may recall, used to be an unparsable, unpardonable sin. Now it's porn" (2007), while Owen Gleiberman of *Entertainment Weekly* was similarly disturbed over the aestheticization of extreme violence and its availability to a mass audience when he said that "it can be said that the most disturbing thing about the *Saw* films is the way that they turn torture into a wink of megaplex vengeance. They're made, and consumed, as a big bloody joke, and that's scary" (2010). The enjoyment of sadistic spectacle was previously marked out by Peter Hartlaub of the *San Francisco Chronicle* who equated a debased, possibly psychotic, audience with the explicit violence of the *Saw* films: "The success of the 'Saw' franchise shouldn't be a huge surprise to anybody. It's the perfect movie for people who spent their childhood pulling the wings off flies and incinerating ants with a magnifying glass—but never got around to becoming serial killers themselves" (2006).

What the above critical reception highlights, albeit in abridged form, is that the *Saw* films are either dismissed out-of-hand or shown contempt that marks them out as disreputable and unworthy of serious consideration. To this end, the term "torture porn" has engendered a reluctance to engage in serious analysis due to the base connotations of the label that clearly demarks "intense bodily acts and visible bodily representations" (Tziallas, 2010) that produce uneasy reactions and associations. However, one cannot leave the *Saw* films in such an unexplored state, regardless of what one may think of the genre or of the blood and gore on display and how it is presented to an audience. The *Saw* franchise highlights a dissonance between critic and fan, which should be explored rather than elided. For example, Jeffrey Sconce has pointed out the importance of confronting such reception with regards to the equally vilified *The Human Centipede 2: Full Sequence* (Six, 2009) when he wryly commented "You know how this game is played. Anytime you see such a consensus of disgusted outrage [...], something very interesting must be going on" (2012). The same is true of the *Saw* films, and a series *that* popular with audiences demands to be taken seriously. Doing so will uncover the reasons why the *Saw* series has been so maligned by film critics and challenge the growing resistance to the study of disreputable and lowbrow films. Films which often act as conduits for society's most troubling fears and anxieties are uncovering a mind-set that increasingly circulates through various socio-cultural configurations and of which the genre of horror becomes the most popular form of representation. Therefore, it is necessary to confront approaches that have downplayed or even circumvented the role of contemporary horror in "reflect[ing] the world as we perceive and experience it" (Wetmore, 2012:97) as has been underlined by the updated introduction to the seminal *Planks of Reason: Essays on the Horror Film* first published in 1985, but reissued in 2004. Here, the editors bemoan the modern horror film as an empty spectacle not worthy of discussion alongside the likes of the original *Texas Chainsaw Massacre* (Hopper, 1974), *Alien* (Scott, 1979) and *The Shining* (Kubrick, 1980), pointedly saying that "horror's situation in the new century reflects merely the increased intellectual impoverishment and neoconservatism of the New Hollywood, the fading of a relatively independent, oppositional cinema (in which horror flourished at the end of the studio system), and the replacement of script and concept with special effects undergirding the 'rollercoaster' experience of the new multiplex cinema" (Grant & Sharrett, 2004:x). Yet, horror has never been more vibrant in American cinema than in the past decade and has circulated through mainstream, independent, exploitation, underground and alternative indices and connected with audiences worldwide. It has been both progressive and conservative, spectacular and displeasurable, fantastical and authentic. In short, twenty-first century horror has represented "a wide range of different forms and cultures [as well as] a heterogeneity of inputs and developments" (Gledhill, 2007:348) that has positioned this contemporary strain of horror as ideal to explore and comment upon the form and content of genre and its ability to comment upon society. That is, "to confront and vicariously conquer something frightening that we do not fully understand" (Barsam & Monahan, 2007:92). In a decade dominated by war and terrorism, torture and religious fundamentalism and ever increasing powers and controls of governments over its people, the horror film in general, and the *Saw* films in particular, offer audiences opportunities to confront, understand and possibly work through the traumatic nature of a post–9/11 America.

Therefore, this book aims to situate the *Saw* franchise as a key case study of American horror in the new millennium. Not just in approaches to the form, content and iconographical detail of horror but in addressing how the films reflect upon and comment on a society in which they were made. As previously stated, to elide such academic scholarship on the premise of distaste is to provide a disservice to a serious engagement of film, especially as the horror genre is a multifaceted development of multiple traditions, cultural influences and visual spectacle, which often resists a cohesive and legible categorization. With that in mind, this book is concerned with peeling back the various layers of the franchise to not only account for how essential building blocks of the horror genre are constructed but how the myriad themes, ideas and issues engendered in the *Saw* films connect with the network of anxieties circulating in American society in the post-millennium, post–9/11 era. Kevin Wetmore, in his book, *Post-9/11 Horror in American Cinema*, clearly positions the *Saw* films as a "conflicted exploration of what it means to be an American in the world today" (2012:20) that offers "no redemption, no hope, no expectation that 'we're going to be OK'" and ultimately leaves characters "in anguish, both physical and psychological, and trapped in a situation that will only end in their agonizing death" (2012:131). In this respect, *Saw* visualizes our demons in a stark light from Jigsaw as the transparent symbol of the external/internal threat/monster to the hidden malevolence in our neo-liberal, capitalist society, such as surveillance control and correction, which have been exacerbated by 9/11 and the ensuing War on Terror. Ultimately, *To See the Saw Movies* utilizes the *Saw* films to provide an important and much needed addition to the film studies discourse on horror. In doing so, the book will show the intricate, protean and complex strands to how the films represent the fears and anxieties circulating in contemporary society but will also remedy the stigma associated with the franchise in terms of its disreputable status by showing what a rich source of material the franchise can provide for academic discussion and analysis.

The first essays examine the *Saw* series as part of post–9/11 American popular culture. James Aston and John Walliss argue, in "'I've never murdered anyone in my life. The decisions are up to them': Ethical Guidance and Cultural Pessimism," that the films can be seen as representative of a shift in American popular culture post–9/11 towards increasing pessimism. The *Saw* franchise, they suggest, exemplifies this trend in several ways, most notably in its emphasis on the corrupted state of humanity. Human beings, the series shows, are riddled with vice and invariably cannot, even when put in a life or death situation, develop the self-awareness to overcome it. Indeed, humans have become so debased and disconnected from life that liberal, progressive attempts to help them and legal attempts to sanction them are doomed to failure. In the end, the only way in which they can be "saved," and by extension the social order be protected from them and thus restored, is through vigilantism and a never-ending cycle of torture. However, they argue, the series undercuts this view thereby offering a critique of American foreign policy post–9/11 and the War on Terror. That is, unlike in other cultural forms such as the western or the war film, within the *Saw* series there is no meaningful renewal through violence for Jigsaw, his apprentices, or their "test subjects." Rather, those who participate in Jigsaw's "games" either die or are left psychologically traumatized, while Jigsaw is shown in terminal decline throughout the franchise, dying in *Saw III*. Indeed, even those individuals Jigsaw believes have "won" their games and thereby overcome their previous weaknesses, his apprentices Hoffman and Amanda, are shown to have fundamentally misunderstood Jigsaw's philosophy, seeing the games as a means to punish, rather than redeem. At the end of the series society is still shown as corrupt, debased, violent and sinful, replete with weak and ineffectual institutions. Thus, violence serves no redemptive or regenerative function for Jigsaw (or society) and as such revokes the "heroic action" of the outsider vigilante who through aggressive male agency restores the status quo. Jigsaw's ultimate ineffectuality as social avenger and redeemer of a fallen and lost society/world thus casts doubt on the neoconservative, right-wing perspective on the necessity of violence undertaken outside the visible sphere of law and order.

Similar themes to Aston and Walliss are explored in Ben McCann's essay, "Body Horror." Drawing on the anthropological work of Mary Douglas on ritual purity and notions of pollution, he argues that the *Saw* series and other forms of contemporary horror featuring extreme forms of bodily harm may be seen to reflect contemporary concerns post–9/11. For Douglas, the physical body operates within primitive ritual as a metaphor for the social body, with dirt and other threats to the physical representing real and perceived threats to the society. Within the *Saw* series, McCann suggests, a similar dynamic is explored with the physical body of Jigsaw's test subjects being constantly jeopardized by traps that both engulf the human body and threaten its integrity. The threat to the body, however, does not stem from "outside" forces, but, rather, internal threats; the series representing, he argues, through its fragmenting and dismembered bodies, a collective nightmare of a nation undergoing political fragmentation while a "barbarian at the gate" pushes at the edges. In this way, he suggests, the violent and bloody spectacle of Jigsaw's tests articulate more than just the mechanics and machinery of gore and guts.

Thus, McCann concludes, the franchise expertly positions violent entertainment alongside contemporary socio-political issues such as the fear of the Other and the fear of invasion and how, ultimately, they use the allegory of the transgressive body to underline their traumatic status.

One leitmotif of the War on Terror is the increasing use of forms of surveillance against real or perceived threats to the social order. The role of surveillance in the *Saw* series is explored in Evangelos Tziallas' essay, "The Spectacle of Correction: Video Games, Movies and Control"; he argues that *Saw* and, more broadly, the genre of torture porn in which it is often placed by critics are concerned centrally with the fear of surveillance; the series's visual and narrative strategies presenting viewers with meditations on both the invasiveness of new surveillance technologies and their ability to both correct and control populations and producing forms of entertainment. Tziallas' use of gamification as an approach to analyze *Saw* is particularly effective in that it explores the growing interconnectedness between cinema and games, especially in the production of spectacle, and examines how game theory can provide a critical discourse with which to address horror in general and the *Saw* films in particular. That is, by utilizing gamified narrative and mise-en-scène *Saw* produces a heightened sense of interactivity which enables viewers to negotiate the ethical and moral implications of *Saw*'s "critical dystopia," thus engendering a friction whereby critical reflection and contemplation can occur.

The next two essays examine the way in which the *Saw* series may be framed in terms of broader theological debates. In "From Jigsaw to Phibes: God, Free Will and Foreknowledge in Conflict," Fernando G. Pagnoni Berns and Amy M. Davis address Jigsaw's seeming omnipotence in the franchise by asking two interlinked questions: firstly, why do all the characters in the series act as Jigsaw predicts, even when he is dead; and, secondly, why do the traps invariably operate correctly, attracting and testing those people they are designed to test? What, in other words, is the role of free will in the franchise? Indeed, they suggest, Jigsaw's test subjects are punished for their past free actions and enjoined to take responsibility for them, while his traps seem to contradict the possibility of free will. To answer these questions, Pagnoni Berns and Davis compare Jigsaw with the character of Dr. Phibes from the 1971 film *The Abominable Dr. Phibes*. Both, they suggest, believe themselves to be delivering divine justice, using highly sophisticated instruments to commit their respective murders, although Phibes, in contrast to Jigsaw, acts as though he were a god, hiding his true face from the world. Jigsaw, moreover, does not see himself as punishing his victims, but, rather, believes that he is giving his test subjects the opportunity to (re)learn how to value their lives, thus emphasizing the role of free will. If at times it appears that Jigsaw is a divine figure, Pagnoni Berns and Davis conclude, it is because he ensures in his plans the complete absence of chance since, as he claims in *Saw VI*, his superior knowledge of human behavior allows him to predict unerringly every action that his subjects will perform. Jigsaw's seeming omnipotence is, in other words, not of divine origin, but rather the result of his acute knowledge of how human beings act, using (or, from his perspective, abusing) their free will.

In his essay "A Voice and Something More: Jigsaw as Acousmêtre and Existential Guru," Brian H. Collins draws on the work of Kierkegaard, Sartre, Chion and Dolar to explore the continuities between the series and Christian and existential morality, in particular the idea of the *acousmêtre*. The series, he argues, is built around the idea that, in the absence of an existential ethics, human freedom is more terrifying than the inevitability of extinction. Each of Jigsaw's test subjects is thus tested not for breaking some form of transcendent morality, but rather, for their inability to bear up to the twin burdens of freedom and responsibility that define human existence (or what Sartre would term "bad faith"). Placed in a life or death situation, each is thus forced to make a choice — the same choice that Kramer/Jigsaw made when he crawled out of the wreck of his car following his attempted suicide: to choose life over death. Collins then explores the parallels between the character of Jigsaw and the life of Kierkegaard, such as a fixation with mortality, the use of pseudonyms, and the transition from the aesthetic to a religious mode of existence where he takes the place of a testing and judging God. Within Jigsaw's existential religion, he suggests, the role of the Jigsaw's acousmatic voice, that is Jigsaw as an unseen but heard figure, creates a ritualized state of emergency in which his test subjects can pass from un-life to freedom and life, but more often choose death or end up dead reinforcing the contention that freedom, not death is what strikes fear into the subjects of *Saw*.

Continuing the themes of applying philosophical arguments to the *Saw* series, Steve Jones' essay, "Twisted Pictures: Morality, Nihilism and Symbolic Suicide," positions a Nietzschean perspective to address the confused sense of ethics in the series, specifically looking at how morality operates through the seven films. Jones re-evaluates Jigsaw's position as torturer in terms of whether this can be seen as presenting a central character who is either a passive or radical nihilist. That is, according to Nietzsche, a person "who judges of the world as it is that it ought not to be and of the world as it ought to be that it does not exist" (1967: 318). This world view is broken down into two intertwined forms of nihilism — passive and radical — in which passive nihilists seek to change prevailing value-systems while keeping the world order intact and radical nihilists adhere to supreme values that cannot exist in the world-as-it-is. Thus, the world cannot be ideal, and so must ultimately be destroyed. By exploring the conception of nihilism in *Saw*, Jones does not set out to simply categorize Jigsaw, but to better comprehend his moral mission, which is vital if we are to understand *Saw*, since Jigsaw's morality drives the series. Ultimately then, Jones refutes the majority of critical reception that focused on Jigsaw's "muddled" morality and hypocritical behavior with regards to his test subjects. Instead, Jones contends that Jigsaw's values are not as confused as have been reported and that rather than being about his proclamation to save others, his actions instead reveal another agenda. That is, following the loss of his unborn son and his failed suicide attempt, Jigsaw seeks to symbolically eradicate himself: the victims he selects reflect and reify his own obsessive personality traits. Therefore, in keeping with the series' narrative twists — which are designed to reverse initially "obvious" meanings — Jones concludes that Jigsaw's mission statement has misdirected critics. His nihilism may be manifested as coerced suffering and articulated as distaste with the world, but the series' symbolic target is Jigsaw himself.

The next two essays, by Jacob Huntley and Dean Lockwood, both apply a Deleuzian perspective to the *Saw* series. In Huntley's "The Jigsaw Assemblage," he develops Deleuze and Guattari's term of *machinic assemblage* to describe the individuals, locations and traps of the *Saw* mise-en-scène alongside wider elements such as discourse, meanings and forms of expression that are associated with Jigsaw's world or sphere of interaction. Huntley notes that while the main icons of the Jigsaw assemblage can be easily identified, what is less clear is the purpose of these components and how they are interconnected and relate to each other. In this respect, Huntley applies Deleuze and Guattari's work in order to account for how the mixture of the Jigsaw assemblage provides ways of analyzing how the franchise comments on the contemporary period, especially one dominated by capitalist forces. That is, Jigsaw's games are meant to reinvigorate an appreciation of life yet he chooses to achieve this through subjugation and bodily pain. The project's philosophical underpinnings and its realization seem to be fundamentally mismatched as enjoyment of life is gruelingly and proscriptively enforced. Given that the ideological position appears to be at variance with the methodology, it indicates that either individuals within the Jigsaw assemblage have suffered a collapse of a stable and cohesive social and psychic body by instead articulating new directions for self and identity through the machinic assemblage of a trap, or subjectivity/identity is being taught afresh, to be read via these textual bodies. It is this reading of the *Saw* films that Huntley attempts to interrogate and in the process explores the tensions and consequences of the project by considering the complexity of the Jigsaw assemblage. For Huntley, two key questions emerge, Firstly, what exactly is at stake for those involved in the games? Secondly, what are the demands made by those enacting this project of revitalization and rehabilitation?

Similarly, Lockwood's essay, "Work Is Hell: Life in the Mannequin Factory," implements Deleuze and Guattari's work by developing Matt Hills' notion of "fantastic psychology" in terms of how we view Jigsaw's monstrosity. Lockwood acknowledges that Hills' work is important with regards to the *Saw* films in terms of how Jigsaw's contention that he is trying to better the world when in actuality he positions himself with the sickness he is trying to alleviate echoes the collapsing of terrorized and terrorist in the post–9/11 context. However, Lockwood sees *Saw* as much more to do with the late twentieth century networking of capital and Deleuze and Guattari's understanding of new "societies of control" that have also emerged in the contemporary period. For Lockwood, therefore, what we seem to be dealing with here is not so much fantastic psychology itself as the way fantastic psychologies are produced or conscripted to abet a new, monstrous form of fantastic *power*. *Saw*'s use of fantastic power takes many forms, most pertinently notions of surveillance, control and correction. Not only does it destabilize the space in *Saw* so that characters are seen as both guilty and innocent but it also blurs the distinction between who is the subject or object of violence, thus establishing the victims of the torture as somehow guilty in their own way. For Lockwood though, this violence or torture is not to destroy the subject but to affect control that has close links to the processes of contemporary capital and labor. Here Lockwood proceeds to analyze the *Saw* films in terms of how they represent the conditions of Capital-Life whereby capitalism no longer exploits labor in an industrial sense, but also the creative, inventive capacities of the body. The resulting "society of control" is writ large on *Saw*'s canvas and Lockwood suggests that we can approach the import of the films in terms of mapping, creating a semblance, of the sense life comes to acquire in conditions of Capital-Life. In *Saw*, Jigsaw's game plan maps out the transformation, under conditions of Capital-Life, of individuals, workers — always defined by their occupation as much as their "sin"— into affective puppets. Puppets that end up dead more often than not.

Madeleine Smith's essay, "Monstrous Bodies and Gendered Abjection," follows the preceding three essays in applying a clear theoretical model to the *Saw* films. In this case, Smith analyses *Saw* through a psychoanalytical framework to interrogate Barbara Creed's work on abjection in the horror film. Creed's highly acclaimed theory posits that abject bodily displays are predominantly associated with the feminine body. However, Smith counters that in contemporary U.S. horror, of which *Saw* is positioned as the most visible presence, abject bodily displays have shifted toward the masculine body, which is not only positioned alongside the female body as abject but is foregrounded as the primary site of abjection throughout the series. By providing a close analysis of the various abject representations, such as the monstrous feminine, the monstrous masculine and the male as possessed monster, Smith cogently challenges Creed's theory surrounding abjection and the monstrous-feminine. For Smith, the series displaces the primacy of the female in Creed's discussions of the abject by presenting males as overtly linked to abjection. Scenes of dead, mutilated and abject men are abundant and prevalent in all of the *Saw* films, suggesting that male displays of abjection are regarded as more monstrous and horrifying than those of females, most evident in the character of Jigsaw. Thus, the franchise undermines the notion that abjection is solely rooted in femininity by presenting gender ambiguous and fluid characters who subvert rigid gender roles to present new ways of interpreting gendered relationships with the abject. With this in mind, Smith concludes that the male body in *Saw* is presented as unstable, vulnerable and subject to extreme abject displays and bodily disintegration, presenting an attitude towards gender in the series that depicts the American male as under threat post–9/11 and following U.S. involvement in Iraq and Afghanistan, suggesting a crisis in confidence over powerful and authoritative displays of patriarchy.

Finally, Jeffrey Bullins, in "Hearing the Game: Sound Design," turns our attention to the role of sound design within the series. The role of sound within film, he notes, is often underappreciated in a medium that has historically been visual-centric. He suggests that the *Saw* films represent a culmination of decades of sound design in the horror genre, presenting a sonic environment that is more experiential rather than representational. The non-diegetic sounds that characterize the film—such as, for example, the sounds accompanying flashbacks or the "whooshing" sound effects associated with camera pans and zooms—do not mimic those of the real world, but are, he suggests, a product of the stylistic conventions established within the horror genre. Therefore, sound in *Saw* becomes a series of sonic motifs that create a hyperreal space which the viewer inhabits and which manipulates their emotional responses. In this respect, the *Saw* series acts as a vital case study to account for how audiences receive horror films and how sound, in particular, can provide an immersive environment where both physical and emotional reactions are manipulated by the complex and innovative use of sound within each film.

References

Barsam, R., and D. Monahan (2010). *Looking at Movies: An Introduction to Film*, New York: W.W. Norton.

Edelstein, D. (2006, January 28). "Now Playing at Your Local Multiplex: Torture Porn," *New York Times*, http://nymag.com/movies/features/15622/.

Ebert, R. (2004, October 29). "Saw." *Chicago Sun-Times*, http://rogerebert.suntimes.com/apps/pbcs.dll/article?AID=/20041028/REVIEWS/40923005/1023.

Gledhill, C. (2007). "The Horror Film." in P. Cook (Ed.). *The Cinema Book*, London: BFI.
Gleiberman, O. (2010, October 29). "Saw 3-D." *Entertainment Weekly*, http://www.ew.com/ew/article/0,,20438035,00.html.
Grant, B.K., and C. Sharrett (2004). "Introduction," in B.K. Grant and C. Sharrett (Eds.), *Planks of Reason: Essays on the Horror Film*. Lanham, MD: Scarecrow (originally published 1985).
Hale, H. (2010, October 29). "Ending a Lethal Game and All Its Gory Details," *New York Times*, http://movies.nytimes.com/2010/10/30/movies/30saw.html.
Hartlaub, P. (2006, October 29). "'Saw III' Could Be Breaking Point for Many Fans." *San Francisco Chronicle*, http://www.sfgate.com/bayarea/article/Saw-III-could-be-breaking-point-for-many-fans-2467514.php.
Lee, N. (2008, October 24). "Grand Guignol, by Way of the Tool Shed." *New York Times*, http://movies.nytimes.com/movie/453137/Saw-V/overview.
Nietzsche, F. (1967) *The Will to Power*. New York: Vintage.
O'Hehir, A. (2010, October 29). "'Saw 3-D': Horror's self-help franchise comes to an end." *Salon*, http://www.salon.com/2010/10/29/saw_3d/.
Savlov, M. (2007, November 2). "Saw IV." Austin Chronicle, http://www.austinchronicle.com/calendar/film/2007-11-02/553186/.
Sconce, J. (2012). "Inhuman Centipede." *Ludic Despair*, http://ludicdespair.blogspot.co.uk/2012/07/inhuman-centipede.html.
Strong, B. (2005, October 18). "Saw II." *The Village Voice*, http://www.villagevoice.com/2005-10-18/film/saw-ii/.
Tziallas, E. (2010). "Torture Porn and Surveillance Culture." *Jump Cut: A Review of Contemporary Media*, http://www.ejumpcut.org/currentissue/evangelosTorturePorn/index.html.
Wetmore, K. (2012). *Post-9/11 Horror in American Cinema*. New York: Continuum.
Wood, R. (1979). "Introduction," in A. Britton, R. Wood, R. Lippe and T. Williams (Eds.), *The American Nightmare: Essays on the Horror Film*. Toronto: Festival of Festivals.

"I've never murdered anyone in my life. The decisions are up to them": Ethical Guidance and the Turn Toward Cultural Pessimism

James Aston and *John Walliss*

The *Saw* franchise of films is the largest-grossing horror franchise of all time. Over the course of seven films (2003–2010), the series has grossed, as of July 2010, $872 million at the box office and more than $30 million on DVD, earning an entry in the Guinness Book of Records (www.boxofficemojo.com, Kit 2008). It has also spawned two video games (*Saw*, 2009; *Saw: Flesh and Blood*, 2010), an amusement ride (*Saw: The Ride* at Thorpe Park Theme Park, Lincolnshire, UK), several mazes, and a comic book (*Saw: Rebirth*, 2005). Despite its commercial success, however, the series is often dismissed, along with films such as *Hostel* (Roth 2005) and *Captivity* (Joffé 2007), as "torture porn," a sub-genre of films characterized, it is claimed, by excessive violence for the sake of titillating audiences and a sense of amorality, if not extreme nihilism (Lockwood 2009). For David Edelstein (2006), the *New York Times* writer who invented the term, the genre — in which he also, perhaps controversially, includes *The Passion of the Christ* (Gibson 2004) — is "so viciously nihilistic that the only point seems to be to force you to suspend moral judgments altogether." Such a partisan position over the negative qualities of the franchise has been reinforced by a majority of critics including David Hiltbrand (2005) of the *Philadelphia Inquirer*, who described *Saw II* (Bousman 2005) as "vilely violent ... the Phnom Penh of splatter movies," and Mike Hale (2010) of the *New York Times*, who bluntly dismissed the franchise as "meretricious garbage, with a claim to moral complexity that serves as a fig leaf while we enjoy the sight of limbs being hacked off and heads exploding." *LA Weekly*'s Nick Pinkerton (2009) intimated that the films should not even be allowed to exist by denouncing *Saw VI* (Greutert 2009) as "gray, grisly, solemn, stupid ... the most dismal thing I've ever laid eyes on, the argument against film preservation." But it was Michael Phillips, writing in the *Chicago Tribune*, who perhaps best exemplifies the majority position of critics when, talking about *Saw II*, he opined:

> [It is] not a film; it's an excuse to show victims bleeding at the mouth, or getting shot in the eye, or plucking out their own eyeballs.... No point in labelling this a horror film. This is a sadism film, and while all good and great horror films know what sadism tastes like, a sadism film settles for nothing of lasting, imaginative horror [Phillips 2007].

Such views were also echoed by film scholars, the most prominent being Christopher Sharrett and Douglas Kellner. Sharrett (2009, 32) complained that the series was characterized by both a "total exclusion of context ... intellectual bankruptcy and retrograde politics," while Kellner (2010, 9) saw the unprecedented and continuing success of the franchise as exhibiting a worrying trend in moviegoers that engendered a "pathological society riven with unmastered aggression and violence." Although both responses clearly perceive the *Saw* franchise as artistically lacking, they concede that the films nonetheless provide a social commentary on the United States in the twenty-first century. For Sharrett (2009, 32), the series critiques "capitalist society from a decidedly conservative position"; positing the figure of a vigilante — "a perfect emblem of the recent era's rightist ideology" — as the means to religitimate the "fallen world" of contemporary capitalist society. Kellner equally finds social worth in the transgressive use of violence and torture in the *Saw* films, arguing that the series

> puts on display the demented illusions, grotesque hypocrisy, obscene violence, and utter lunacy of the Bush-Cheney era, which finds its true face in the sick and twisted killer-ex-machina Jigsaw ... the lunatic killer Jigsaw can therefore be read as a metaphor for Dick Cheney and his subordinates, a group of fanatical, warped, and vicious advocates of torture and murder, believing that their torturing and murdering is in the cause of good because it is punishing evil [Kellner 2010, 7, 8].

The series' producers, however, were much more unequivocal on their position that not only did the series promote a strong moral message but that it did so through innovative uses of the horror genre. Rejecting many accusations found in the critical reception of the franchise, *Saw VI* director Darren Lynn Bousman (*Saw VI* Press Conference 2009) claimed that at its core, the series promotes a moral message. While acknowledging that his film, and by extension the series, is not a "critics' darling," it nonetheless "has a bigger moral message than a lot of the films that do win [Academy Awards]." In contrast to horror films that are merely "just blood and violence and, you know, you get hot teenagers and get them naked and having some sex and doing some killing," he argued that in the *Saw* series "there's a moral message underneath them ... so I would just challenge [critics and audiences] to look beneath the surface." Cast member Cary Elwes (*Saw* Special Edition Audio Commentary

2005) echoed this, describing *Saw* (Wan 2004) as "a morality tale that was twisted, the most twisted morality tale ever." Going further, series star Tobin Bell claimed in one interview that the series could serve as a pedagogical tool in schools:

> Y'know those kids, a teacher could sit them in a classroom and tell them not to move and say "today we are going to talk about appreciating your blessings" and they'd be like [pretends to fall asleep] "oh god." That kind of thing. For some reason in *Saw* there is so much energy and mayhem going on around it and then all of a sudden out of the blue comes this little message that comes through and they remember that. People learn in different ways and the environment in which something is said makes it resonate sometimes, and sometimes it just puts you to sleep [Artisan News Service 2007].

With this in mind, this essay will examine the ethical vision presented in the *Saw* series, focusing in particular on how it represents a trend within post–9/11 popular culture toward increasing cultural pessimism.[1] In doing so, we will draw on our own previous work (Walliss & Aston 2011 and Aston & Walliss 2011) and the work of others such as Mervyn Bendle (2005), John Stroup and Glenn Shuck (2007), and Douglas Kellner (2010), who have argued that post–9/11 cinema is characterized by a fundamental sense of pessimism. In particular, we will situate our argument within Bendle's (2005, 4) claim that popular culture, echoing wider shifts within American culture, has witnessed a movement from what he terms a Promethean view of human nature that sees human beings as able to be improved, to a more pessimistic, Augustinian view emphasizing "human sinfulness and weakness ... a dystopian vision ... anti-humanism ... [and] conservatism." We will locate the *Saw* films within this cultural trajectory, in particular focusing on the "games" and the use of torture and how these rituals disturb a clear moral and ethical vision as the franchise moves unsteadily between conservative and liberal ideologies. To put it another way, human beings, the films show, are riddled with vices and invariably cannot, even when put in a life-or-death situation, develop the self-awareness to overcome them. Indeed, humans have become so debased and disconnected from life that those liberal, progressive attempts to help them and legal attempts to sanction them are doomed to failure. In the end, the only way in which they can be "saved," and by extent the social order be protected from them and thus restored, is through vigilantism and a never-ending cycle of torture.

Reconnecting with Your "True" Self: Ethics in Saw

Within the *Saw* films, individuals, either alone or in combination with others, are placed in ingenious and lethal traps. These traps, referred to as "games" by their creator, John Kramer (aka Jigsaw), are designed to encourage the re-emergence of what Kramer believes is the survival instinct within his "test subjects," with each test reflecting their particular vices or perceived failings. At the beginning of each game, the test subjects find a Dictaphone nearby with a recorded message from Kramer — his voice slowed and distorted to mask his identity — in which they are cryptically told why they are where they are through a series of instructions that they have to follow in order to "win" their game. Alternatively, Kramer may deliver this information via a videotaped message, the message given via a sinister puppet known in the franchise as "Billy." For example, in *Saw IV*, a multiple rapist [Ivan Landsness], who has been freed through the actions of his lawyer, is placed in a game that will rip the limbs from his body unless he pushes two buttons, which in turn will drive two knives into his eyes. Via a Dictaphone message, Jigsaw tells him:

> Hello Ivan. As a voyeur you've kept photos of those you have victimized. Can you see the pain that you have brought them? You have torn apart their lives. You have used your body as an instrument of abuse. Now I give you the chance to decide what is more important: your eyes that have led you blindly astray, or your body which has caused those around you endless suffering. You have been handed the tools which can save your life. Decide quickly though. In 60 seconds the choice will be made for you.

In this example, the rapist has to willingly blind himself in order to escape, thus performing a symbolic castration that directly aligns the trap to his past actions. In *Saw III* (Bousman 2006), a man (Jeff) who has become obsessed with punishing the drunk driver (Tim) who killed his son is put through a series of games designed to see if he can overcome his sense of vengeance by forgiving and saving from death a witness who did not come forward to the police and the judge who, Jeff believes, did not sentence Tim to a long enough prison term. These games eventually culminate in one wherein Jeff can either help free Tim or watch him be slowly torn to pieces in a machine to which he is strapped and thus satiate his desire for vengeance. These "games" supply the narrative with both agency and direction, though each film, and the series as a whole, characteristically ends with a twist; the final scenes of the film revealing via flashback a different interpretation of the series of games or the meta-reason for why a particular test subject was chosen. For example, at the finale of *Saw III*, the viewer is shown through flashbacks that Jeff's games were part of a larger game that Kramer was putting his accomplice, Amanda, through to test whether she had overcome her own violent tendencies and self-destructive behavior.

Kramer's motivation for his actions is left implicit within *Saw* (Wan 2004), although it is subsequently explored, again in flashback, throughout the remaining films in the series. As the films progress, the audience gradually becomes aware of Kramer's backstory and how he assumed the mantle of Jigsaw. Kramer is a civil engineer who, among other projects, designs a community project that is intended to provide homes to low-income families, while his pregnant wife (Jill) runs a drug clinic named Cherish Your Life. Both characters are thus established as members of the liberal middle class exemplified in their intent on helping those less fortunate than themselves. Kramer's liberal values, however, begin to unravel when a drug addict robs the clinic, seriously injuring his wife who subsequently has a miscarriage. Reacting to the death of his son, who was to be called Gideon — presumably in reference to the Old Testament judge — Kramer falls into depression and abandons his housing project as an overwhelming pessimism of humanity takes hold. Shortly afterwards, he is diagnosed with an aggressive cancerous brain tumor and attempts suicide by driving his car off a cliff. While Kramer survives the attempt, it is, he claims in *Saw IV*, "a different person [who] crawled out of the wreckage":

> It was the moment that I decided to end my life that started me in my work and brought meaning to it. I had literally driven myself to suicide and I had failed. My body had not been strong enough to repel cancer cells, yet I had lived through a plunge off a cliff. But to my amazement, I was alive and I was determined to spend the rest of my days testing the fabric of human nature.

Kramer is thus reborn as Jigsaw, beginning his new life by putting Cecil, the drug addict who injured his wife, through his first game. Cecil's ordeal establishes a clear pattern that is continued throughout the franchise, both in the rationale of the games and in their execution. That is, Kramer tells Cecil that his "life is a lie" and that the device that encases his head with knives is a "tool, to reclaim your life, to discard the vices that have so corrupted your soul." Here, Kramer clearly articulates the raison d'être behind his philosophy — namely, that Cecil must reconnect with life, to "cherish your life," and thus relinquish previous wrongs, vices, and transgressions. Or, as Steve Jones (2010, 234), in his article "Time Is Wasting: Con/sequence and S/pace in the *Saw* Series," pithily sums it up: "Be what I say or die." This "reconnection" or renewed appreciation of one's own life is usually only possible through self-inflicting injury and pain onto one's body, which is overwhelmingly the case for most of the devices utilized in Jigsaw's games. In the case of Cecil, he has to push his face against the knives in order to escape, thus making visible the "ugliness of his soul," as Kramer rationalizes it. Cecil does escape but learns nothing from his ordeal, choosing instead to attack Kramer, only to fall to his death in a pit of razor wire.

Kramer's rejection of his own previous life is predicated on the same guiding principle that he admonishes others for — namely, reconnecting to the "true" self. Sharrett (2009, 34) outlines this figure that Kramer embodies as "the disgruntled, middle-class white male professional, [who] fits in a long tradition of male characters fed up with democratic institutions, determined to set their own rules," such as, for example, Paul Kersey in the *Death Wish* series of movies (1974–1994) and Harry Callaghan in the *Dirty Harry* series (1971–1988). Rather than continue his help at a communal, grass-roots level, Kramer turns to rightist ideology and vigilantism, selecting those individuals who he believes are responsible for the decline in societal standards as his test subjects. Indeed, expressing his change of philosophy and shift into vigilantism, Kramer explains to Cecil:

> Things aren't sequential: good does not lead to good, nor bad to bad. People steal, don't get caught, live the good life. Others lie and cheat and get elected. Some people stop to help a stranded motorist and get taken out by a speeding semi. There's no accounting for it. How you play the cards you've been dealt is all that matters.

The morality of Kramer and the franchise as a whole is thus predicated along these lines of restoring fairness back into a world where the innocent suffer and the criminal and miscreant receives little or no punishment for his or her actions. However, Kramer's use of apprentices in the film, necessitated by his increasing debilitation through cancer, undermines his clear moral imperative articulated to Cecil. While Kramer's games are ultimately "winnable," those designed and implemented by his apprentices — Amanda, a former drug addict with a history of violence both against herself and others, and Hoffman, a corrupt and brutal police detective — are designed instead to singularly kill the people they entrap. They thus reflect a nihilistic and sadistic game-playing that contravenes Kramer's original approach. While Kramer's application of the games is horrific and unlawful, the games nonetheless present a clear moral framework that attempts to recoup the "dysfunctional system" that he believes has befallen contemporary American society (Sharrett 2009, 35). Conversely, the traps and games designed by Kramer's protégés represent a sadistic application of the philosophy, and both are subsequently punished within the series' diegesis for failing to heed Kramer's advice and reconnect with and value their own lives. It is the ethical dimension of *Saw*'s morality that this article now addresses.

Saw and Post-9/11 Cultural Pessimism

The ethical vision of the *Saw* series is fundamentally a pessimistic one, emphasizing a form of moral social Darwinism. For Kramer, human beings have lost their survival instinct typically as a consequence of moral weakness of indulging in some form of vice and so have to (re)learn to appreciate their life through being forced to play one of his games. By demonstrating their will to live, often through enduring some form of mutilation symbolic of their weakness/vice, Kramer's logic goes, human beings thus demonstrate their will to live and regain their lost survival instinct. In contrast, Kramer removes a jigsaw-piece section of flesh from the bodies of those who fail as a symbol of their lack of survival instinct (Huntley 2007). As Dean Lockwood observes,

> The torture scenarios ("games") in the *Saw* movies are conceived by their creator as jolts necessary to arouse people irresponsibly sleepwalking through their lives ... in the expectation of torture, the victims are exposed not to the possibility of death, or not only to the possibility of death, but to an ecstatic transformative, self-altering moment which opens up a revitalized, more intense engagement with life [Lockwood 2009, 42, 46].

Such a morality is also clearly a highly individualistic one. Having abandoned his former liberal values, Kramer reborn as Jigsaw would seem to have embraced a more rightist ideology emphasizing personal choice and responsibility. Indeed, as Sharrett has observed, in many ways Kramer — and more broadly the series as a whole — can be seen as fundamentally conservative and reactionary. Those individuals deemed by Kramer to have lost their survival instinct are not capable of regaining it through any standard means, but have, in contrast, to be tortured and undergo physical mutilation in order to do so. However, even when placed within a life-or-death situation and given the opportunity of demonstrating their will to survive, most of Kramer's "subjects" are unable to do so. Indeed, even those individuals who Kramer believes have overcome their former vices — his apprentices Amanda and Hoffman — eventually relapse into their selves, thus undermining Kramer's rationale and moral vision (Jones 2010).

Nevertheless, what is arguably the most significant ethical question raised within the series is whether Jigsaw's tests should be understood as murder. Within the series' diegesis Kramer is often referred to as "the Jigsaw killer" and as a serial killer. However, when confronted with this accusation at several times in the series, Kramer denies this, telling a police detective during his interrogation in *Saw II* (Bousman 2005), "I've never murdered anyone in my life. The decisions are up to them." While, as Jake Huntley (2007) wryly observes, such a defense "probably wouldn't stand up in court," Kramer's reply does have a degree of truth. Kramer's tests are designed in principle to be winnable by his test subjects, and, indeed, Kramer wants his test subjects to pass the test and survive, although he arguably expects that they will not. Kramer, after all, invariably finishes his Dictaphone message to subjects by telling them that the choice of whether they live or die is theirs. In this way, as Jones (2010, 235) suggests, Kramer's games may be seen to be founded less on "rehabilitation per se, but [rather] on punishing people for not transforming."

Even so, Kramer's motivations can be compared with those of his apprentices. Whereas he seeks to reform his test subjects, offering them a possibility to win his games, both Amanda and Hoffman in contrast seek instead to punish their subjects, giving them tests that are impossible to win. As Kramer tells Hoffman later in the series in a flashback scene:

> Vengeance can change a person; make you into something you never thought capable of being. But unlike you I have never killed anyone. I give people a chance.... You can dispense justice and give people a chance to value their lives in the same moment ... killing is distasteful to me. There is a better, more efficient way.... You see it's a different method that I'm talking about. If a subject survives my method, he or she is instantly rehabilitated.

For Kramer, then, violent self-injury is a means to an end ("rehabilitation"), whereas for his apprentices it is the sadistic end in itself. The ethical switch toward a more pessimistic and nihilistic use of violence and aggression can be seen to reflect the series' critical treatment of U.S. politics. As Kellner (2010, 8) has observed, Jigsaw's approach to his test subjects may be read as metaphor for American war on terror and foreign policy post–9/11 in terms of its "Vengeance-Outside-the-Law morality" of pre-emptive war, racial and ethnic profiling, the surveillance state of Homeland Security, and the use of torture by American personnel. Elizabeth Swanson Goldberg (2001, 251) outlines that the use of torture in American cinema, particularly in the 1980s cycle of "counterhistorical" dramas of *The Killing Fields* (Joffé 1984) and *Salvador* (Stone 1986), ultimately supplies "the occasion for advancement of an idealized Western or U.S. political identity in a global context." In Goldberg's analysis, scenes of torture are carried out via the "national or cultural other" so that the act itself is distanced and that both the victim and the perpetrator are rendered unthreatening for Western audiences (Goldberg 2001). Indeed, Jason Middleton (2010) observes that this representational strategy is carried through to the *Hostel* films, the other key proponent of the contemporary "torture porn" cycle along with the *Saw* franchise. However, in the *Saw* films the figure of the "Other" is much less pronounced, making the outcome of the recurring scenes of torture and violence more unsettling as boundaries between the Self and the Other become less defined. As such, the violence is only partially successful in eliminating the fears and anxieties connected to issues of torture, surveillance, and vigilante justice within American audiences. Although Jigsaw can be viewed as Other in his remoteness and detachment from the actors engaged in his various forms of rehabilitation, he is still clearly identifiable as a white, male American. Similarly, the largest proportion of victims are white males and the location where these victims endure their fate is always clearly situated as being on American soil. That is, even though the abandoned warehouses and disused factories that the "games" take place in exist in a kind of liminal zone, these locations nonetheless oppose the exotic and foreign nature of the Eastern European–based *Hostel*, thus providing a more immediate, visible, and unsettling examination of contemporary American foreign policy and the war on terror.

Therefore, *Saw*'s use of (white) American actors who carry out and are subjected to torture brings the issue closer to "home" for American audiences and is further developed through Jigsaw's recourse to vigilantism. Specifically, in the games, subjects have to inflict pain and damage onto their bodies in order to "win" and thus become better, more connected citizens. The notion of redemption, or regeneration, through violence is a founding American myth that, as Slotkin (1973, 5) has argued, has become a "structuring metaphor of the American experience." For Slotkin, the use of a regenerative violence, so prevalent in American cultural forms such as the Western and the war film, enables a clear moral and religious certitude to coexist with an ethical use of force. Such a narrative was applied to the twin wars of Iraq and Afghanistan and has largely been replicated in recent American horror films.[2] However, in the cycle of *Saw* films, the belief of regenerative violence in structuring national character and identity is compromised by a pessimistic and increasingly nihilistic application. In the *Saw* franchise, there is no meaningful renewal through violence for either the perpetrator or the test subjects. The people who participate in the games either die, survive but are left psychologically traumatized as we are shown in *Saw 3D* (Greutert 2010) with the "Jigsaw survival group," or become sadistic and unhinged apprentices. Kramer is shown in terminal decline during the series due to an inoperable brain tumor and is eventually killed by Jeff in *Saw III*. Also, at the end of the series, society is still shown as corrupt, debased, violent, and sinful, replete with weak and ineffectual institutions. Thus, violence serves no redemptive or regenerative function for Kramer (or society) and as such revokes the "heroic action" of the outsider vigilante who through aggressive male agency restores the status quo. Kramer's ultimate ineffectuality as social avenger and redeemer of a fallen and lost society/world thus casts doubt on the neoconservative, right-wing perspective on the necessity of violence undertaken outside the visible sphere of law and order. Here, the scenes of torture in the *Saw* films provide a stark critique of America's war on terror suggesting that its use, for both victim and perpetrator is destructive, providing real concerns over how such political uses of violence will impact national consciousness and the American character.

The *Saw* franchise also markedly delineates the shift from pre-millennium optimism to post-millennium, post-9/11 pessimism in its bleak and often nihilistic worldview characterized by broken social institutions, ineffectual (male) authority, and violent death. This move to a more anxious and misanthropic cultural expression can be seen in a variety of cinematic genres — from the shift in the "belief in human self-determination to a conviction of human sinfulness and weakness" in apocalyptic sci-fis such as *Children of Men* (Cuarón 2006) and *Cloverfield* (Reeves 2008) to patriarchal anxiety in Westerns such as *The Assassination of Jesse James by the Coward Robert Ford* (Dominik 2007) and *There Will Be Blood* (Anderson 2007) (Bendle 2005, 4). Indeed, in these films, the private sphere of the individual or the family is mapped out over larger, public issues circulating in contemporary society such as terrorism, war, the environment, and pandemic disease. The horror genre in general, and the *Saw* franchise in particular, continues this shift, key within which is the representation of the family, which according to Williams (1996, 14) in *Hearths of Darkness*, play "a significant role in any society determining everyone's psychic and social formation according to changing historical, political, and ideological dimensions."

The family in the *Saw* franchise is under assault from the start, either internally through the breakdown of familial relationships or externally through the machinations of Kramer and his apprentices. Instances of the ruptured family, or the family in crisis, are present throughout the series and are usually connected to the loss of patriarchal authority. For example, in *Saw II*, Detective Matthews (Donnie Wahlberg), who is investigating the Jigsaw Killer, is portrayed as a corrupt, unstable, and violent figure, divorced from his wife and estranged from his son. He is singled out by Kramer, who has kidnapped and imprisoned his son and who offers Matthews a simple challenge in order to get him back. Rather than just listening to what Jigsaw has to say, which is the only rule of his game, Matthews instead attacks his tormentor and in the process unwittingly incarcerates himself in a new game Jigsaw has devised, which ultimately leads to his death in *Saw IV*. Indeed, the irony of the Matthews test is that the son was actually hidden in a box in the same room as he and Jigsaw, and that if he had played the game faithfully not only would his son have been returned to him as Jigsaw promised, but he would have also still had Jigsaw in custody. The family under crisis is continued throughout the series with a later example taking place in *Saw VI*. In this film, the traditional nuclear family moves from a unified and stable unit to one that is ripped apart and subjected to physical and mental torture due to the father's complicity as the head of a corrupt and unethical insurance company. That the father ends up being pierced with needles and filled with hydrofluoric acid so that his body literally becomes unstable and out-of-control as it breaks apart is a clear indication of the loss of patriarchal order and the strong, male body that is traditionally associated with such an authoritative position.

The overly pessimistic representation of the family in the *Saw* franchise predominantly links the breakdown of the family unit to an errant, ineffectual, or morally debased father. This crisis in masculinity, exposed within the narratives of family breakdown in the *Saw* films, serves two larger purposes. First, the weak father, whether physically, emotionally, or morally, connects in the diegesis to the motivations and rationale of John Kramer; in particular, Kramer's attempts to recover and sustain both a "rigid morality" and a strong, primarily male individualism to rescue a "fallen" society (Sharrett 2009, 34). Here, Kramer, in the guise of Jigsaw, reinstates himself as the strong father, encouraging morally conflicted, disconnected, and weak people to make what he sees as the "correct" individual choices in order to enable them to become stronger, more active subjects. Similarly, Kramer's transformation into Jigsaw and his use of "games" enables him to recoup his own past masculine weaknesses when he failed to protect his unborn son and subsequently attempted suicide. Second, the breakup of the family, and more importantly the lack of patriarchal order, reflects changing dynamics post–9/11 where male authority has been brought into question over events such as Abu Ghraib, Guantanamo Bay, alleged state-sanctioned torture, and the general military and government conduct and leadership in the wars in Iraq and Afghanistan. For example, Kramer's use of elaborate torture chambers and physical tests of endurance to punish those whom he sees as representative of "evil" or at least morally dubious can be seen on one level as a veiled critique of the Bush-Cheney administration post–9/11, as they were, according to Kellner (2010, 9), "constructing apparatuses of torture in Afghanistan, Iraq, Guantanamo, and other sites throughout the world to punish its alleged enemies and 'evil doers.'" In this respect, the type and rationale of violence in the *Saw* films directly addresses the fear and anxiety circulating in America of unchecked and out-of-control masculinity, especially from those in power. Thus, the *Saw* films offer up an indictment of masculinity that mirrors uncertainty and anxiety over male agency within American culture. Furthermore, Jigsaw's reconstitution of a moral and ethical framework is undermined by highlighting his male agency and power as crazed and demonstrably excessive, which is combined with the sadistic motivations of his apprentices. Both forms reaffirm *Saw*'s rampant and violent masculinity that is unchecked and uncontrolled in its actions. This unregulated masculinity that is on display in the *Saw* films also faces little opposition as any restorative masculinity is withheld through a host of impotent and ineffectual characters. The ending of *Saw*, for example, has the typical male hero alone in a sealed room screaming for help as the screen fades to black. In *Saw 3D*, an entire SWAT team is wiped out trying to rescue victims of one of Jigsaw's "games."

On its own terms, the *Saw* franchise seems to offer little or no possibility for the restoration of the sanctity of the family or of a strong and moral patriarchal order. The assault on the social body of the family and the male figurehead is further compounded by another of the recurrent motifs in the series of films, namely the prolonged, bloody, and destructive attack on the corporeal body. Just as the family comments on the social health of a nation, so too does the body as Mary Douglas (1970, 70) has presciently argued in *Purity and Danger*, where she analyzes the concept of purity and its importance in everyday society. One of the key themes Douglas discusses is that the physical body acts as a metaphor for the social body. That is, rituals used to control the body can be mapped onto the desire to control the social body so that "bodily control is an expression of social control" (1970:70). Therefore, representations of the body as unregulated and out-of-control indicate traumatic ruptures within the social fabric if, as Douglas contends, "there is no natural way of considering the body that does not involve at the same time a social dimension" (*ibid.*). In this respect, the *Saw* franchise's examination of the excessive and brutalized body is able to offer "incisive social critiques, portraying contemporary society as isolating, unpredictably horrific and threatening, a nightmarish series of encounters in which personal relationships — families, couples, friendships, partnerships — disintegrate and fail, often violently" (Palmer 2006, 22). Similar to Douglas's contention about the traumatized body signifying ruptures within the social fabric, so too does blood symbolically comment on the health of society. For example, the philosopher Rene Girard (1995, 34), in his turn toward anthropology and the origin of violent rivalry and victimhood in society, has outlined how spilt blood is usually associated with the impure and that "when men are enjoying peace and security, blood is a rare sight. When violence is unloosed, however, blood appears to be everywhere — on the ground, underfoot, forming great pools." If we are to apply this to the *Saw* films, whose tagline for the promotional campaign for *Saw II* was "there will be blood," then the excessive amount of blood coupled with the brutalized body adds another signifying layer to the fears and anxieties circulating in contemporary American society.

Each film in the *Saw* franchise opens with a particularly violent and bloody "game" which results in the death of the "player." The games range from crawling through razor wire in order to escape a dungeon-type room in *Saw* to two men choosing to dismember their mutual lover rather than cause injury to themselves in *Saw 3D*. These games are not only excessive and bloody but predominately feature the body under threat through a variety of external implements such as hammers, fish hooks, and axes (*Saw IV*), a razor-sharp pendulum (*Saw V*), and metal bolts (*Saw VI*). To a large extent, this is replicated through many of the games featured during the ensuing narrative development of each film, although external threats to the body are often combined with internal threats represented through self-injury or mutilation in order to "win" the game. For example, the opening game in *Saw VI* acts as a significant illustration of the body under threat as it features both an external threat and self-injury by the player. The game features Simone and Eddie, who have been selected by Jigsaw due to their unscrupulous financial practices as lending bankers. In order to "win" the game, the two players must — in a clear reference to Shylock in Shakespeare's *The Merchant of Venice*— extract a "pound of flesh" from their own bodies in order to stop steel screws from boring into their skulls. Both administer self-injury with Eddie cutting off flesh from his stomach and Simone cutting off her arm in a final victorious act of bloody self-mutilation. Needless to say, as the loser, Eddie is subjected to the external threat of the contraption secured to his head that bores the steel screws through his head in a horrific and bloody climax. In the *Saw* series, self-injury is recurrent in many of the games instigated by Jigsaw. While such action may originally be conceived by Kramer as a means of rehabilitation, it nonetheless clearly forwards the crisis in masculinity (as most of the subjects are male) that was developed within the representation of the family and the patriarchal father.

If the lack of patriarchal authority and power within the family in the *Saw* franchise can be seen to comment on the weakening of American strength post–9/11 and the body under threat corresponds to Douglas's formulations over the interconnectedness of the physical and social body, then the *Saw* films forward a very distinct "collective nightmare." On one hand, the weak father figure offers a critique of the scandals carried out under George W. Bush's leadership. While on the other hand, the bloody and brutalized body brings home the trauma of American people who were "faced with tortures, brutality and harm in far more graphic and realistic manners than in Jigsaw's games, losing limbs, being ambushed and blown apart with improvised explosive devices (IEDs), and suffering from post-traumatic syndrome" (Kellner, 2010:8) in the twin wars of Iraq and Afghanistan. Thus, rather than redeeming American identity by using the Other, the exotic, or the foreign as agents of abuse, torture, and murder, the *Saw* films directly indict the contemporary context of the "war on terror" and the fall out it has caused in places spanning the Middle East to Guantanamo Bay. In bringing scenes of torture "back home" and making the figure of the white, male American implicit in its execution, American bodies are no longer exempt from narratives of torture and thus the moral and ethical dimensions of such acts cannot be completely expelled in favor of the non–American and the foreign. In this respect, the *Saw* franchise is able to address "our shifting fears and aspirations, and our sense of what constitutes the prime moral, social, and political problems facing us individually and collectively" (Waller, 1987:12). That is, torture and similar forms of aggression are never necessary and if carried out have no progressive impact on society or the body politic, instead producing considerable psychic damage manifest in *Saw*'s pessimistic treatment of both the family and the brutalized, defenseless, and bloodied body. As the mutilated Simone violently declares to one of the policemen who questions her after surviving the game in *Saw VI*, "What the fuck am I supposed to learn from this?"

Conclusion

Kramer's rationale in the *Saw* films was to restore a strong moral and ethical code in people who, through vice, crime, and weakness, had withdrawn from being productive, well-rounded members of society. Kramer's method of reconnecting the individual to life was through a series of games involving "excruciating forms of torture and free-form bloodletting" (Sharrett 2009, 32). Thus Kramer can be seen to embody the "right-wing fantasy" of the vigilante figure epitomized by Dirty Harry in his extralegal and violent methods (Kael 1973, 385). In that film, as in *Saw*, illegal and unethical actions are legitimized as offering a panacea for a society in which liberal institutions are held responsible for society's breakdown. The strong, male social avenger reverses the decline and ineffectual nature of society by operating outside the law and as such appeals to the "conservative spectator" in the reassertion of right-wing, individualist, male ideology (Lev 2000). However, Kramer, as the vigilante figure in *Saw*, does not repair the "fallen" society as he sees it, but ultimately makes things worse. Through his apprentices, Amanda and Hoffman, the games become sadistic and murderous and as such embody unregulated and out-of-control aggression.

The change in the games to a more pessimistic and even nihilistic outcome moves toward a more hostile and critical account of American politics post–9/11, a system that has covertly sanctioned detention, interrogation, and torture outside of the legal sphere of law and order. The shift from an initial conservative position, which represented Kramer as the strong, male individual entrusted with stemming the tide of a bankrupt society, to the liberal critique of the American government's sanctioning of torture in the "war on terror" represents a very real crisis over conservative male agency and politics. On the one hand, Kramer takes the "extreme individualism of a [vigilante] hero with no use for established authority" in getting the job done and restoring male agency and authority to a directionless society (Lev 2000, 37). On the other hand, Kramer's upholding of a right-wing and conservative masculinity combined with a clear moral and ethical code is critiqued as excessive, debilitating, and destructive through characters such as his apprentices and symbols such as the (male) body and the family.

The schizophrenic nature of the films' ideological stance thus mirrors the crisis over conservative politics in America since 9/11. The franchise's increasing pessimism ultimately undermines the restorative figure of the vigilante, offering instead a thoroughly nihilistic worldview. In *Saw*, humanity and society are doomed, trapped in a never-ending circle of violence, degradation, and alienation with no one to come to the rescue. As such, it brings us back to the critical reception of the *Saw* films that lamented the nihilism of the films or the unremitting sadism contained in the violent set-pieces. While true, critics aligned these approaches to the high level of bloody and horrific violence suggesting *Saw* as another example in a long line of debased cultural expressions obsessed with outrage and controversy. What was not addressed was how the pessimistic development of the *Saw* franchise uncovered a crisis in meaning and representation in conservative political ideology that rather than lamenting the existence of the films in fact shows how suitable horror cinema is in articulating "our sense of what constitutes the prime moral, social, and political problems facing us individually and collectively" (Waller 1987, 12).

Notes

1. An earlier version of this essay was published as "I've never murdered anyone in my life. The decisions are up to them.": Ethical Guidance and Cultural Pessimism in the *Saw* Series" in the *Journal of Religion and Popular Culture* 24, no. 3 (2012). Reprinted with permission from University of Toronto Press (www.uptjournals.com).

2. See for example the Hostel films but also the remakes of 1970s American horror such as *Texas Chainsaw Massacre* (Nispel 2003) and I Spit on Your Grave (Monroe 2010) in which excessive violence by the victims is justified by the greater acts of atrocity committed by the perpetrators.

References

Artisan News Service. 2007. "*Saw IV* (4) An Educational Experience, Says Tobin Bell." http://www.youtube.com/watch?v=yiySjzpXz7U&feature=related. (27 September 2012).

Aston, James, and John Walliss. (2011) "The (Un)Christian Road Warrior: The Crisis of Religious Representation in The Book of Eli." *Journal of Religion and Film* 15 (1). http://www.unomaha.edu/jrf/Vol15.no1/WallissBookEli.html. (27 September 2012).

Bendle, Mervyn. 2005. "The Apocalyptic Imagination and Popular Culture." *Journal of Religion and Popular Culture* XI. http://www.usask.ca/relst/jrpc/art11-apocalypticimagination.html. (27 September 2012).

Douglas, Mary. 1970. *Purity and Danger: An Analysis of Concepts of Purity and Taboo*. Middlesex. Harmondsworth, Penguin.

Edelstein, David. 2006. "Now Playing at Your Local Multiplex: Torture Porn." *New York Times*, 28 January. http://nymag.com/movies/features/15622/. (27 September 2012).

Girard, Rene. 1995. *Violence and the Sacred*. London: Althone.

Goldberg, Elizabeth Swanson. 2001. "Splitting Difference: Global Identity Politics and the Representation of Torture in the Counterhistorical Dramatic Film." In *Violence and American Cinema*, ed. J. David Slocum, 245–270. New York: Routledge.

Hale, Mike. 2010. "Ending a Lethal Game and All Its Gory Details." *New York Times*, 29 October. http://movies.nytimes.com/2010/10/30/movies/30saw.html. (27 September 2012).
Hiltbrand, David. 2005. "The Ickiest Ick That Movie Money Can Buy." *The Philadelphia Inquirer*, 28 October. http://articles.philly.com/2005-10-28/entertainment/25441891_1_sarin-tobin-bell-first-film. (27 September 2012).
Huntley, Jake. 2007. "'I Want to Play a Game': How to See *Saw*." *The Irish Journal of Gothic and Horror Studies* 3. http://irishgothichorrorjournal.homestead.com/SawHuntley.html (accessed 16 May 2011). (27 September 2012).
Jones, Steve. 2010. "'Time Is Wasting': Con/sequence and S/pace in the *Saw* Series." *Horror Studies* 1 (2): 225–239.
Kael, Pauline. 1973. *Deeper into Movies*. Boston: Little-Brown.
Kellner, Douglas. 2010. *Cinema Wars: Hollywood Film and Politics in the Bush-Cheney Era*. Oxford: Wiley-Blackwell.
Kit, Zorianna. 2008. "'Saw' Movie to Get Guinness Record." Reuters, 22 July. http://www.reuters.com/article/2010/07/23/us-saw-idUSTRE66M02F20100723 (16 May 2011).
Lev, Peter. 2000. *American Films of the '70s: Conflicting Visions*. Austin: University of Texas Press.
Lockwood, Dean. 2009. "All Stripped Down: The Spectacle of 'Torture Porn.'" *Popular Communication* 7 (1): 40–48.
Middleton, Jason. 2010. "The Subject of Torture: Regarding the Pain of Americans in Hostel." *Cinema Journal* 49 (4): 1–24.
Palmer, Tim. 2006. "Style and Sensation in the Contemporary French Cinema of the Body." *Journal of Film and Video* 58 (3): 22–32.
Phillips, Michael. 2007. "Review of *Saw II*." *Chicago Tribune*, 16 June. http://events.gazette.com/reviews/show/7957-review-saw-ii. (27 September 2012).
Pinkerton, Nick. 2009. "Movie Reviews." *LA Weekly*, 21 October. http://www.laweekly.com/2009-10-22/film-tv/movie-reviews-amelia-astro-boy-saw-vi/3/. (27 September 2012).
Saw VI Press Conference. 2009. http://www.ugo.com/ugo/html/article/?id=17961 (accessed 16 May 2011).
Sharrett, Christopher. 2009. "The Problem of *Saw*: 'Torture Porn' and the Conservatism of Contemporary Horror Films." *Cineaste* 31 (1): 32–37.
Slotkin, Richard. 1973. *Regeneration Through Violence: the Mythology of the American Frontier, 1600–1860*. Norman: University of Oklahoma Press.
Stroup, John M., and Glenn W. Shuck. 2007. *Escape into the Future: Cultural Pessimism and Its Religious Dimension in Contemporary American Popular Culture*. Baylor, TX: Baylor University Press.
Waller, Gregory A., ed. 1987. *American Horrors: Essays on the Modern American Horror Film*. Chicago: University of Illinois Press.
Walliss, John, and James Aston. 2011. "Doomsday America: The Pessimistic Turn of Post-9/11 Apocalyptic Cinema." *Journal of Religion and Popular Culture* 23 (1): 53–64.
Williams, Tony. 1996. *Hearths of Darkness: The Family in the American Horror Film*. London: Associated University Press.

Movies Cited

The Assassination of Jesse James by the Coward Robert Ford. 2007. Directed by Andrew Dominik. Warner Bros.
Captivity. 2007. Directed by Roland Joffé. Lionsgate Films.
Children of Men. 2006. Directed by Alfonso Cuarón. Universal Pictures.
Cloverfield. 2008. Directed by Matt Reeves. Paramount Pictures.
Hostel. 2005. Directed by Eli Roth. Lionsgate Films.
I Spit on Your Grave. 2010. Directed by Stephen R. Monroe. Anchor Bay Entertainment.
The Killing Fields. 1984. Directed by Roland Joffé. Warner Bros.
The Passion of the Christ. 2004. Directed by Mel Gibson. Icon Productions.

Salvador. 1986. Directed by Oliver Stone. Hemdale Film Corporation.
Saw. 2004. Directed by James Wan. Lionsgate Films.
Saw II. 2005. Directed by Darren Lynn Bousman. Lionsgate.
Saw III. 2006. Directed by Darren Lynn Bousman. Lionsgate.
Saw IV. 2007. Directed by Darren Lynn Bousman. Lionsgate.
Saw V. 2008. Directed by David Hackl. Lionsgate.
Saw VI. 2009. Directed by Kevin Greutert. Lionsgate.
Saw 3D. 2010. Directed by Kevin Greutert. Lionsgate.
The Texas Chainsaw Massacre. 2003. Directed by Marcus Nispel. New Line Cinema.
There Will Be Blood. 2007. Directed by Paul Thomas Anderson. Paramount Vantage.

Body Horror
Ben McCann

> *"What is being carved in human flesh is an image of society"*—Mary Douglas

A man is covered in flammable jelly, and burned alive. One detective's rib cage is torn out, and another's head is crushed by two ice blocks. Someone else is decapitated by a razor blade collar. So far, so *Saw*—a world of slicing, dicing, mutilation, and dissection. This world is a series of ingenious exploitative exercises in shock and schlock that seemingly taps into the "demented illusions, grotesque hypocrisy, obscene violence, and utter lunacy of the Bush-Cheney era" (Kellner, 2010: 7). With each new *Saw* film (released over seven successive Halloween weekends, from 2004 to 2010) came increasingly imaginative deaths and sustained gruesome imagery. Of course, horror films have always traded in this imagery of sustained corporeal degradation, but especially so, it seems, in this blockbuster franchise. Beneath *Saw*'s intricate mythology, its elaborate plot twists, and its moral seriousness lies a series of set pieces in which both male and female bodies are ripped and torn, and great pleasure is taken in the showing of the wound. Via a series of lethal Rube Goldberg traps, blood flows, bones snap, and flesh is rended. The *Saw* series is rhythmically structured around these traps, and their grisly ingenuity and ghastly precise engineering satisfies the core horror audience. But there is something else going on here as well against the backdrop of the series' tonally bleak *mise en scène*: the playing out of embedded coded anxieties about the malleability and permeability of the human body. On one level, the body horror in *Saw* appeals to gore fans (through websites such as *Bloody Disgusting.com* and fan sites replete with lists such as "The Top 10 Best Traps from the *Saw* Series"). This sustained horrific imagery is also a rich storehouse of allusion and historicized context. For instance, the consistent scenes of corporeal mutilation — and the powerful emotional charge we feel when watching them — recall Freud's notion (2003) that lost "organs" (140) and "severed limbs" are "highly uncanny" because of their "proximity to the castration complex" (150).

The films symbolically chart a crisis in masculinity; male characters are rendered powerless and impotent at the hands of Jigsaw (at the end of *Saw* [2004], Adam [Leigh Whannell] is locked in a sealed room screaming for help as the screen fades to black) and there is none of the cathartic, restorative moral recalibration that occurs in most traditional horror narratives. Moreover, it has long been accepted that horror films deal with the body on both a literal and figurative level; in *Saw*, beneath the splatter and the gore, there reside frequent allegorical interpretations of the porosity of the body and its susceptibility to foreign invaders.

This essay will examine the body horror in the franchise which is centered on both external and internal threats to the body and as such represents fears and anxieties circulating in contemporary American society. The body in *Saw* has both a corporal and social function whereby attacks on the physical nature of the body allegorize fractures in the national body politic. By looking at both examples of recent body horror films in France and Mary Douglas' key anthropological text *Purity and Danger: An Analysis of Concepts of Pollution and Taboo* (1966), the essay will examine the correlation in the *Saw* franchise between the corporeal and social body to see how the films articulate state-of-the-nation preoccupations while coterminously producing a violent and bloody visual spectacle. An examination of the current French body horror tradition is especially useful, for it emphasizes the transnational reach of contemporary American horror cinema (via genre recycling and reworking within a specific national context) and indicates how politically coded horror texts — whether *Saw*, or a near contemporary French equivalent such as *Sheitan* (Chapiron, 2006) — can function as barometers of domestic uneasiness.

"A payload of delicious nastiness": Body Horror and Reflectionist Readings

Traditional body horror, as Kelly Hurley defines it, is

a hybrid genre that recombines the narrative and cinematic conventions of the science fiction, horror, and suspense film in order to stage a spectacle of the human body defamiliarized, rendered other. Body horror seeks to inspire revulsion — and in its own way pleasure — through representations of quasi-human figures whose effect/affect is produced by their abjection, their ambiguation, their impossible embodiment of multiple, incompatible forms [Hurley 1995: 203].

Different directors have interrogated this ambiguation in various ways — David Cronenberg's *Videodrome* (1983) and *Existenz* (1999) explore the fusion of flesh and technology, and highlight how the body is subjected to — and vulnerable to — many external factors, such as science, media, and digital environments. The extremities of Japanese body horror, most familiar to Western audiences in *Tetsuo: The Iron Man* (1988), are exemplified by Sato Hisayasu's delirious *Muscle* (1988) and *Naked Blood* (1995), which frame the body as a flexible, perpetual site of biological reimagining and thriving social codes. Brian Yuzna's *Society* (1989) is a satire of the wealthy Beverly Hills set that mixes Dali-esque physical contortion with a savage critique of commodification and the Reaganite nuclear family. Broadly speaking, body horror features the graphic depiction, destruction or degeneration of the human body. There is a frequent fascination with the wounding and opening up of the body, so that — via progressive taboo-breaking representations — the body "display[s] itself as a visual feast" (Magistrale 2005: 16).

Linda Williams has labeled particular film genres — particularly horror, pornography, and melodrama — as "body genres" because they violate the classical realist paradigm of "efficient, action-centered, goal-oriented linear narratives" and offer gratuitous scenes of uncontrollable sensation, such as terror, arousal, and despair (Williams 1991: 603). These gratuitous scenes in *Saw* are legion.[1] The directors of the first film in the *Saw* franchise, Leigh Whannell and James Wan, point to 2004 as the year that "extreme horror" like the earlier, ghettoized *Cannibal Holocaust* (Ruggero, 1980) or *The Evil Dead* (Raimi, 1981) became palatable to mainstream audiences. After the self-reflexivity of *Scream* (Craven, 1996), the teen-targeted *I Know What You Did Last Summer* (Gillespie, 1997) and the parodic *Scary Movie* (Wayans, 2000), films such as *House of 1000 Corpses* (Zombie, 2003), the remake of *The Texas Chainsaw Massacre* (Nispel, 2003), *Dawn of the Dead* (Snyder, 2005) and *The Hills Have Eyes* (Aja, 2006) as well as *Saw* and *Hostel* (Roth, 2005), were seen as the standard bearer of a new, commercially driven body horror genre, in which the malleability of the human body and its violent, traumatic breaching could be displayed both as a physical manifestation of the fear of corporeal attack and the promise of an almost-pornographic pleasure in seeing the body opened up in increasingly graphic ways. If body horror privileges the body as the focal point of both pleasure and pain, then *Saw* bridges these two conflicting responses, appealing to the spectator on a fundamentally visceral level.

Saw represented the reemergence of a visceral horror style in American cinema, and its arrival was accompanied by a vigorous ongoing commentary on its meaning, its political persuasions, and its role as an explicit cultural response to a particular moment in American politics. Many critics have argued that the *Saw* franchise reflects prevalent social attitudes and cultural fears and concerns; tapping into what horror novelist Stephen King once called "national phobic pressure points" (King 1981: 5). In a 2010 interview, Whannell recalls the political climate that formed the backdrop to the release of the first *Saw*:

I think at the time *Saw* came out, the world was a very anxious place [...] I think people were being confronted, especially here in America, with things that are difficult to face up to. Like the American government being accused of these backroom dealings, and giving orders to soldiers about how to treat detainees. Guantanamo Bay, all that stuff was really beginning around that time, 2004, 2005. [...] Maybe people subconsciously vent about things they can't bear to think about, and maybe horror films do reflect that. I guess it can't be a coincidence that all these extreme horror films were popular at a time when there was all this extreme stuff going on in the world [Tobias 2010].

To be sure, this idea that films reflect particular political contexts has been around since Siegfried Kracauer's *From Caligari to Hitler* (1947), and has since guided much social film history. Kracauer argued that the cinema of the 1920s Weimar Republic (incidentally, horror films like *The Cabinet of Doctor Caligari* [1920], *Nosferatu* [1922], and *Dr. Mabuse the Gambler* [1922]) offered a unique insight into the collective mindset of post–World War I Germany, and that by dint of their collective conception and mass consumption, such films reflected society more accurately than other arts forms and offered insights into the mindset of their audience. Kracauer's conclusions, that "what films reflect are not so much explicit credos as psychological dispositions— those deep layers of mentality which extend more or less below the dimension of consciousness" (Kracauer 1947: 6), represents the classic reflectionist model.

Horror cinema's ability to tap into national trauma and its capacity to function as a politically charged allegory is a familiar discursive paradigm, and one that has been applied persuasively to many different types of horror films. As Andrew Tudor reminds us, the most common assumption about the specificity of the horror film is that their "thematic features can be treated as articulations of the felt social concerns of the time" (Tudor 2002: 50). Tudor's example is one well-known to the horror discourse— that 1950s American science-fiction horror films (*The Thing from Another World* [1951], *Them!* [1954], *Invasion of the Body Snatchers* [1956]) are on the surface a thematic treatment of alien invasion or the risks of nuclear power, but also mount a deeper interrogation of specific contemporaneous fears, such as "xenophobia, anti-communism, [and] anxiety about technocracy and mass society" (Tudor 2002: 51). David J. Skal goes back even further in American horror film history, and noticed that the makeup used by Lon Chaney in *The Hunchback of Notre Dame* (1923) and *The Phantom of the Opera* (1925) "bore more than a passing resemblance to the faces of the *mutilés de guerre* that haunted Europe and America" following World War I; a multitude of men "with smashed features, missing noses, and mouths full of broken teeth" (Skal 1993: 66). Robin Wood also applied this discourse to the popularity of the slasher film in 1970s

America, reading the resurgence of horror in *Last House on the Left* (1972) and *The Texas Chainsaw Massacre* (1974) as a return of the culturally and politically repressed in post–Vietnam War society.

More recently, David Edelstein, commenting on the upsurge in extreme, prolonged graphic torture, abduction, rape and dismemberment in films such as *The Devil's Rejects* (2005) and *Hostel* (2005) — as well as the first *Saw* film — coined the term "torture porn" to describe how these films consciously reflected post–9/11 and post–Abu Ghraib anxieties. As part of a post–9/11 American horror subgenre, these works combine "explicit scenes of torture and mutilation [with] terrific production values and a place of honour in your local multiplex" (Edelstein 2006) to confront willing audiences with visceral, grotesque imagery and implicit political content. Evangelos Tziallas also sees the torture porn sub-genre as representative of a post–9/11 anxiety, arguing that it has more to do with surveillance and the cultural consequences of surveillance. For Tziallas, Jigsaw is a metaphor for the Bush-era conservative panopticon; "He is 'judge, jury and executioner' rolled into one" (Tziallas 2010). Whether consciously inserted or not, such image-appropriations of Abu Ghraib, extraordinary rendition, and the torture of terror suspects by successive directors meant that both *Saw* and *Hostel* rapidly became fertile literal and figurative sites; on the one hand they abided by strict generic rules and framed their horrors in increasingly imaginative ways; on the other, they barometrically indicated specific national concerns and afflictions, deconstructing the perceived integrity of the human body to symbolic effect.

Body Horror à la française

The return of the body horror genre in recent times has not only been confined to America. Other international cinemas, in Japan, Britain, Australia, Korea and Latin America, have explored, often extremely, the realms of biological dystopia and corporeal impairment. This wave of body horror can be contextualized within the increasing cross-cultural nature of contemporary horror cinema (remakes, industrial migration, commercial viability of genre), but there are also political inflections. Contemporary body horror films frequently express a deep suspicion of the "outsider," generally personified by the malicious individual(s) whose motives remain inexplicable or pathologically brutal. Such films — whether *Wolf Creek* (McLean, 2005) or *Eden Lake* (Watkins, 2008) — serve as a bellwether reflecting a fearfulness of the ramifications of flows and movements across and through national frontiers and "bodies."

Indeed, before looking more closely at *Saw* and its sustained deployment of the body horror aesthetic, it is worth looking across the Atlantic, to France, where at roughly the same time as the *Saw* franchise, an equally visceral strain of body horror was developing, and was layered with political codings. Anyone observing the fluctuating trends in recent French cinema will have noticed the emergence of a corpus of films that thrives on unsettling the audience on a visceral, violent level. According to Tim Palmer, the agenda of this aggressive *cinéma du corps*, "is an on-screen interrogation of physicality in brutally intimate terms" (Palmer 2006a: 171). The narratives in films like *La Vie Nouvelle/ A New Life* (2002), *Trouble Every Day* (2001) and *Irréversible/Irreversible* (2002) blend the high art elements associated with their auteur directors (Philippe Grandrieux, Claire Denis, Gaspar Noé) with images of the pornographic and the abject, provocatively exploring issues of sexual, gender, and body politics within a global post-modern culture, and seek to engage in new modes of conceptually dynamic film-making. James Quandt (2004) has described these types of film as examples of the "New French Extremity," or a "cinema suddenly determined to break every taboo, to wade in rivers of viscera and spumes of sperm, to fill each frame with flesh, nubile or gnarled, and subject it to all manner of penetration, mutilation, and defilement." While other critics in France have suggested that these films do not reproduce images of "body horror" in the Cronenbergian or J-Horror sense (but rather embrace images of the corporeal and the abject in order to interrogate issues such as sexual violence, female emancipation, and the crisis of masculinity), it is clear that these films are combining a purely sensational *mise en scène* with a move towards framing the body within a sensuous, almost transcendental register.

There is another branch of *cinéma du corps* that trades far more aggressively in the kinds of imagery familiar to the *Saw* franchise — the French gore/ slasher cinema, or *nouveau splatter*. These pure genre films, which include works like *Martyrs* (Laugier, 2008), *La Meute/The Pack* (Richard, 2010), *Mutants* (Morlet, 2009), *Ils/Them* (Moreau & Palud, 2006), *À l'intérieur/Inside* (Bustillo & Maury, 2007) and *Frontière(s)/Frontiers* (Gens, 2007) form the vanguard of a new horror movement that has been enthusiastically greeted by both French and non–French audiences and has maneuvered itself into a position to overtake comedy as the genre best equipped to challenge consensual, recuperative versions of recent French socio-political debates. Matt Smith has noted that these films represent the French equivalent of the *Saw*-style body horror genre, and are obsessed with the body both social and corporeal:

> As the French seem intent to prove, it is not our corporeal existence that should be held sacred — [their] insistence on showing anything and everything is evidence of this. The body is meant to be examined, explicitly and externally, to deepen our understanding of our own humanity ... and what we hope lies in wait for us at the end of it all [Smith 2011].

In particular, the three films *Ils*, *À l'intérieur* and *Frontière(s)* are each unrelenting in their tonal and narrative components and are engaged in a fascinating dialogue with recent political and social events in France, grafting metaphors of border porosity and domestic invasion onto their narratives of visual excess. What characterizes these horror films are claustrophobic atmospheres of anxiety, events taking place within naturalistic surroundings, and a sense of unease emanating from the supposed normality of the diegetic world. Moreover, they are profoundly nihilistic, bespeaking an ideological emptiness at the heart of modern French society. The monsters in these films, whether murderous children (*Ils*), a female serial killer (*À l'intérieur*), or neo–Nazi cannibals (*Frontière[s]*) are all projections of a particular set of fears that does not correspond with the dominant paradigms of modern existence (stability, civility, orthodoxy) but rather embody modes of disruption that threaten the consensual frameworks of modern French society. If the blood and gore in *Frontiere(s)* is designed "to satiate even the most ravenous gore hounds" (Dargis 2008), then it, via this precise appropriation of generic codes and archetypes, enables the recent French films to traumatize audiences by juxtaposing images of the unwatchable and the unspeakable with uncomfortably familiar sociopolitical nuances.

Modern French horror films — like their American counterparts — all share a deep suspicion towards the outsider, generally personified by the malicious individual(s) whose motives remain inexplicable, contradictory or pathologically brutal. As such, they serve as a bellwether reflecting a profound skepticism towards the broadening of the European Union and a fearfulness of the ramifications of flows and movements across and through French frontiers. Horror films have now emerged as a new means of projecting particular fears and threats that destabilize the perceived dominant consensual paradigms of contemporary existence in France. What they finally suggest is that those paradigms of stability, civility, orthodoxy and superiority are in fact a fallacy, and that modern France is an increasingly paranoid realm subtended by the atavistic, the irrational, and above all, the primal.

This New French Extremity, which incorporates the *cinéma du corps* and the slasher film both offer, according to Palmer, "incisive social critiques, portraying contemporary society as isolating, unpredictably horrific and threatening. [...] In the age of the jaded spectator, the cynical cinéphile, this brutal intimacy model is a test case for film's continued potential to inspire [...] raw, unmediated reaction" (Palmer 2006b: 22). *Ils*, *À l'intérieur* and *Frontière(s)* mark the incorporation of an aggressively politically inflected discourse into a popular genre, in turn imbuing it with ideologically progressive or recuperative resonances. These horror films situate their horrors in the immediacy of contemporary France — both *À l'intérieur* and *Frontière(s)* contain images of the autumn riots of 2005 that engulfed the nation for nearly a month — and suggest that the physical destruction of the body in these films allegorizes fractures in the national body politic.

Both *Ils* and *A l'intérieur* conform to Andrew Tudor's definition of paranoid horror (1989). Tudor suggests that there are two traditions of horror fiction — secure and paranoid. Secure horror is structured around clear oppositions: the threat is external, human action is meaningful, the "monster" is defeated and narrative closure is guaranteed. Paranoid horror, on the other hand, is patterned around less clearly marked binaries: the threat is internal, human action is unsuccessful, doubt is pervasive and the narrative remains unresolved, implying a continuing spiral of escalation.[2] Thus France's own fears of excessive immigration and social destabilization are encoded in the narrative patterns of paranoid horror. Both films refuse traditional resolution, restoration or a cathartic overpowering of horror, and instead destabilize audience expectations and promote discourses of nihilism and rupture.

Mary Douglas, Saw, and the Transgression of Boundaries

As Gabrielle Murray notes, critics have seen the horror genre as historically "functioning like a Richter scale, charting the unease in society of generational subconscious fears" (Murray 2008). In both the aforementioned French films and the *Saw* series, the breachability of borders and boundaries is a fundamental fear, and one that is relentlessly exploited both on a narrative and a visual level. The work of British anthropologist Mary Douglas is useful in conceptualizing this cultural and corporeal role of boundaries and borders. In her seminal work *Purity and Danger: An Analysis of Concepts of Pollution and Taboo* (1966), Douglas writes about ritual cleanness and uncleanness, and the role that rituals of purity and pollution have played, and continue to play, in both advanced and primitive societies. She also notes that abominations, restriction, and punishment represent the power of social boundaries, and argues that ritual pollution reinforces the society's structure and sense of order, and comes to the defense of the boundaries of that structure whenever they are under threat.

For Douglas, the idea of pollution seeks to maintain the status quo in spite of whatever forces threaten it. She also explores the meaning of dirt in different social and linguistic contexts, and argues that dirt is matter considered out of place:

> [D]irt is essentially disorder. There is no such thing as absolute dirt: it exists in the eye of the beholder. If we shun dirt, it is not because of craven fear, still less dread or holy terror. Nor do our ideas about disease account for the range of our

behaviour in cleaning or avoiding dirt. Dirt offends against order. [...] For I believe that ideas about separating, purifying, demarcating and punishing transgressions have as their main function to impose system on an inherently untidy experience [Douglas 1966: 2–4].

Douglas's arguments are developed over ten chapters, with titles such as "Ritual Uncleanness," "Secular Defilement," and "The System at War with Itself." She writes that bodily orifices sometimes seem to represent points of entry or exit to social units and that any structure of ideas is vulnerable at its margins. Because the margins of the body are the areas of greatest breachability, it is normal to expect the body's orifices to symbolize its most vulnerable points. In the chapter "External Boundaries," Douglas proposes a model of the body that is a metaphor for society. The body is a microcosm of the social body, and thus a symbol of society:

> The body is a model which can stand for any bounded system. Its boundaries can represent any boundaries which are threatened or precarious. The body is a complex structure. The functions of its different parts and their relation afford a source of symbols for other complex structures [Douglas 1966: 115].

Thus the ordering and arranging of the physical body replicates the mechanisms of social structuring: the control of the corporeal body is an expression of social body, and concerns with bodily orifices duplicates social concerns. As Douglas wrote in her later work, *Natural Symbols*,

> Interest in its (the body's) apertures depends on the preoccupation with social exits and entrances, escape routes and invasion. If there is no concern to preserve social boundaries, I would not expect to find concern with bodily boundaries [1973: 98–99].

Therefore, representations of the body as unregulated and out-of-control indicate traumatic ruptures within the social fabric. Douglas contemplates the margins of the bounded body as representative of any boundary, border or threshold that is threatened. Because the margins define the social structure, they must always be protected to preserve the integrity of the whole. Holes in the boundary (or orifices in the body) are particularly vulnerable. In the context of *Saw*, Douglas' ideas are particularly revealing, for they attest to the ways in which particular groups and individuals under threat will always attempt to preserve the integrity of individual and social body. Bodily boundaries and openings are a major preoccupation of the films — each of Jigsaw's traps place the body in a position of peril, and many of their intricate mechanisms eventually pull the body apart. The most frightening aspect of *Saw* is that the bodies' internal boundaried structures are persistently jeopardized by the traps that engulf the body and threaten its integrity. No protection is offered: the fleshy body — like the social body at risk from what Douglas sees as pollution and contamination — is at risk from invasion.

The *Saw* series undoubtedly extends the "domestic invasion" trope that has long been a common expository element in American horror cinema (*Halloween* [1978], *When a Stranger Calls* [1979], *A Nightmare on Elm Street* [1984]). Such scenarios are always politically charged, for, as Steffan Hantke suggests, "The privacy of the home also stands for the integrity of the bourgeois patriarchal family [...] will the family stand up to the pressure? Can it be defended [...] is it even worth defending?"³ Jigsaw is a threatening force imposed on the inside from without, and works seemingly at random and without warning. This tendency throughout *Saw* to focus on an internal destabilizing domestic threat brings into focus Douglas' observations on the transgression of boundaries. While most of these threats in the series take place in hermetically sealed rusting warehouses or deserted, post-industrial backrooms, *Saw IV*'s main action takes place in the outside world. Rigg's "game" involves the torture of six citizens. By now, Jigsaw's contagion — or "pollution," to cite Douglas — has spread from the fictional world to the real world; we are all potential victims now. Dana B. Polan has argued that much of the significance of modern horror lies in the suggestion that "horror is not something from out there, something strange, marginal, *ex*-centric, the mark of a force from out there, the inhuman." Rather, he continues, contemporary horror films suggest "that the horror is not merely among us, but rather part of us, caused by us" (Polan 2004: 143). Jigsaw is no exception to Polan's schema.

Following on from Douglas" thinking on the transgression of boundaries, two other interlinked theoretical approaches centered on the horrific are worth mentioning. Noël Carroll in *The Philosophy of Horror* (1990) argues that the horror monster disturbs the natural order by being interstitial and impure. Jigsaw's monstrous status fits this template of the monster who is able to seemingly appear and reappear at will (even when he "dies" in *Saw III*, he returns, like all archetypal monsters, to wreak havoc in the four subsequent sequels), refusing to honor the sanctity of borders and barriers and disseminating himself seamlessly through time and space. Throughout the series, Jigsaw is presented as omnipresent and unstoppable — an implacable monster.

Julia Kristeva's "Powers of Horror: An Essay on Abjection," observes that

> It is thus not lack of cleanliness or health that causes abjection but what disturbs identity, system, order. What does not respect borders, positions, rules. The in-between, the ambiguous, the composite. The traitor, the liar, *the criminal with a good conscience*, the shameless rapist, *the killer who claims he is a savior* [Kristeva 1982: 4; my emphasis].

This serves as a useful description of Jigsaw's motivations, as well as his symbolic role as the disturber of order and rules. He is a transgressive figure whose identity remains a secret for much of the franchise. In *Saw II*, he states "I've never murdered anyone in my life. The decisions are up to them" (so, strictly speaking, he is not a serial killer). Here he fits Kristeva's description of a killer who tests his victims' will to live. For Kristeva, we are both drawn to and repelled by the abject, and it is because of this sensation that "one thus understands why so many victims of the abject are its fascinated victims — if not its submissive and willing ones" (Kristeva 1982: 9). In the *Saw* franchise, this combination of desire and disgust emerges over and over again, as we endlessly watch excessive and dehumanizing attacks on the body. Douglas, Carroll and Kristeva each obliquely clarify Western horror cinema's continual obsession with the notion of the body, both corporeal and social. Body horror "graphically enact[s] perhaps the most dreadful apocalypse of all — the perpetual intimate apocalypse of the human body revealed not as a consolidated and impregnable citadel, but as a flexible assemblage that disallows for illusions of corporeal integrity or of the sovereignty of the human form" (McRoy 2005: 6). It is this fear, of borders transgressed, and bodies ruptured, that highlights Douglas's central concern, that "bodily control is an expression of social control" (Douglas 1970: 70). Once that bodily control breaks down, the social fabric is terrorized — and that is where Jigsaw steps in, to fill the void.

Saw *and the* Mise en Scène *of Body Horror*

> *We humans [...] hide from the frightening reality of our fragile innards by believing in the strength of plastic and supermarkets. Yet we [are] fascinated, as we have always been, by blood and tissue and bone.* —Vivian Sobchack

If the traumatized or distressed body signifies a rupture within the social fabric, then spilt blood is a symbolic marker of the health of society. French historian René Girard has outlined how spilt blood is usually associated with the impure and that "when men are enjoying peace and security, blood is a rare sight. When violence is unloosed, however, blood appears to be everywhere — on the ground, underfoot, forming great pools" (Girard 1995: 34). *Saw* positively drowns in blood; it pours out of brutalized bodies, which in turn reflects masculine ineffectuality and impotence and, in the words of Douglas, the "enfeebling" of the whole system (Douglas 1966: 126).

Because the *Saw* films "use excess to express the trauma inflicted on the American national consciousness" (Tziallas 2010), many of the traditional genre elements of the horror film are incorporated into their narrative and tonal structure. Before each film begins, the words of the production company — Twisted Pictures — are tangled by a coil of barbed wire and then impaled by a metal spike. The spike is then rotated, tightening the barbed wire and gouging deep scars into the letters. These are films, it appears, in which primitive instruments will be deployed to wreak simple, effective violence. Muted color tones dominate — this is a gloomy world of browns, grays, and greens, and as typifies a world of invisible foes and bodily apocalypse, *mise en scène* functions as a marker of the forthcoming inevitability of corporeal disintegration. The films take place in predominantly deserted industrial buildings — an abandoned mannequin factory in *Saw* and an old steelworks in *Saw II* — that are precise locations for the performing of explicit, exploitative acts on the body. Far away from the civilizing, normative spaces of urban centers, the body horror in *Saw* takes place in liminal, post-industrial sites (similar to the deserted farms and rural woods of *Deliverance* [Boorman, 1972] and *The Texas Chainsaw Massacre* [Hooper, 1974]).

The murky *mise en scène* in *Saw* is designed to evoke dread both in the characters shortly to be subjected to torture and in the spectator. In Elaine Scarry's seminal work on torture, *The Body in Pain*, she discusses this issue: "The room, both in its structure and its content, is converted into a weapon, deconverted, undone. Made to participate in the annihilation of the prisoners, made to demonstrate that everything is a weapon, the objects themselves, and with them the fact of civilization, are annihilated: there is no wall, no window, no door, no bathtub, no refrigerator, no chair, no bed" (Scarry 1985: 41). Body horror takes places in the most banal of settings — and is part of a graphic film tradition which uses excessive imagery of torture and corporeal degradation to express a series of traumas inflicted on the national consciousness.

Saw and Post-9/11

"Each era," writes Frank McConnell, "chooses the monster it deserves and projects" (1975: 137). Post-9/11, the monster is Jigsaw. As we have already mentioned, critics have been eager to draw parallels between the *Saw* series and contemporary historical circumstances; namely, that *Saw* is "about" a post-9/11 America. If, as we have suggested, body horror deploys the annihilation of the flesh to critique the social fabric, the events in *Saw*, *Hostel*, and *Captivity* (Joffé, 2007), in which people are kidnapped for reasons beyond their knowledge, and then summarily detained, confined, and tortured, seems to resonate all too loudly with contemporary domestic geo-political debates. Such diagrammatic connections between horror and reality certainly have some validity — Matt Hills reminds us of the orange jumpsuit Donnie Wahlberg wears in *Saw IV* that is a visual echo of Guantanamo Bay prisoners, or the threats of torture to extract information in *Saw II* — but Hills continues by noting how there is no one, clear, unambiguous reading of the *Saw* films: Jigsaw can stand "both for the Bush administration's defense of 'righteous torture' and for terroristic radicalization" (Hills 2011: 118). Such doubling pervades the *Saw* series, and suggests that singular cultural contexts via which we can read the films and interpret what they are about needs to be replaced with a more nuanced appreciation of the multiple meanings of *Saw*.

However, these reflectionist readings persist, and critics have identified numerous horror films that have attempted to anatomize how America has responded to 9/11. Tracing the iconography of recent horror films, Kevin J. Wetmore argues that the depiction of planes falling from the sky in *Vanishing on 7th Street* (Anderson, 2010), falling bodies in *The Happening* (Shyamalan, 2008), and malevolent clouds in *The Mist* (Darabont, 2007) are all conscious requisitions of images of 9/11 by filmmakers that allow audiences the opportunity to "re-experience [9/11] under safer conditions or with a different ending" (Wetmore 2012: 24). Evangelos Tziallas maintains that the *Saw* series exemplifies contemporary discourses on surveillance, and "allegorizes larger cultural and political trends in panoptic (the few watching the many) and synoptic (the many watching the few) subjectivities" (Tziallas 2010). Read allegorically, the former may be read as anti–American terrorists (who may or may not have, at some point since 9/11, breached national borders and plotted an attack on the body politic from within) and the latter as the American governmental response to 9/11 via the Patriot Act and other surveillance protocols and policies which granted governmental agencies unprecedented freedom to surveil and investigate individuals they suspected of being involved with terrorism. This use of surveillance to break down privacy and to bolster institutional power runs through *Saw*, via the use of technology (cameras, mobile phones, computers, tape recorders) and the all-seeing techniques of CCTV surveillance.

Conclusion

The *Saw* films situate horror in the everyday world of contemporary America but do not project that horror onto a foreign invader. To borrow Robin Wood's phrase, these films represent the "collective nightmare" (Wood 1978: 19) of a nation undergoing social and political fragmentation, condemning itself to annihilation while the "barbarian at the gate" pushes at the edges. Certainly the emotional and ethical resonances of *Saw* suggest consonances with the French *cinéma du corps* of the late 1990s and early 2000s, but whereas those films were deliberately, almost archly, philosophical in their explorations of physicality, the corporeal and the abject, the *Saw* franchise — like some of the more delirious entries in the French splatter canon — cleave much closer to the conventional body horror tropes of American cinema. The franchise may seek to interrogate deeper cultural and political anxieties, but they are also careful to satisfy their core audience, offer up graphic spectacle, seek worldwide distribution for their films, and gain praise (or notoriety) as proponents of popular genre cinema in a cinematic climate that has always jealously guarded the psychological and intimate concerns of *auteur* cinema. Ultimately, *Saw* articulates more than just the mechanics and machinery of gore and guts. As those bones crunch and the screams rise, the fear of the Other, the fear of invasion, and the fear of corporeal pollution all come into sharp focus. As surgeon Lawrence Gordon reminds us, Jigsaw "doesn't want us to cut through his chains; he wants us to cut through our feet." Body horror, like Jigsaw, has its own set of rules.

Notes

1. For a full list of the all of the deaths in the seven *Saw* films, go to http://horror-movies.wikia.com/wiki/List_of_deaths_in_the_Saw_series.
2. For Tudor, "secure horror" covers the 1930s to the 1950s, while "paranoid horror" is the dominant trend from the 1970s onwards.
3. Hantke is writing about Michael Haneke's *Funny Games* (1997), in which a bourgeois family is terrorized and eventually murdered by two boys.

References

Dargis, Manohla. "After Making It Out of Paris, There's No Escape." *New York Times*, 9 May 2008.
Douglas, Mary. *Natural Symbols*. New York: Vintage, 1973.
_____. *Purity and Danger: An Analysis of Concepts of Pollution and Taboo*. London: Ark, 1966.
Edelstein, David. "Now Playing at Your Local Multiplex: Torture Porn: Why Has America Gone Nuts for Blood, Guts and Sadism." *New York Magazine*, 6 February 2006.
Freud, Sigmund. "The Uncanny," in *The Uncanny*. New York: Penguin, 2003, pp. 123–162.
Girard, René. *Violence and the Sacred*. London: Althone, 1995.
Hantke, Steffan. "Funny Games," in *100 European Horror Films*, edited by Steven Jay Scheider, London: BFI, 2007, p. 92.
Hills, Matt. "Cutting into Concepts of 'Reflectionist' Cinema?: The *Saw* Franchise and Puzzles of Post-9/11 Horror," in *Horror After 9/11: World of Fear, Cinema of Terror*, edited by Aviva Briefel and Sam J. Miller, 107–23. Austin: University of Texas Press, 2011.
Hurley, Kelly. "Reading Like an Alien: Posthuman Identity in Ridley Scott's *Alien* and David Cronenberg's *Rabid*," in *Posthuman Bodies*, edited by Judith Halberstam and Ira Livingston, 203–224. Indianapolis: Indiana University Press, 1995.
Kellner, Douglas. *Cinema Wars: Hollywood Film and Politics in the Bush-Cheney Era*. Oxford: Wiley-Blackwell, 2010.
King, Stephen. *Danse Macabre*. New York: Everest House, 1981.
Kracauer, Siegfried. *From Caligari to Hitler: A Psychological Study of the German Film*. Princeton, NJ: Princeton University Press, 1947.
Kristeva, Julia. *Powers of Horror: An Essay on Abjection*. New York: Columbia University Press, 1982.

Magistrale, Tony. *Abject Terrors: Surveying the Modern and Postmodern Horror Film*. London: Peter Lang, 2005.
McConnell, Frank. *The Spoken Seen: Film and the Romantic Imagination*. Baltimore: Johns Hopkins University Press, 1975.
McRoy, Jay. "Introduction," in *Japanese Horror Cinema*, edited by Jay McRoy, 1–11. Edinburgh: Edinburgh University Press, 2005.
Tim Palmer, "Style and Sensation in the Contemporary French Cinema of the Body," *Journal of Film and Video*, 58(3), 2006b, pp. 22–32.
_____. "Under Your Skin: Marina de Van and the Contemporary French *cinéma du corps*." *Studies in French Cinema*, vol. 6 (3), 2006a, pp. 171–181.
Polan, Dana B. "Eros and Syphilization: The Contemporary Horror Film: in *Planks of Reason: Essays on the Horror Film*, edited by Barry Keith Grant and Christopher Sharrett, 142–52. Lanham, Toronto and Oxford: Scarecrow, 2004.
Quandt, James. "Flesh and Blood: Sex and Violence in Recent French Cinema." *Art Forum*, February 2004. http://findarticles.com/p/articles/mi_m0268/is_6_42/ai_113389507 (accessed 20 May 2008).
Scarry, Elaine. *The Body in Pain: The Making and Unmaking of the World*. New York: Oxford University Press, 1985.
Skal, David J. *The Monster Show: A Cultural History of Horror*. New York: W.W. Norton, 1993.
Smith, Matt. "Confronting Mortality: 'The New French Extremity,'" the *Hostel* Series and Outdated Terminology." *The Split Screen* (Part 2 of 3), http://thesplitscreen.wordpress.com/2011/06/28/confronting-mortality-the-new-french-extremity-the-hostel-series-and-outdated-terminology-part-2-of-3/ (accessed 12 September 2012).
Tobias, Scott. "Interview with Leigh Scannell and James Wan." *AV Club*, 29 October 2010 http://www.avclub.com/articles/saw-creators-leigh-whannell-and-james-wan,46975/ (accessed 12 September 2012).
Tudor, Andrew. *Monsters and Mad Scientists: A Cultural History of the Horror Movie*. Blackwell: Oxford, 1989.
_____. "Why Horror? The Peculiar Pleasures of a Popular Genre," in *Horror: The Film Reader*, edited by Mark Jancovich, 47–56. New York: Routledge, 2002.
Sobchack, Vivian. "The Violent Dance: A Personal Memoir of Death in the Movies." *Graphic Violence on the Screen*. Ed. Thomas R. Atkins, 79–96. New York: Monarch, 1976.
Tziallas, Evangelos. "Torture porn and surveillance culture." *Jump Cut*, http://www.ejumpcut.org/currentissue/evangelosTorturePorn/index.html (accessed 12 September 2012).
Wetmore, Kevin J. *Post-9/11 Horror in American Cinema*. London: Continuum, 2012.
Williams, Linda. "Film Bodies: Gender, Genre, Excess." *Film Theory and Criticism*, 7th ed., edited by Leo Braudy and Marshall Cohen, 649–657. New York: Oxford University Press, 2009.
Wood, Robin. "Gods and Monsters." *Film Comment* 14:5 (1978), 19–25.

The Spectacle of Correction: Video Games, Movies and Control
Evangelos Tziallas

In a previous publication titled "Torture Porn and Surveillance Culture,"[1] I argued that the "torture porn" subgenre was engaging with the praxis of political and cultural surveillance. In this essay, I would like to revisit my earlier publication and revise, further contextualize and rearticulate some of my previous observations, sentiments and arguments, honing in on how the series uses the spectacle of correction to anxiously engage with the discourse and experience of control as it is configured in contemporary surveillance saturated control societies. Most importantly, I would like to focus on how the series discursively incorporates "gamification" as a conduit and consider some of the negative and positive ramifications which arise from this absorption.

I argue that what differentiates the *Saw* series from other "torture porn" films and the horror genre in general is its emphasis on correction, rather than simple punishment and death. Unlike other horror films where the goal is to kill as a way to punish, in the *Saw* series, the goal is to correct, to discipline people back into proper order. But this correction is contingent upon surveillance expressed through technology, becoming the grammar of informatics. The series' visual and narrative strategies present viewers with anxious meditations on both the invasiveness of new technologies and their, at times, less than obvious abilities to correct and control under the guise of creating new forms of interactivity and entertainment. Although the series is an offspring of the serial killer detective genre and capitalizes on the genre's puzzle-solving formula,[2] the *Saw* series evolves the game playing narrative by structuring it according to video game logic and by absorbing video game iconographies and aesthetics into its mise-en-scène. What makes the series an important contemporary popular cultural artifact to be further studied is the way it merges the discourse, representation and function of gamification and surveillance (/-technologies). As Catherine Zimmer argues, "The more obvious *intent* of the [surveillance] video technology for the Jigsaw character is to function as an organizational methodology serving to produce and control responses."[3] Building on this, I argue that as the series evolves, it intensifies its emulation of video games, deploying gamification as a critical allegory, visualizing and attempting to simulate contemporary control society's capabilities to correct and control via seemingly innocuous entertainment technologies.

But if the goal is to reveal contemporary forms of control and correction, if the spectacle of excessive bodily violence is a product of playing twisted games which are meant to leverage visceral affect as a form of a critique, is this goal inherently undercut by the series' status as a spectacle? I wish to use this paradigm as a framework to explore the series' ambiguities, ambivalences and engagements, rather than simply point out its failings and limitations. I argue that although the films are not "resistant" in the traditional sense,[4] if we frame them as "critical dystopias," it creates a space for thinking about the critical potentials of the series, as well as films and genres of similar liking, alongside its shortcomings and complicities.

Surveillance, Control and the Spectacle of Correction

In the last few years, there has been an influx of publications on the torture porn sub-genre circulating through academic and intellectual circles. Works in *Jump Cut*,[5] *Cine Action*,[6] *Cinema Journal*,[7] *CineEast*,[8] *Critical Quarterly*,[9] and *Popular Communication*,[10] to name a few, testify to the sub-genre's seductiveness and ability to provoke. Broadly speaking these investigations revealed a rich source of criticism about contemporary American cinema and culture, likewise revealing deeply rooted anxieties in the American social consciousness about the future of America and American culture.

My study attempted to address these concerns, but filtered through the discourse of surveillance. I argued that the sub-genre was about the fear of surveillance, expressing intense anxieties over the spread of invasive and ubiquitous recording and monitoring technologies, their respective political rhetoric which buttress them as necessities, and their refashioned uses as sources of, and methods for producing, entertainment. In my previous article I talked extensively about surveillance, pan/synopticism and discipline, but much less so about control. Here, I would like to continue to talk about surveillance as a system which, when reconfigured through computer technology and reformatted as informatics, evolves disciplinarity to a system of virtual, mobile, and loose control, and its relationship to the discourse and spectacle of correction. Of particular interest to me was how the sub-genre appropriated kidnapping as a narrative strategy, capitalizing on the broader social "threat of being constantly, unknowingly watched and monitored, [and] the looming threat of potential 'correction' and punishment via abduction or torture."[11] Unlike typical slasher or horror films the goal is not death but calculated, elongated pain as a method of correction. It is this observation I would like to focus and expand upon.

It was Foucault's champion, Gilles Deleuze, whose short "Postscript on the Societies of Control"[12] sought to continue Foucault's line of reasoning about the disciplinary society as it evolved throughout the late twentieth century. Foucault's work focused exclusively on the modern era with nary a reference to contemporary configurations of surveillance or the role recent technology has played in these configurations. I argue the spectacles of corrections we witness in the *Saw* films highlight the tensions between traditional systems of surveillance and disciplinarity and new formations of control. Importantly, the series attempts to make transparent and confront us with the invisible networks which propel and expand the control society,[13] revealing how the prevalence and power of disciplinarity and panopticism are still retained in these new configurations.

In *Discipline and Punish*, Michel Foucault argued that during the Modern era, Western societies transitioned into "disciplinary societies." The "spectacle of the scaffold" was replaced with a system of observation and documentation which carefully balanced visibility and invisibility, conditioning individuals to perpetually monitor themselves. Foucault used Jeremy Bentham's Panopticon prison to demonstrate not just how modern society was structured according to similar principles, but, conversely, to highlight how his architectural utopia was the incarnation of modernity's reigning ideology. Building on his arguments and observations about surveillance, Foucault's *The History of Sexuality Vol. 1*, challenged the "repressive hypothesis" arguing that sexuality was contingent upon confession and western medicine/psychiatry, and inherently predicated on a system of surveillance. Sexuality's configuration as "biopower" was a key method for disseminating surveillance throughout modern society. Biopower inscribes a hierarchical organizing system of observation and documentation, tracking and producing normalcy and deviancy, efficiency and waste, injecting the will to knowledge and the need and ability to "correct" into every facet of existence. It is through knowing and controlling bodies, sex, procreation, pleasure and desire where everything can be defined and corrected.

For Deleuze, however, the industrial disciplinary society was a pre-computerized/ digitized society; we, however, are "societies of control," demarcated by "modulation," an endlessly adaptable system which has replaced modernity's spaces of enclosure. The system of modulation is maintained by the *password* and by (data-)*banks*, and rather than disciplining individuals into docile bodies, it is the formation of *dividuals*,[14] the creation of loose networks of control and the anchor of debt which sustain the control society. Post-industrial society is not organized the way industrial society was: the factory has been shipped off to China; the guard tower replaced by a camera (which may or may not be actually recording); spaces of enclosure replaced by GPS tracking devices; the archive and file cabinet by digital information banks housed in discreet warehouses; and institutions with neoliberal consumerism. Biopower and surveillance melded into machinery giving rise to the control society and its discursive tools. In the *Saw* films, technology penetrates and deforms the body in order to use the body to correct the victim's "soul." The films are visual and auditory pornographies of the implicit and often invisible violence of biopower as they are configured by technology in contemporary society. This highlights the collision between, and recent collusion of, traditional methods of corporeal medical/psychiatric observation which were subservient to human authority and neoliberal methods which emphasize helping one's self and making use of new technologies to empower and correct one's self.

The *Saw* series tells the story of the Jigsaw killer, an older man (John Kramer) diagnosed with terminal cancer who survives a suicide attempt and then sets about trying to teach others to "cherish your life," and his accomplices/converts Amanda Young and detective Mark Hoffman.[15] Prior to his crash, Jigsaw essentially gave up on life; it was only after he crashed his car and was forced to endure excruciating pain and save himself did he develop a newfound appreciation for it. Inspired by this method for rejuvenation verging on reincarnation, he decides to offer people drowning in their own malaise a similar opportunity. Jigsaw scopes out and monitors individuals, sets up elaborate, individualized, time contingent scenarios where people choose to either suffer extreme pain (and later on, difficult ethical situations about choosing who lives or dies) and live, or do nothing and die.

The revenge narrative allegorizes how surveillance functions in the control society. Jigsaw is the panopticon: he knows all and sees all and once the object of his gaze your newfound placement in his field of vision lands you in a literal trap. Like in the panopticon, characters never know they are being watched and yet they, along with audiences, know very well that there is always the looming presence of the surveillance gaze[16]; it is this anxiety which the series taps into and uses as both a narrative strategy and to critically engage. Victims end up in an enclosed space, under total observation, where the system of panopticism which was meant to instill self-surveillance as an automatic, self-regulating/disciplining process is spectacularly visualized; the ideology of panopticism and its implicit violence and violation is rendered transparent. Yet in making the process transparent it speaks to the failure of contemporary disciplinary mechanisms; had they functioned properly there wouldn't be a need for such graphic and overt correction. These extreme forms of correction are clearly not just about the individuals, but aimed at society's weak disciplining systems which have failed to properly instill self-surveillance.

The sense of the "individual succeeding against all odds," coupled with the "types" of people Jigsaw chooses to punish (drug users, self-mutilators, traitors of family/friends/justice, the over sexed) also makes Jigsaw a representative of both neoliberal and neoconservative values. A figural representative of the Bush Administration and biopower, Jigsaw seeks out those who are "victims" of "liberal culture," and gives them the opportunity to *correct themselves*. Jigsaw doesn't kill and neither does he correct; he simply puts people in a situation where they, of their own free will and muster, "pick themselves up by their own bootstraps." What we as spectators bear witness to is a series of intricately crafted sadistic behavior modification therapies; the entire *Saw* series turns the process of correction into a spectacle. True to torture's intention of "forced confession" and a perverse refashioning of psychotherapy's "free association," Jigsaw via a tape-recorder "confesses" on behalf of his patients. Victims have individualized therapies, sadistically tailored to reflect their failings and areas of needed improvement.[17] Successful completion of their therapy, however, does not bring them back to a prior state of being, but to a whole new one; they "are reborn." In many respects, Jigsaw is also a symbolic evangelical preacher on a mission to force various sinners to confess and repent for their sinful ways, become born again, and add converts to his congregation. The prevalence of vaginal weaponry[18] and coding of these torture/clinical spaces as vaginal transform torture into sinister gateways to salvation. The fusion of science, surveillance and religion speaks to the triumph of conservative rhetoric endemic in American politics after 9/11, and the violence of administering biopower in the name of social progress and cohesion.

As Jigsaw tries to justify his means to the police, he is likewise trying to both justify his position to the characters and audience, as well as point to the police's failings. This is similar to how superheroes supersede the law in order to justify their actions, with the series implicitly critiquing America's resurgent need for superheroes and zest for superhero blockbuster films during a period of social and political unease.[19] In this respect Jigsaw is also a vigilante, or perverse anti-superhero; instead of watching over the city and protecting citizens from villains, it is the citizens themselves who are the villains. Jigsaw intervenes in order to protect society from itself. Like the robots of *I Robot* whose job it is to kill humans in order to protect humans, contemporary society is committing suicide vis-à-vis of liberalism; liberalism is the disease, conservatism is the cure, and Jigsaw is the superhero-psychiatrist-priest who will save us from ourselves by forcing us to save ourselves from ourselves. This not only replicates the Bush Administration's dictum of partially turning the surveillance gaze from outside America's borders to inside America's borders, but intensifies the general "movement from external to internal surveillance [which occurred] throughout the seventies" in American society.[20] Importantly, it is also during this period (the 1970s) where computer, military and entertainment technologies were developing and advancing at a rapid rate, giving rise to the control society.

The process of bearing witness foregrounds the process of identification through observation, inviting audiences to contemplate their relationship to the images they see and the meaning of their experience. This invitation, however, is somewhat truncated as our gaze is inextricably filtered through Jigsaw, the figural panopticon, fusing his gaze and the cinematic camera's gaze. Although these spectacles may attempt to visualize how conservative rhetoric and politics are trying to correct us (the audience/spectator) their spectacularized presentation and affective goal has the potential to transplant this corrective discourse; a dialectical tension between "this is what is happening to you, wake up!" and "this is you and if you don't change yourself, this will happen to you!" is produced. The process of correction is inextricably bound to the process and discourse of cinematic identification and the changing nature of visual pleasure and narrative cinema[21]; in the case of the *Saw* films, the cinema's gamification as a process of potential new control, as correction is tethered to gamification. This correlation is made quite explicit in the third, but especially fourth film, where individual protagonists are forced to decide whether they will save a person of low moral character or someone who did them wrong, or let them die. We are invited to go through the protagonists' torturous situation, experiencing what they experience, seeing what they see, feeling what they feel. As detective Rigg makes his way through Jigsaw's games in *Saw IV*, Jigsaw's accomplices have left painted notes at various torture sites asking Rigg to "See What I See" in order to "Feel What I Feel." These notes are reflexive instructions. This is Jigsaw telling both the character and the spectator to see the world through his eyes in order to experience how his perceptions of the world make him feel. By filtering our experiences through him we will "see" how his games are justified and necessary; these are Jigsaw's true goals. By transparently announcing his control over the characters he likewise reveals his attempts to control the audience; as we identify and bear witness, we too are placed in this game world, forced to go along as well. There is a collapse between the cinematic spectator and the film's protagonist cum gamer.

But if we are forced to go along and if we can be convinced of Jigsaw's position, then we too become one of Jigsaw's converts. In essence, the tension between immersion and potential correction, and distanced observation and criticism crystallizes the paradox of the cinematic spectacle and its potential complicity with the thing or things it seeks to render transparent and neutralize. By using spectacle as a tool for confrontation, the series potentially renders it symptomatic. This is particularly problematic as the discourse, deployment, and representation of surveillance is a growing cultural, social and political reality. If concerns about surveillance are increasingly forming the zeitgeist, to what degree can films about surveillance and control, such as the *Saw* series, offer an alternative to that discourse which the cinema itself is so intimately bound to; as John Turner has argued, "The very medium of cinema itself can be understood as hyper surveillant."[22] This is particularly problematic since "many of the films that address the practice of surveillance or use of surveillance technologies in their narratives do so as an opportunity to celebrate the spectacle elements invested in surveillance or to integrate the use of surveillance as a narratival device to promote suspense and, subsequently, violence."[23] Surveillance can become a simple spectacle which is integrated into the narrative as a strategic device for inducing pleasure nullifying criticism.[24] Instead of critiquing surveillance we simply become accustomed to it.

For Guy Debord, "the spectacle" is controlling with this sentiment responding to the West's post-war rapid transformation into a consumer society where objects became idols and everyone was to willfully submit to the enslavement of capitalism and its images.[25] Years later, however, Foucault would famously argue that "our society is one not of spectacle, but of surveillance."[26] This ideological contention, as Martin Jay points out, is the difference between being the subject of the gaze (Debord) and the object of the gaze (Foucault),[27] with Deleuze seeking a middle ground, recognizing that the corporation's, the post-industrial control society's factory, "soul" is marketing.[28] In control societies spectacle, surveillance and marketing become a synonymous intersubjective experience.

Since Guy Debord and the Situationist International's socialist intervention, the "society of the spectacle" have increasingly been a point of contention amongst academics and the intelligentsia; this is particularly true in Film Studies as mainstream cinema is, essentially, a money making spectacle. In the 1970s, formal alternatives to Hollywood's studio system filmmaking were upheld as primary ways to resist the cinematic apparatus' complicity in implanting bourgeois capitalist ideology into the minds of its audiences (where it can be unconsciously replicated from within each subject, ensuring its hegemonic continuation). But the various strategies offered by film theorists and critics in the 1970s and 1980s no longer really apply as the cinema they spoke of no longer exists as such, and the "apparatus" as it was theorized has been thoroughly challenged and dismantled.[29] It is not my desire to advocate on behalf of, or reassert, apparatus theory's "imprisonment thesis," for as Alexander Galloway notes, "Flexibility is one of the core political principles of informatic control."[30] Rather, I wish to think about how the apparatus of gaming, how hardware figuratively, and at times literally, penetrates the cinematic apparatus and the consequences of this absorption. I argue that there is enough formal and narrative friction to open up a productive space to think about the series as something which is struggling with this current, or concurrent, transformation; the series is, in essence, almost struggling *with itself.* I believe that beyond the scenes of spectacular corrections the series both bedazzles and shocks us with, it is its complex engagement and intermingling with video games, their hardware, their software, their power, and their pleasures which simultaneously reveals an anxious, frustrated reaction to its own ambivalence. It revels in this new technology's pleasure as it struggles to resist its consuming seductiveness.

Video Games, Cinema, Gamification

> *"If* Pac-Man *had affected us as kids, we'd all be running around in dark rooms, munching pills and listening to repetitive electronic music."*[31]

Studies about video games have been around for decades, with research often coming from media studies and/or sociology, but it is only recently that it has become its own interdisciplinary field. As one of the latest manifestations of the moving image's technologically inspired evolution, it is no surprise that the field takes cinema "as an important point of reference."[32] It is commonplace that video games are largely inspired by the cinema, particularly early text-based and VGA adventure games, and later on "interactive movie" games such as *Phantasmagoria* and *Gabriel Knight 2*.[33] The success of early adventure games made narrative a cornerstone of the gaming experience and soon other genres — Shooting, Action and Simulation — made narrative an integral component of their quality, pleasure and thus critical and economic success. However, as many have argued and continue to argue,[34] video games are not simply extensions or reworkings of the cinema, but rather, unique forms in their own right which carry on certain cinematic legacies. Video/computer games are, after all, a product of computer language, of software, rather than cinematic language. But there has been increasing interest in academia about how video games have been potentially impacting the cinema, specifically, narrative-fiction film's structure, or, language. In his chapter, "S/Z, the 'Readerly' Film, and Video Game Logic," in *Studying Contemporary American Film: A Guide to Movie Analysis*, Warren Buckland and Thomas Elsaesser, using *The Fifth Element*, explore this reverse osmosis, fleshing out how contemporary narrative cinema's digitization has "adopted the rules and strategies of video games."[35] Building on Simon Gottschalk's "videology"[36] proposition, Buckland and Elsaesser lay out seven principles of video game logic that "only when combined together [do] they begin to dominate a film's narrative structure." It is precisely this logical system which simultaneously informs the *Saw* series' narrative structure, and as I will argue later, its mise-en-scène, cinematography and iconography, affording it an opportunity to reflect upon this integration's symbioses and frictions. If we breakdown their seven points, the *Saw* series' video game logistics become clearer:[37]

1. *Serialized repetition of actions (to accumulate points and master the rules).* Protagonists, and various victims, must unravel a personalized narrative as a way to contextualize themselves and piece together a map of sorts. Players must learn the rules of the game as they play the game in order to beat the game. Each death awards those who survive knowledge as "points."
2. *Multiple levels of adventure.* The solving of each clue or completion of each game leads to the next game and opens up new areas for exploration, ultimately guiding one to the end.
3. *Space-time warps.* The game spaces themselves are time warps; at once timeless and meticulously timed, and at once present, yet entirely invested in the past. Characters are playing these games under carefully monitored conditions and are forced to play these games because of something they did in the past; they are, in a sense, brought back in time in order to "correct" their errors or be punished for them. The multiple, and at times, confusing use of flashbacks, and Jigsaw's gamemaster voice-over likewise confuse a stable space-time continuum. Additionally, their existence is squarely within reality, yet perplexingly almost outside reality, mark the spaces as hyperreal, as *virtual*, only further confounding their space-time linearity and cohesion.
4. *Magical transformations and disguises.* Although by no means "magical," throughout the series, new victims-turned-accomplices are continuously revealed (Amanda, Detective Hoffman and even Dr. Gordon). Importantly, Jigsaw's "forced confessions" are meant to remove each character's "disguise" and render them transparent; to forcibly reveal their "true" selves. In addition, the various physical and emotional transformations characters go through during their "treatment" verge on the fantastical. In *Saw*, Dr. Gordon cuts off his foot (and survives), in *Saw V*, Brit saws her hand in half to survive, and the final *Saw 3D* revolves around characters recounting their personally designed torture games and their subsequent emotional/physical transformations cum deformations; and let's

not forget all the failed "transformations" we witness of those who can't/ don't correct themselves.

5. *Immediate rewards and punishment (which act as feedback loops).* Failure to win a game is instantly punished with death; winning a game is immediately rewarded with life. However, for those who do win, failure to learn from their victory, that is, failure to be corrected is immediately punished. Importantly, when characters "win," they, like video game players, are rewarded with a "cut-scene;" their "cut-scene" is their live witnessing of the torture and death of their opponent. Typically, game players are rewarded with a spectacular "cut-scene," a high-powered, cinematic mini film, when they beat a level or "boss," or achieve some major goal.[38] Spectacles of corrections as well as failures in the series further marry the characters-as-gamers and cinematic spectator.

6. *Pace.* Buckland and Elsaesser quote Nicholas Luppa's assertion that "pace is one of the most important features of video games" because video games "require pacing and the beats that are being counted in that pacing are the beats between interactions."[39] Pacing in the *Saw* films vary. Although time is always of the essence, how that is represented and experienced differs. At times, "music video" style rapid editing is used to disorient viewers and bridge emotional relations between those in the diegesis and spectators. At others points, we experience the "countdown" scenarios in real-time along with the characters; editing is less frenetic, with affective duration being the goal.

7. *Interactivity.* Building on the importance of pacing, Buckland argues "that the player controls the beats via interaction, which confers upon the player the feeling of control — the manipulation of a character in a usually hostile environment."[40] Control, interaction and pleasure are contingent in video games. In the *Saw* series, it is the heightened *sense* of interactivity which is important, a necessary component of its gamified narrative and mise-en-scène. Although we do not control the characters in the films, the film's ethical implications are enmeshed within the gamified narrative, forging a more intimate sense of interactivity as we negotiate our alliances and allegiances.[41] It is also at the level of our gaze, our desire or inability to bear witness which *simulates* interactivity as well.

The entire series is structured around Jigsaw's desire to "play games" with his victims, and as the series develops, its narrative logic and mise-en-scène increasingly reflects its affinity to gaming. In the original *Saw*, Jigsaw plays an extended mind game with two victims, Adam and Dr. Gordon, who must figure out how they know each other while discovering various clues to help them solve intricate puzzles in order to escape their imprisonment from a dilapidated bathroom. In the first film, the main "torture scenario" is slowly teased out while flashbacks to previous tortures and the supporting storyline are intercut throughout. However, as the series develops, the initial one-on-one scenario is replaced with multiple victims; from player (victim) vs. computer (Jigsaw) and player vs. player, to players vs. players configured in variable ways.

In *Saw II*, Jigsaw kidnaps eight victims and places them in a sealed house to compete for immunity, the antidote to the poison slowly seeping into the boarded up house. The allusions to reality television are hard to miss as these "contestants" play various "mini games" scattered throughout a surveillance-camera rigged house. In *Saw III*, Jeff, the film's protagonist, finds himself in a sealed warehouse where he must play three "mini-games," while in the fourth film detective Rigg must, in under 90 minutes, play numerous mini-games scattered throughout the city. The key transition here is the movement from a "space of enclosure" to GPS monitoring; a shift from the panopticon to that of networked control.

In the first four films, it is video game logic which dominates, while the fifth, sixth and final films make clearer affinities to video games themselves. Capitalizing on the series' success, game developers opted to turn the films into a video game; a relatively common Hollywood marketing strategy and source of additional revenue. *Saw: The Video Game* was to be released in tandem with *Saw IV*; however, it wasn't released until 2009 when *Saw VI* was playing in theatres. Hollywood's horizontal marketing strategies make it difficult to ascertain whether the continual "gamification" of the *Saw* series inspired the creation of a video game, or whether producers had the creation of a game on their radar from the very beginning, hoping to potentially launch a new lucrative series.[42] Regardless, *Saw V* is reflexive of itself as a game. The film returns to the enclosed space but denies the characters the greater degrees of flexibility characters in *Saw III and IV* had as the five kidnapped players move from game room to game room competing directly against each other. After each mini-game, one player dies. It is revealed in the end that if all the players cooperated, if they played as a team rather than as opponents, they would all have been able to survive. The sixth and final films are hybrids of *Saw V* and *Saw III*, with protagonists trapped in a large space and forced to make their way from enclosed game space to enclosed game space, playing mini games against single or multiple opponents. Regardless of the configurations though, the ultimate goal, like in any horror film or video game, is to survive.

In "Match Made in Hell," Richard Rouse III argues that "the goal of video games and the goals of horror fiction directly overlap, making them ideal bedfellows,"[43] a union which has no doubt aided in making horror related video games both popular and financially successful, especially the "survival horror" genre.[44] Rouse notes that "games have inhabited the horror genre for almost as long as they've been in existence."[45] Recently, this phenomenon has been reversed with horror movies being adapted from horror video games,[46] as well as "video game versions" of popular films being used to not only make more money, but further sell a high stock brand or franchise (*Batman, Star Wars*, etc.). Importantly, Buckland and Elsaesser argue that when "discussing the popularity and pleasures of video games, we should not leave out their content and themes, which can in fact be summarized in one word — violence."[47] Violence is an important source of horror and video games' pleasure. It is, therefore, not surprising that the increasingly intimate relationship between video games and cinema holds the horror genre as their conduit of choice.

Bernard Perron argues that "the survival horror can be defined as an 'extended body genre,'"[48] as survival horror's strategy is to make viewers feel the characters' panic, and the intensity of the video game's diegesis within the players themselves.[49] "Body genre" was a term coined by Linda Williams which defined certain genres (horror, melodrama, pornography) as being entirely invested in not just the characters' bodies, but the audience's bodies.[50] These genres are defined by their need to physically affect their viewers, with their desire and abilities to agitate bodies marking them as "low," rather than "high," as "high" genres/art would affect only the mind. Importantly, the *Saw* series is not just part of the survival horror video game genre and a "body genre," but also a revision of "body horror;" the sub-genre of horror cinema which holds the body as *the* site of horror. Thus it is at the level of the body, of bodily experience, which centripetally blends survival horror, body horror, video games, "'torture' (and) 'porn.'" Video game and film characters along with video game players and cinematic spectators all collide into each other.

Buckland's exploration of how the logic of video games is increasingly bleeding into and restructuring contemporary fiction cinema's "language" is an important early study, as are works which have highlighted genre and ideological affinities, such as those mentioned above. But recent works have also sought to further this line of inquiry by fleshing out how the language and logic of hardware, of operating systems, affect and evolve representation, pleasure and our interaction with media.[51] The body as a representation and as a corporeal being experiencing those representations aligns horror, pornography, cinema and video games in crucial ways, pointing to the importance the body plays as a conduit of information; one which *absorbs* and evolves *as* it mediates. The body is a crucial site for hegemonic replication, but also resistance.

At a very basic level, it is tempting to frame the affinities between the large enclosed spaces of the panopticon as a metaphor for the "enclosed worlds" of video games, and players as guards in the guard tower invisibly controlling characters (prisoners); but that would be a reductionist and overly simplified simile. Although there are formal affinities to surveillance (such as the ability to control and change camera views [in some games] giving a *sense* of total observation, or the fact that the most common camera positions are located just behind the character giving a sense of ceaseless tracking, and of course the above the diegesis shot where we watch down over it from a bird's eye view mimicking aerial surveillance/military reconnaissance, or the high angle, high level shots which appropriate the surveillance angle)[52] it is the experiences which make these formal affinities pleasing, popular and now, *natural*, which are important.

It is vital here to make the distinction between being controlled and being used clear. Building on William Burroughs' beliefs, Wendy Chun points out that "without resistance, one is 'used' rather than controlled. This implies that control requires free will, and so what we take to be freedom, the ability to decide, is the basis for control."[53] That is, if one is being used, they do not know they are being controlled, thus control entails the knowledge that one is being controlled thus producing the knowledge of an "alternative," or "escape": freedom. Characters in films have the same type of mobility/freedoms and limitations/restrictions as characters in video games. Film and video game characters are able to freely move around within their allotted spaces, or, diegesis within certain, predetermined parameters, with those parameters being defined by the type of diegesis and medium. Video game characters are not imprisoned, but they are *controlled*. Although they are stand-ins for the gamer, video game characters differ in that they are being used[54] while gamers are being controlled. In similar respects, moviegoers and video gamers are also not imprisoned, but they too, to varying degrees, are controlled, but a recognized control; moviegoers and video gamers give permission to the apparatus and its output to exercise a certain amount of control over them. However, as gaming and moviegoing, and as movies and video games, penetrate and impregnate each other, the line between being controlled and being used becomes more and more diffused.

In *Gaming: Essays on Algorithmic Culture*, Alexander Galloway argues that video games are "actions" and must be understood as things to be played and not texts to be read.[55] Galloway wanted to expand on the relationships between video games and other media, by exploring how algorithms organize electronic games, video and computer games, engendering an "algorithmic culture." Galloway wanted to think about the effects and overlaps games have with other media, but also intervene in the ways these electronic pleasures were being discussed in film and media studies. Rather than setting clear distinctions, Galloway looks at the porous nature of media.[56] In his chapter, "Origins of the First-Person Shooter," Galloway explores how POV shots in the cinema influenced the ubiquity of POV embodiments in video games, arguing that although there are similarities, "in film, the subjective perspective is marginalized and used primarily to effect a sense of alienation, detachment, fear, or violence, while in games, the subjective perspective is quite common and used to achieve an intuitive sense of motion and action in gameplay."[57] That is, although the cinematic POV popularized that way of seeing and experiencing moving image dieseges, their purposes and affects differ: in cinema, alienation; in video games, intimacy. What is important here is that Galloway emphasizes the embodied gazing and experiences of the cinema and video games as permeable points of contact which overlap action and observation, immediacy and distance.

In a later chapter, "Allegories of Control," Galloway, building on arguments Frederic Jameson made in *Signatures of the Visible*, argues that video games, unlike cinema, "don't attempt to hide informatic control; they flaunt it."[58] Because cinema "sublimates" political control into representation and hides the "boring minutiae of discipline and confinement that constitute the various apparatuses of control in contemporary societies," video games, which "do nothing but present contemporary political realities in relatively unmediated form, ... achieve a unique type of political transparency."[59] Building on this bold observation he argues that contemporary "knowledge-reversal" films (films who have their history in the "whodunit" genre and 1970s "conspiracy films") such as *eXistenZ*, *The Usual Suspects*, *Fight Club* and *The Game* (to which I would add *Memento* and *Identity*), fetishize narrative "knowledge triumph;" having everything solved for you by the end is a form of control itself as the ending which ultimately reveals the narrative as a lie is a false empowerment of "disingenuous informatics." Because the narrative's reorganization is influenced by knowledge technologies, the falsified thrill ride continues to conceal the controlling potentials of these technologies which create epistemophilic narratives; thus the "transparency" of power in video games cannot be attained by the cinema.

But what about the *Saw* films? Although they as "puzzle films" play with information and create "false narratives" in the way movies such as *Fight Club* and *The Game* do, I believe their foregrounding of informatics through the body not just at the level of representation, such as in *eXistenZ*, but through calculated visceral affect, in conjunction with their gamified narrative and, most importantly here, mise-en-scène, afford them a higher degree of dialectical tension and more leeway to reflexively engage. Unlike films which shuffle narrative conventions and information, the *Saw* films foreground discourse and technology which influence cinematic play. The recent anthology *Puzzle Films: Complex Storytelling in Contemporary Cinema* (published three years after *Gaming*) has attempted to flesh out the history and current contexts which enable and even necessitate these new, complex methods of storytelling. Crucially, Thomas Elsaesser has, in "The Mind-Game Film," reasserted how video games and new technologies are important phenomena which influence how we tell stories, and what kind of stories we want to tell and be told. He writes:

> The popularity and profitability of computer games has nonetheless given rise, among film and humanities scholars, to a renewed interest in mathematical game theory. Especially "new media" theorists have begun to rethink the logic of traditional narratives, arguing that the storytelling we know and are familiar with from Homer to Homer Simpson may itself be historically specific and technology-dependent — and thus a doubly variable — way of storing information and of organizing direct sensory as well as symbolic data. It would therefore be not altogether unreasonable to assume that new technologies of storage, retrieval, and sorting, such as the ones provided so readily and relatively cheaply by the computer or internet servers, will in due course engender and enable new forms of "narrative."[60]

My intention is not to challenge Galloway's argument, but, in line with Elsaesser's assessment of recent thought, to suggest that the *Saw* series, although part of the "knowledge reversal" genre, is also reflexively engaging and challenging the material reality, the hardware, as much as the software, which gives rise to these new ways of telling stories, rather than simply symptomatically replicating these shifts.

Although there has been more work produced on software, and the effects of software,[61] there is a poverty of research on the power and effects of hardware. Brad Millington in "Wii Has Never Been Modern: 'Active' Video Gamers and the 'Conduct of Conduct,'" explores how Nintendo's Wii console enacts a system of control through leisure entertainment. Although his paper focuses on Wii's incredibly successful *Wii Fit* "video game," Millington's observations are likewise meant to speak about the Wii console as a whole.[62] He is interested in exploring the "ways in which new video game systems potentially foster variegated forms of surveillance and control."[63] His study is meant to fill in a gap in video game research, arguing that "video game scholars have yet to investigate the ways in which human/non-human hybridity might permit control over corporeality."[64] Focusing on *Wii Fit*, the exercise program gamifies biopower by getting you to correct improper habits in order for you to return to a normal, or "healthy," body weight/size. The entire "game" is based on a system of normalized biopower (statistics, health informatics), with the software *and hardware* "empowering" you as an individual to "change yourself." Most importantly, *Wii Fit* not only visualizes biopower but the general process of control and the effects this hardware technology has on the body as a tool of correction; it crystallizes how the hardware and its other, more inconspicuous output produces similar types of control. As Millington bluntly puts it, "Wii creates new articulations of technology-mediated control,"[65] in that, during gameplay, your body is subservient to the limitations and desires of the Wii. Although you exercise a certain amount of control over the game with your controller (and various hardware appendages such as the Balance Board for the *Wii Fit*) and, in many of the games, bodily movements, your success requires you to *synchronize* your body with the machine, with *its* logical processing.

Discussing the now classic simulation game *Civilization II*, Ted Friedman makes some insightful and provocative arguments about how video games produce pleasure:

> The way computer games teach structures of thought — the way they reorganize perception — is by getting you to internalize the logic of the program. To win, you can't just do whatever you want. You have to figure out what will work within the rules of the game.... The pleasure of computer games is entering into a computer-like mental state: responding as automatically as the computer.... The result is an almost meditative state, in which you aren't just interacting with the computer, but melding with it.[66]

For Friedman, it is the logic of the computer, the hardware, which is important, as the video game is, in essence, a graphic user interface; it is the visual manifestation of not just source code, but protocol. Gaming can be a means of control and therefore, correction, and the *Saw* series makes a spectacle of gamification as a form of potential correction and control, likewise reflecting on its own compromised engagement with this increasingly normalized reality.

Alexander Galloway's earlier book, *Protocol: How Control Exists After Decentralization*, ambitiously argued against the belief that "new communication technologies are based on the elimination of centralized command and hierarchical control" and that we are "witnessing a general disappearance of control," arguing instead that "protocol is how technological control exists after decentralization."[67] Although "protocol referred to any type of correct or proper behavior within a specific system of conventions ... now protocols refer specifically to standards governing the implementation of specific technologies ... thus protocol is a technique for achieving voluntary regulation within a contingent environment."[68] As social, economic and cultural spheres increasingly rely on computers and electronic information technologies, we must invariably adapt to their way of thinking and processing. The logic of new technologies produce new forms of surveillance, and it is through new technologies where we learn and enact self-surveillance. The *Saw* series' gamification, its "if X then Y" systemization, speaks to how the logic of informatics is continuously manifesting culturally, artistically and politically in contemporary society.

Galloway's work was influenced by Lev Manovich's assertive intervention, *The Language of New Media*. In this new media opus, Manovich traces the history of "new media," producing a cartography of "computing and media technologies[']"[69] symbioses, outlining how their complementary organization built the path toward new media, likewise arguing that new media is not "new," but a continuation of this relationship which is decades in the making. Manovich's brilliant study cannot be fully accounted for here, but what are important are his arguments that we are a "society of the screen"[70] and that once entertaining screen, the cinematic screen, is now being overtaken by the computer screen, a screen synonymous with military-surveillance. In this sense, "cinema becomes a slave to the computer,"[71] yet, paradoxically, "virtual technology's dependence on cinema's mode of seeing and language is becoming progressively stronger."[72] For Manovich, "The area of computer culture where the cinematic interface is being transformed into a cultural interface most aggressively is computer games."[73] It is not only this transformation which is being realized in the *Saw* series but the anxiety over this conflated *history* and current rapid transition's effect on the present, and future.

In *The Simulation of Surveillance: Hypercontrol in Telematic Societies*, William Bogard argues that surveillance in contemporary society is often expressed through simulation and simulation technology, with simulation technology manifesting and attempting to realize the *fantasy* of total observation and control. He writes, "technologies of simulation are forms of *hypersurveillant control*, where the prefix 'hyper' implies not simply an intensification of surveillance, but the effort to push surveillance technologies to their absolute limit"[74]; Bogard specifically points out "gaming"[75] as a key example of simulated surveillance. For Bogard, "Simulation, we could say, is the *panoptic imaginary*."[76] Synthesizing Baudrillard and Foucault, Bogard argues that discussions of surveillance and simulation must take into account the role of fantasy and the imaginary; that the synthesis and symbiosis of surveillance and simulation are contingent upon desire and the future, and in many respects, the collapse between the present and the future.[77] Thus in many respects, simulation carries on the utopian dream of modernity and the fantasy of technology's progressive teleology: that technology will move us toward a better future. Simulation runs on modernity's utopian impulse, but as a phenomenon of post-industrial and postmodern society, it likewise taps into contemporary society's dystopic impulse. It is because "simulated surveillance ... [is] a paradox of control ... [as] it is a fantasy of absolute control and the absence of control at the same time,"[78] where anxieties about surveillance rub up against the desire for simulation, stimulating friction. I believe it is this friction which is being *emulated* by the *Saw* series as it grapples with the cultural politics of technology, and specifically entertainment technology, as a tool, if not weapon, of utopia and dystopia.

The Saw Series, Intimacy, and Critical Dystopia

The *Saw* series was not the first to present a horrific vision of contemporary culture's gamification as a warning about where this path will lead us to; the Canadian film *Cube* predated the first *Saw* film by seven years. In the film, seven strangers awake to find themselves in a giant metal Rubik's cube. To escape they must figure out the space's internal mathematical logic in order to chart a safe path out of the cube. This bleak dystopia visualizes the oppressiveness of algorithmic logic by placing its characters inside a mechanical panopticon; a computational space of enclosure where the space itself is always watching and waiting to punish any misstep. Our obsession for virtual immersion turns a benign game, a Rubik's cube, into a gamified prison space where systemic mathematical logic, the language of computers and console gaming, is the source code of our own suicidal desire for simulation. The film, a technological re-vision of Luis Buñuel's *The Exterminating Angel*, contemplates the complexities and consequences of desire's fusion with technology, and thus algorithm, protocol and surveillance cum control. While Buñuel's film focused on the bourgeoisie and the imprisonment of decadence and civility, *Cube's* far more pessimistic aesthetics and narrative present us with a dystopic vision of where our desire to immerse ourselves in virtual worlds can lead us to. The twentieth century has been called the "age of ideology," and the function of utopia is often meant to shatter the illusion of ideology and offer a better alternative.[79] Juxtaposing *The Exterminating Angel* to *Cube* we not only see how the twenty-first century is moving beyond the concern over ideology *as* control, but that cultural artifacts, films *and* video games, are increasingly choosing dystopia as their critical method for engagement.

A recent *South Park* episode which parodies the film *The Human Centipede*, entitled *Humancentipad*,[80] provides a humorous, but no less biting critique of how technologies, specifically Apple's "i" products (iPhone, iPad, iTouch, iPod) invade our privacy and individuality, by forging far too intimate relations between machines and bodies. Briefly, *The Human Centipede* is about three people, two female friends (the front and middle links) and one man (the last link) whose mouths are sewn onto each other's rectum producing one long human digestive tract with multiple appendages, thus creating a "centipede" made of humans. The *South Park* episode uses and brings to surface the film's underlying critiques of our loss of individuality and privacy that our confession-obsessed, hypervisible culture facilitates, tailoring it to directly criticize Apple's hidden power agenda. While on the surface the company (a stand in for telecommunication in general) sells us products designed to "bring us closer together" as a community, they paradoxically sell us products meant to produce (in)dividuals (thus the ingenious use of the "i" prefix). Technology is bringing us closer and closer together, but how close is too close? How intimate does our relationship with strangers or technology really *need* to be?

Both *The Human Centipede* and *South Park*'s *HumancentIpad* express deep-seated anxieties about new technologies' controlling potentials and are not just extensions of body genre, but "torture porn" and the dystopic endpoint of body-horror as well. It is the film and episode's use of bodily violence and the languorous witnessing of said violence as allegorical critiques of surveillance and control technologies which place these texts in dialogue. In the *South Park* episode, Steve Jobs is the figural stand-in for *The Human Centipede's* mad scientist/doctor, framing Jobs as a genius "gone too far," and Apple's "i" products as tools of control masquerading as communication-entertainment technologies. The episode ends with Gerald Brofloski announcing that "this is the future," and pleading, "but can't we just slow down and enjoy the present a little longer?" Not only does this set up a *postmodern* technological teleology, that technology *is* dystopia, but it aligns current communication-entertainment technologies as gateways to that dystopia. But of interesting reversal here is how *intimacy*, rather than alienation, is the experience of dystopia simultaneously collapsing future and present: "the future is here." Although most accounts of dystopia hold the intimacy of the omniscient gaze as invasive, with bodies often isolated and banned from physical touch, here it extreme tactility, rather than distanced observation, which is terrifying. In this sense, the *Saw* series as well as *The Human Centipede/HumancentIpad* are more inspired the tradition of Aldous Huxley's *Brave New World* than George Orwell's *Nineteen Eighty-Four*. The global village never seemed so crowded.

The term "critical dystopia" was coined by Tom Moylan in his study *Scraps of the Untainted Sky: Science Fiction, Utopia, Dystopia* and referred to "a textual practice first emerging in the late 1980s in response to the conservative political retrenchments of the Reagan-Thatcher era," with their "'strongly and more self-reflexively 'critical' stance" actively retrieving and refunctioning "the most progressive possibilities inherent in dystopian narrative."[81] Building on this, Constance Penley, discussing James Cameron's *The Terminator*, has argued that the critical dystopia "tends to suggest causes rather than merely reveal symptoms,"[82] with Peter Fitting arguing that the adjective "critical" "implies an explanation of how the dystopian situation came about as much as what should be done about it."[83] The diegesis is meant to critically reflect the anxieties and hopes of the publication's current cultural context, with the author(s) often offering solutions to move us off our path towards the dystopic future, and towards a utopic, or at least better one.

When framed as a critical dystopia and as torture porn, the *Saw* series offers a unique reversal of the utopic and intimate sexual interludes Linda Williams, building on Richard Dyer's arguments about musical numbers in musicals,[84] identified in narrative (heterosexual) pornography.[85] This is particularly important as Williams' groundbreaking 1989 study *Hard Core: Power, Pleasure, and the "Frenzy of the Visible"* framed (1970s heterosexual narrative) pornography as the latest manifestation of sexual "knowledge-power," or surveillance. In the *Saw* films, torture scenes are dystopic interludes. Williams and Dyer's accounts refer to the genres' hegemonic, if negotiated, reassertions of heteronormative gender couplings as utopia; here the interludes are dystopic fusions between human and machine. This subversion of Vertov's "peace between man and machine" takes on additional critical force considering Vertov, Dyer and Williams are likewise speaking about the intimate union forged between the cinema and spectators, with the *Saw* films engaging with the impact gaming and gaming technologies are having on these phenomena and their intermingling.

Speaking specifically about cinema and utopia, Richard Dyer writes, "Utopiannism is contained in the feelings it embodies. It presents, head-on as it were, what utopia would *feel like* rather than how it would be organized."[86] Dyer himself recognizes the limitations of this pleasure[87] as most accounts of the cinema's "power to condition" are contingent upon its pleasure economy, with critics often taking a Brechtian approach, arguing that pleasure is an anesthetic and that what is needed is agitation and displeasure to shock people out of their pseudo-coma; thus displeasure rides the utopic impulse by challenging ideology, opening up a space for charting a path toward utopia.[88] Much more recently, however, Peter Ruppert has argued that since movies are designed for mass consumption they cannot "be expected to be overtly critical of the industrial and ideological apparatus on which their *existence depends*,"[89] reasserting Dyer's position by arguing that the "utopian film ... is better gauged in terms of what a film does: its functions and effects on the audience."[90] Dean Lockwood has also argued that "torture porn taps into a 'nightmarish cybernetic dystopia,' but ... also promises metamorphosis and [thus also] constitutes a "utopian impulse."[91] Since the films offer images of correction, or, "solutions" they too, in a sense, ride the utopic impulse of "making things better." The *Saw* series' mixture of bodily agitation and pleasure which poach utopic impulses in order to pervert them, critically questioning the meaning of "correction," cum "improvement"; after all, dystopias are all about ruling ideology wielding technology as a way of correcting and controlling the body, as a way to organize biopower and thus society at large.

Although not the typical dystopic text I argue the *Saw* series' mise-en-scène and emulation of extreme tactility and intimacy aligns itself with the tradition of critical dystopia by exerting visual extremity, visceral affect and play as its critical weapons. The *Saw* series' gamified narrative and mise-en-scène mark the films as science fiction or even as extreme reimaginings of magical realism, as much as horror or detective films; their gamification makes them hyperreal, makes them *all too* real, and futuristic. *Saw II* and *VI*'s metallic color palette recall David Fincher's *Alien 3*,[92] and the drained, darkly tinted color scheme of the *Saw*, *Saw III* and *V* films speak to a bleak, dehumanized existence, with the foregrounding and fusing of machinery, information technology and bodily control appropriating elements of "cyberpunk" and "biopunk" engendering a unique hybrid. Although the series does not "explain" the development of dystopia in the way *The Terminator* or traditional critical dystopias do, the series does use flashbacks and Jigsaw's tape-recorded voice-overs as a way to explain how and why the characters have ended up in the situations they find themselves in. Importantly, we should not consider the lack of a unified vision of resistance or clear path toward an alternative as a failure: we should instead see the "solutions" the films offer (correction, control, death, disfigurement) as perverse reflections engaging with the limitations and powers of their media as a way to invite personal and social contemplation after the films have ended.

Conclusion

The *Saw* series and this essay are part of a growing dialogue about the representations and potential effects of surveillance and control in (new and old) media.[93] I laid out three initial goals: to demonstrate that the *Saw* films make spectacles out of correction; to show how the films are structured by video game logic and bring the borders of video gaming and movie watching/making into more intimate contact; and to argue that the films align themselves with the energies of critical dystopias as a way to engender friction and affect for further reflection and contemplation. By fleshing out this three part dialogue I hope that I have further opened a space for contemplating contemporary cinema's symbiosis with surveillance, correction, control, and gameplay, and the effects these engagements have on experiences both inside and outside the theater and on the medium/art form itself.

Notes

1. Evangelos Tziallas. "Torture Porn and Surveillance Culture," *Jump Cut: A Review of Contemporary Media* 52 (Summer 2010), http://www.ejumpcut.org/currentissue/evangelosTorturePorn/index.html. I invite readers to peruse the online article and use it as a visual reference as it contains hundreds of images.

2. Jennifer Reburn's recent dissertation "Watching Men: Masculinity and Surveillance in the American Serial Killer Film 1978–2008," dedicates an entire chapter to exploring the torture porn sub-genre as an offspring of the serial killer sub-genre; she argues that puzzles bridge the two sub-genres. See pages 229–231, 238.

3. See Catherine Zimmer's "Caught on Tape? The Politics of Video in the New Torture Film" *Horror After 9/11: World of Fear, Cinema of Terror*, Ed. Aviva Briefel and Sam J. Miller (Austin: University of Texas Press, 2011), 87.

4. Here I'm referring to traditionally conceptualized frameworks á la Peter Wollen's "Godard and Counter Cinema: *Vent D'Est*," and the avant-garde as strategies for resisting dominant ideology. The questions: What is resistance? How does the cinema resist? And more recently, what should be resisted? are not only too grand to flesh out, let alone adequately engage with and provide meaningful critiques of and answers to, but are historically contingent; most of the dialogue was created as an attempt to resist the oppressive cinematic apparatus' implementation of bourgeois, capitalist ideology. Besides the obvious problem of setting up the cinema as an automatically evil disseminator of ideology and something which needs to be resisted, the process by which one resists and more importantly, their effectiveness, are indeterminate to say the least. As most research which held the issue of "resistance" at its core was produced well over 30 years ago, my approach will engage with resistance as something which, in contemporary society, is bound to complicity. See Philip Rosen's various introductions in *Narrative, Apparatus, Ideology: A Film Theory Reader* for a concise dialogue.

5. Gabrielle Murray, "*Hostel II*: Representations of the Body in Pain and the Cinema Experience in Torture-Porn." *Jump Cut: A Review of Contemporary Media* 50 (Spring 2008), http://www.ejumpcut.org/archive/jc50.2008/TortureHostel2/index.html.

6. Gregory A. Burris. "Shocked and Awed: Hostel and the Spectacle of Self-Mutilation," *CineAction* 80 (2010) 2–12; Jerod Ra'del Hollyfield, "Torture Porn and Body Politic: Post-Cold War American Perspectives in Eli Roth's *Hostel* and *Hostel: Part II*," *CineAction* 78 (2009): 23–31.

7. Jason Middleton, "The Subject of Torture: Regarding the Pain of Americans in Hostel," *Cinema Journal* 49.4 (Summer 2010): 1–24.

8. Christopher Sharrett, "The Problem of Saw: 'Torture Porn' and the Conservatism of Contemporary Horror Films," *Cineaste* 35.1 (2009): 32–37.

9. Adam Lowenstein, "Spectacle Horror and *Hostel*: Why 'Torture Porn' Does Not Exist," *Critical Quarterly* 53.1 (2011): 42–60.

10. Dean Lockwood, "All Stripped Down: The Spectacle of 'Torture Porn,'" *Popular Communication* 7.1 (2009): 40–48.

11. Tziallas, p. 4, Text Only, Printable Version.

12. Gilles Deleuze, "Postscript on the Societies of Control," *October* (1992): 3–7.

13. Something Dean Lockwood has likewise recently touched upon. He writes, "I submit that torture porn films can also be understood as allegories of control." P. 45.

14. For Deleuze, we are all databanks ripe with valuable information. It is not so much our labor which is valuable, but the information we implicitly contain within ourselves which make us valuable in the control society. It is our behaviors and desires which must be acquired and analyzed in order to manufacture products and services specifically tailored to tap into those behaviors and desires which make us dividuals rather than individuals.

15. And doctor Lawrence Gordon, one of the two main protagonists from the original *Saw* film, which is only revealed during the last 30 seconds of the series' final film, *Saw 3D*.

16. As the series develops and as Jigsaw's gruesome spree is sensationalized by the media, characters from within the diegetic world express awareness of Jigsaw's surveillance gaze. They

may not know that they themselves are being watched, but they know very well that Jigsaw is watching everyone and it may very well be them.

17. Importantly, Foucault notes how the creation of biography is linked to disciplinary systems of correction. On pages 251–252 of *Discipline and Punish* he writes, "The offender becomes an individual to know … [and] the prison a sort of artificial and *coercive theatre* in which his life will be examined from top to bottom … it is a biographical knowledge and a technique for correcting individual lives." Observing the delinquent must reveal the "the story of his life … [as the] biographical investigation is an essential part of the preliminary investigation" [emphasis mine].

18. See my "Torture Porn and Surveillance Culture" article for a more detailed list (with visuals) and explanation.

19. See my interview with Sarah Boesveld in the Arts sections of *The National Post*, June 6, 2012. http://arts.nationalpost.com/2012/06/06/superheroes-surveillance-who-are-these-masked-men-and-what-do-they-represent/.

20. Stephen Paul Miller, *The Seventies Now: Culture as Surveillance*, p. 1.

21. I purposely used this phrasing to highlight Laura Mulvey's infamous 1975 article, but did not directly reference her article so as to avoid the lengthy discussion of gendered identification and pleasure which was a foundational discourse when film studies was developing as an academic discipline. I address this in further detail, using Carol Clover's analysis of cross-gendered, masochistic identification, in my "Torture Porn and Surveillance Culture" article.

22. Turner, p. 94.

23. Turner, p. 94.

24. Turner's article focused more on films which used surveillance technologies and their visual/audio output as motifs and core narrative elements, and even though the *Saw* films rely on surveillance technologies as methods for telling their stories, it is the discourse and spectacular representation of panopticism, control and correction, rather than surveillance's technological representation/manifestation in the *Saw* films which I would like to focus on.

25. See Guy Debord's opus *The Society of the Spectacle*.

26. Foucault, *Discipline and Punish*, p. 217.

27. Martin Jay, *Downcast Eyes: The Denigration of Vision in Twentieth-Century French Thought*, p. 416.

28. Deleuze, p. 6.

29. Although I could list dozens of articles and books, I will simply point to Barbara Klinger's *Beyond the Multiplex: Cinema, New Technologies, and the Home*.

30. Alexander Galloway, *Gaming*, 100.

31. Although the origin of this now cliché "the medium is the message" observation about the effects of video games on the human psyche and behavior is somewhat vague (British comedian Marcus Brigstocke has claimed authorship and not, as it was presumed, Nintendo CEO Kristian Wilson), its acuteness carries a certain currency about the power of video games as participatory entertainment.

32. King and Krzywinska, "Introduction: Cinema/Video Games/Interface," p. 3.

33. Angela Ndalianis, "'Evil Will Walk Once More': *Phantasmagoria*—The Stalker Film as Interactive Movie," 87–112.

34. See King and Krzywinska's "Introduction: Cinema/Video Games/Interface," *Screenplay: Cinema/Video Games/ Interface*, for a full assessment.

35. Buckland and Elsaesser, p. 161.

36. Simon Gottschalk, "Videology: Video-Games as Postmodern Sites/Sights of Ideological Reproduction," *Symbolic Interaction* 18.1 (Spring 1995): 1–18.

37. Buckland and Elsaesser, pp. 162–163.

38. This is an unplayable moment tinged with pornographic excess; the video game, or at least programmers, are both seducing players and exhibiting their power and skill to do so at the same time.

39. Buckland and Elsaesser, p. 163. As examples, think of how important pacing one's jumps over a series of chasms in a *Super Mario*, or any platform, game is, or think of levels

where the television or computer monitor's frame almost imprisons one's avatar, as the pre-timed mobile frame moves across the screen, limiting and dictating one's mobility and pacing.

40. Buckland and Elsaesser, p. 163.

41. See Murray Smith's "The Logic and Legacy of Brechtianism" in David Bordwell and Noël Carroll's *Post-Theory: Reconstructing Film Theory*. 130–148. Briefly, in this essay, Smith asserts that spectators able to differentiate between being aligned with a character and having an allegiance with that character. The film may construct alliances through formal choices, but that doesn't mean spectators develop attachment to that(/those) character(s).

42. The first and second *Saw* video games were poorly received by critics, fans and gamers alike. There are no plans to continue the game series.

43. Rouse, p. 15.

44. Bernard Perron argues that "the survival horror genre might be the game genre most often compared to film." http://www.aestheticsofplay.org/perron.php.

45. Rouse, p. 15.

46. The *Resident Evil* series is the prime example, but also *Silent Hill* and *Alone in the Dark*.

47. Buckland and Elsaesser, p. 163.

48. Perron, "The Survival Horror: The Extended Body Genre," p. 125.

49. Perron, p. 131. He writes, "The odyssey of self-exploration is veiled in an interesting way in the survival horror genre because the gamer embarks on an adventure through some-BODY else, namely the main character he is required to play ... the gamer forms one body ... with his player character."

50. See Linda Williams, "Film Bodies: Gender, Genre and Excess," *Film Quarterly* 44.4 (Summer 1991): 2–12.

51. See Steve Keane's "From Hardware to Fleshware: Plugging into David Cronenberg's *eXistenZ*," 145–156.

52. A term I use to refer to high angle, high level camera positions often shot from the corners of a room or adjacent to wall, mimicking the placement of a surveillance camera. See my "Torture Porn and Surveillance Culture" article for visual examples and further details.

53. Wendy Chun. *Control and Freedom: Power and Paranoia in the Age of Fibre Optics*, p. 272.

54. Although there are the odd games where characters talk back to the gamer (LucasArts games such as *Day of the Tentacle* and the *Indiana Jones* series are some interesting examples) thus breaking the fourth wall, this is *simulated* recognition of being "controlled," often used as a way to fuse more intimate relations between gamers and characters and heighten the sense of interactivity. The "announcing" of control only further controls the gamer.

55. Galloway, *Gaming*, 2–6.

56. He argues that "It is a cliché today to claim that movies are becoming more and more like video games.... Today video games and film are influencing and incorporating each other in novel ways." P. 39.

57. Galloway, *Gaming*, 40.

58. Galloway, *Gaming*, 90.

59. Galloway, *Gaming*, 91–92.

60. Elsaesser, p. 22.

61. I speak here of the large field of "media effects" research often housed in sociology departments, but also the rising interest in software studies, spearheaded by Matthew Fuller, Lev Manovich, and Noah Wardrip-Fruin and their book series of the same name.

62. These observations are also applicable to Playstation 3 and X-Box 360 as both systems have developed and released their own motion sensor technology additions.

63. Brad Millington, "Wii has Never Been Modern: 'Active' Video Gamers and the 'Conduct of Conduct,'" *New Media & Society* 11.4 (2009): 622.

64. Millington, p. 622.

65. Millington, p. 628.

66. Ted Friedman, "*Civilization* and Its Discontents: Simulation, Subjectivity, and Space," 136–137.

67. Galloway, *Protocol*, p. 8.
68. Galloway, *Protocol*, p. 7.
69. Manovich, *The Language of New Media*, p. 20.
70. Manovich, p. 94.
71. Manovich, p. 25.
72. Manovich, p. 82.
73. Manovich, p. 83.
74. Bogard, p. 4.
75. In addition, Bogard lists "the modeling of complex physical, biological, and social processes" as well as "profiling, cybernetics, miniaturization, tele-presencing, cloning, and stealth technology," p. 3.
76. Bogard, p. 19.
77. Speaking of limits he writes, "That limit is an imaginary line beyond which control operates, so to speak, in 'advance' of itself and where surveillance — a technology of exposure and recording — evolves into a technology of *pre*-exposure and *pre*-recording...." He continues to argue that "simulation technology from the perspective I adopt here, is part of what I will call the *imaginary* of surveillant control — a fantastic dream of seeing everything capable of being seen, recording every fact capable of being recorded, and accomplishing these things, whenever and where possible, prior to the event itself," pp. 4–5.
78. Bogard, p. 22.
79. Lyman Tower Sargent, p. 118.
80. Original air date, April 27, 2011, production code 1501.
81. See Phillip E. Wegner's "Where the Prospective Horizon Is Omitted: Naturalism and Dystopia in *Fight Club* and *Ghost Dog*" for a lengthier discussion of critical dystopia and its negotiated status in the two aforementioned films and films in general.
82. Constance Penley, "Time Travel, Primal Scene and the Critical Dystopia," 117.
83. Pg. 156. Fitting argues that films such as *The Truman Show* and *Dark City*, although offering visions of dystopia, lack self-awareness and introspection, and while *The Matrix* offers some progress by emphasizing community over individuality (or the "lone hacker" so popular in cyberpunk literature), it is *Pleasantville* which comes the closest to representing the essence of the critical dystopia, even though it fails to "offer any instructions for political action." Pg. 164. See his article for a more extensive justification.
84. See Richard Dyer's "Entertainment and Utopia" in *Only Entertainment*, 19–35.
85. See Linda Williams, chapter 6, "Hard Core Utopias: Problems and Solutions," in *Hard Core: Power, Pleasure, and the "Frenzy of the Visible."*
86. Dyer, p. 20. Emphasis mine.
87. Dyer writes, "Professional entertainment is the dominant agency for defining what entertainment is. This does not mean, however, that it *simply* reproduces and expresses patriarchal capitalism ... show business's relationship to the demands of patriarchal capitalism is a complex one ... [but] it does not simply reproduce unproblematically patriarchal-capitalist ideology." P. 20. Dyer argues that "the workforce (the performers themselves) is in a better position to determine the form of its product" and that "subordinate groups" such as blacks, gays and women have played important parts in shaping and evolving entertainment. P. 20.
88. This dialogue, however, must be understood within its cultural context as both Dyer's piece and debates about Brecht, distanciation, alienation and anti-pleasure formed the intellectual *zeitgeist* of the 1970s. See Dana Polan's "Brecht and the Politics of Self-Reflexive Cinema" for a concise discussion of the dialogue as the dialogue was talking place, and see Sylvia Harvey's "Whose Brecht? Memories for the Eighties: A Critical Recovery" for a political and intellectual reassessment.
89. Peter Ruppert, p. 139.
90. Peter Ruppert, p. 140.
91. Dean Lockwood, p. 46.
92. In "Caught on Tape? The Politics of Video in the New Torture Film" Catherine Zimmer argues that the *Saw* series is itself inspired by Fincher's *Se7en*. P. 85.

93. See Catherine Zimmer's "Surveillance Cinema: Narrative Between Technology and Politics." *Surveillance and Society* 8.4 (2011): 427–440; and Jessica Lake's *Red Road (2006) and Emerging Narratives of 'Sub-Veillance,'" Continuum: Journal of Media and Cultural Studies*. 24.2 (2012): 231–240, for an interesting and important discussion about surveillance technology and cinematic spectatorship. In addition, see the popular blog *Film Studies of Free* for a list of recently published, free articles on the subject of "Surveillance Film Studies." Posted by Catherine Grant. September 23, 2011. http://filmstudiesforfree.blogspot.co.uk/2011/09/surveillance-film-studies.html.

Author's Note

Thank you to John Walliss, James Aston and Thomas Waugh for their keen editorial eye and support. Thank you to Michael Keill for allowing me to bounce ideas off of him and providing me with honest feedback and criticism throughout the preliminary and writing stages. And thank you to the Social Science and Humanities Research Council of Canada for providing me with the funding, and thus time, needed to research and write this essay.

References

Boesveld, Sarah. Interview with Evangelos Tziallas. "Superheroes and Surveillance: Who Are These Masked Men, and What Do They Represent?" *The National Post*. June 6, 2012. http://arts.nationalpost.com/2012/06/06/superheroes-surveillance-who-are-these-masked-men-and-what-do-they-represent/.

Bogard, William. *The Simulation of Surveillance: Hypercontrol in Telematic Societies*. Cambridge: Cambridge University Press, 1996.

Buckland, Warren, and Thomas Elsaesser. *Studying Contemporary American Film: A Guide to Movie Analysis*. New York: Oxford University Press, 2002.

Burris, Gregory A. "Shocked and Awed: Hostel and the Spectacle of Self-Mutilation." *CineAction* 80 (2010) 2–12.

Chun, Wendy Hui Kyong. *Control and Freedom: Power and Paranoia in the Age of Fiber Optics*. Cambridge: MIT Press, 2006.

Clover, Carol J. *Men, Women and Chainsaws: Gender in the Modern Horror Film*. Princeton: Princeton University Press, 1992.

Debord, Guy. *The Society of the Spectacle*. Trans. Donald Nicholson-Smith. New York: Zone, 1995. [1967]

Deleuze, Gilles. "Postscript on the Societies of Control." *October* 59 (Winter 1992) 3–7.

Dyer, Richard. "Entertainment and Utopia," in *Only Entertainment*, 2d ed. London: Routledge, 2002. 19–35.

Elsaesser, Thomas. "The Mind Game Film," in *Puzzle Films: Complex Storytelling in Contemporary Cinema*, edited by Warren Buckland, 13–30. Oxford: Wiley-Blackwell, 2009.

Fitting, Peter. "Unmasking the Real? Critique and Utopia in Recent SF Films," in *Dark Horizons: Science Fiction and the Dystopian Imagination*, edited by Raffaella Baccolini and Tom Moylan, 155–166. New York: Routledge, 2003.

Friedman, Ted. "*Civilization* and Its Discontents: Simulation, Subjectivity, and Space," in *On a Silver Platter: CD-ROMs and the Promises of a New Technology*, edited by Greg M. Smith, 132–150. New York: New York University Press, 1999.

Foucault, Michel. *Discipline and Punish: The Birth of the Prison*, 2d ed. Trans. Alan Sheridan. New York: Vantage, 1995.

_____. *The History of Sexuality: An Introduction*, 2d ed. Trans. Robert Hurley. New York: Vintage, 1990.
Galloway, Alexander. *Gaming: Essays on Algorithmic Culture*. Minneapolis: University of Minnesota Press, 2006.
_____. *Protocol: How Control Exists after Decentralization*. Cambridge: MIT Press, 2004.
Gottschalk, Simon. "Videology: Video-Games as Postmodern Sites/Sights of Ideological Reproduction." *Symbolic Interaction* 18.1 (Spring 1995): 1–18.
Grant, Catherine. "Surveillance Film Studies." *Film Studies for Free*. September 23, 2011. http://filmstudiesforfree.blogspot.co.uk/2011/09/surveillance-film-studies.html.
Harvey, Sylvia: "Whose Brecht? Memories for the Eighties: A Critical Recovery." *Screen*, 23.1 (1982): 45–59.
Hollyfield, Jerod Ra'del. "Torture Porn and Body Politic: Post-Cold War American Perspectives in Eli Roth's *Hostel* and *Hostel: Part II*." *CineAction*, 78 (2009): 23–31.
Jay, Martin. *Downcast Eyes: The Denigration of Vision in Twentieth-Century French Thought*. Berkeley: University of California Press, 1993.
Keane, Steve. "From Hardware to Fleshware: Plugging into David Cronenberg's *eXistenZ*," in *Screenplay: Cinema/Video Games/Interface*, edited by Geoff King and Tanya Krzywinska, 145–156. London: Wallflower, 2002.
King, Geoff, and Tanya Krzywinska. "Introduction: Cinema/Video Games/Interface," in *Screenplay: Cinema/Video Games/Interface*, edited by Geoff King and Tanya Krzywinska, 1–32. London: Wallflower, 2002.
Klinger, Barbara. *Beyond the Multiplex: Cinema, New Technologies, and the Home*. Berkeley: University of California Press, 2006.
Lake, Jessica. *Red Road (2006) and Emerging Narratives of "Sub-Veillance." Continuum: Journal of Media and Cultural Studies* 24.2 (2012): 231–240.
Lockwood, Dean. "All Stripped Down: The Spectacle of 'Torture Porn.'" *Popular Communication* 7.1 (2009): 40–48.
Lowenstein, Adam. "Spectacle Horror and *Hostel*: Why 'Torture Porn' Does Not Exist." *Critical Quarterly* 53.1 (2011): 42–60.
Manovich, Lev. *The Language of New Media*. Cambridge: MIT Press, 2001.
Middleton, Jason. "The Subject of Torture: Regarding The Pain of Americans in Hostel." *Cinema Journal* 49.4 (Summer 2010): 1–24.
Miller, Stephen Paul. *The Seventies Now: Culture as Surveillance*. Durham: Duke University Press, 1999.
Millington, Brad. "Wii has Never Been Modern: 'Active' Video Gamers and the 'Conduct of Conduct.'" *New Media and Society* 11.4 (2009): 621–640.
Murray, Gabrielle. "*Hostel II*: Representations of the Body in Pain and the Cinema Experience in Torture-Porn." *Jump Cut: A Review of Contemporary Media* 50 (Spring 2008): http://www.ejumpcut.org/archive/jc50.2008/TortureHostel2/index.html.
Ndalianis, Angela. "'Evil Will Walk Once More': *Phantasmagoria*—The Stalker Film as Interactive Movie," in *On a Silver Platter: CD-ROMs and the Promises of a New Technology*, edited by Greg M. Smith. 87–112. New York: New York University Press, 1999.
Penley, Constance. "Time Travel, Primal Scene and the Critical Dystopia," in *Alien Zone: Cultural Theory and Contemporary Science Fiction Cinema*, edited by Annette Khun, 116–127. London: Verso, 1990.
Perron, Bernard. "Coming to Play at Frightening Yourself: Welcome to the World of Horror Video Game." *Online Conference Proceedings from Aesthetics of Play*, http://www.aestheticsofplay.org/perron.php.
_____. "The Survival Horror: The Extended Body Genre." *Horror Video Games: Essays on the Fusion of Fear and Play*, edited by Bernard Perron, 121–142. Jefferson, NC: McFarland, 2009.
Polan, Dana. "Brecht and the Politics of Self-Reflexive Cinema." *Jump Cut: A Review of Contemporary Cinema* 17 (1978): http://www.ejumpcut.org/archive/onlinessays/JC17folder/BrechtPolan.html.

Reburn, Jennifer. "Watching Men: Masculinity and Surveillance in the American Serial Killer Film 1978–2008," Diss. University of Glasgow. 2012. http://theses.gla.ac.uk/3390/01/2012ReburnPhD.pdf.

Rosen, Philip, editor. *Narrative, Apparatus, Ideology: A Film Theory Reader*. New York: Columbia University Press, 1986.

Rouse, Richard. "Match Made in Hell: The Inevitable Success of the Horror Genre in Video Games." *Horror Video Games: Essays on the Fusion of Fear and Play*. Editor Bernard Perron, 15–30. Jefferson, NC: McFarland, 2009.

Ruppert, Peter. "Tracing Utopia: Film, Spectatorship and Desire." *Utopian Studies* 7.2 (1996): 139–152.

Sargent, Lyman Tower. *Utopianism: A Very Short Introduction*. Oxford: Oxford University Press, 2010.

Sharrett, Christopher. "The Problem of Saw: 'Torture Porn' and the Conservatism of Contemporary Horror Films." *Cineaste* 35.1 (2009): 32–37.

Smith, Murray. "The Logic and Legacy of Brechtianism," in *Post-Theory: Reconstructing Film Theory*, edited by David Bordwell and Noël Carroll, 130–148. Madison: University of Wisconsin Press, 1996.

Turner, John. "Collapsing the Interior/Exterior Distinction: Surveillance, Spectacle, and Suspense in Popular Cinema." 20.4 *Wide Angel* (October 1998): 93–123.

Tziallas, Evangelos. "Torture Porn and Surveillance Culture." *Jump Cut: A Review of Contemporary Media* 52 (Summer 2010): http://www.ejumpcut.org/currentissue/evangelosTorturePorn/index.html.

Wegner, Phillip E. "Where the Prospective Horizon Is Omitted: Naturalism and Dystopia in *Fight Club* and *Ghost Dog*," in *Dark Horizons: Science Fiction and the Dystopian Imagination*, edited by Raffaella Baccolini and Tom Moylan, 167–185. New York: Routledge, 2003.

Williams, Linda. "Film Bodies: Gender, Genre and Excess." *Film Quarterly* 44.4 (Summer 1991): 2–12.

_____. *Hard Core: Power, Pleasure, and the "Frenzy of the Visible."* 2d ed. Berkeley: University of California Press, 1999.

Wollen, Peter. "Godard and Counter Cinema: Vent D'Est," *Film Theory and Criticism: Introductory Readings*, 6th ed., edited by Leo Braudy and Marshall Cohen, 525–533. New York: Oxford University Press, 2004.

Zimmer, Catherine. "Caught on Tape? The Politics of Video in the New Torture Film," in *Horror after 9/11: World of Fear, Cinema of Terror*, edited by Aviva Briefel and Sam J. Miller, 83–106. Austin: University of Texas Press, 2011.

_____. "Surveillance Cinema: Narrative Between Technology and Politics." *Surveillance and Society* 8.4 (2011): 427–440.

From Jigsaw to Phibes: God, Free Will and Foreknowledge in Conflict

Fernando G. Pagnoni Berns and *Amy M. Davis*

"But he knows the way that I take; when he has tested me, I shall come forth as gold."—Job 23:10

"Blessed is the man who perseveres under trial, because when he has stood the test, he will receive the crown of life that God has promised to those who love him."—James 1:12

As the *Saw* franchise has progressed, an intriguing narrative strategy has emerged which is based on two interrelated points. The first point is that all of the characters in the films behave just as Jigsaw/John Kramer (Tobin Bell) predicts. No character performs an action that disrupts the mastermind's carefully-orchestrated plans. In none of the seven films do the characters decide not to listen to the cassette recorder or — eventually — choose not to follow the directives; likewise, characters consistently fail to take the kind of common-sense precautions that would help them to survive their ordeals. For example, in *Saw II* (Darren Lynn Bousman, 2005), Tate Obi (Tim Burd) reluctantly climbs into a furnace to get two syringes containing an antidote to the poison that is slowly killing both him and his companions, all of whom have been trapped within an elaborate "torture" house by Jigsaw. While inside the furnace, Tate fails to take the precaution of blocking open the furnace door, and ends up trapped inside, where he is burned alive. This critique does not imply that the characters in *Saw* necessarily should be aware of how the traps work or how their captor thinks, but it does establish that no character in any of the films commits an action which derails or at least complicates the general guidelines that Jigsaw has planned. In other words, no character can anticipate the thoughts of either John Kramer or his accomplices. Kramer, however, seems to know in advance each of the actions that the people caught in his traps will perform.

The second point is that all of the traps that Jigsaw has designed correctly attract the people they are designed to attract. Thanks to his repeated, uncanny success when it comes to ensnaring his victims and understanding how they will react to particular sets of circumstances, Jigsaw seems to have a supernatural or divine quality of foreknowledge that allows him to predict absolutely all of his subjects' future actions, as well as ensuring the proper functioning of his machines, no matter how long they sit idle, awaiting their quarry. It is for this reason that his traps are so effective. Foreknowledge (the ability to know the future) is often thought to be an essential trait of the very nature of God, since God, in His omniscience, cannot be ignorant of the future. Just like God, Jigsaw seems omniscient. Every plan, every mechanism and device goes just as it was planned. Each automatic door, each spring that pushes a deadly sharp object into the eyes of a poor victim, each hinge fulfills its role in Jigsaw's deadly plans.

Foreknowledge as a Threat to Free Will

The above points have been made not as a criticism of the inherent contradictions that run throughout the *Saw* franchise. Rather, it is this very absence of realism and logic — Jigsaw's seeming omniscience, the fact that no aspect of the traps (from the humans to the machines involved) ever fails to go according to plan — all tie into an important theme which runs throughout the franchise: free will.

It is very important to remember that, according to the narrative, all of the characters are placed in situations (caught and subjected to cruel tests) as a response to their own past actions, be it criminal actions or simply acts of omission. For example, several of the characters tested are there for committing actions that Kramer believes led them to waste the life that was given to them. The characters are punished or, rather, "tested," so that — in Jigsaw's world-view, at least — they can be redeemed by what is characterized as their freely-committed actions in the present. But in a game that seems contradictory, Jigsaw looks like an omniscient being who foresees everything and leaves nothing to chance, just as some argue that God governs our time completely, leaving nothing to chance. Jigsaw/God's foreknowledge of future — and supposedly free — decisions is grounded in Jigsaw/God's own omniscience. Even Kramer's ex-wife, Jill Tuck (Betsy Russell), points out in *Saw IV* (Bousman, 2007), "I didn't just get pregnant. It was carefully planned. Everything with John was." But even within these fatalistic notions, we must distinguish between divine providence — the theological notion that it is God who dictates even the smallest, seemingly most insignificant events taking place in the cosmos — and divine foreknowledge, a theological philosophy in which it is argued that God does not dictate our actions, but instead knows each one of them in advance (Zagzebski 2002).

If God knows beforehand every action that each individual will perform, and since, it must be posited in this scenario, those actions are written even before the birth of the person who will perform them, then every action undertaken by an individual (even if he believes himself to be free) is actually executed under the command of divine determinism. Robert Kane comments in his book *A Contemporary Introduction to Free Will* (2005) that "divine *foreknowledge* would be as much a threat to free will as divine *foreordination*" (150). For Kane, foreordination is when the actions of men are completely directed by God or a divine being. But Kane argues, in accordance with Saint Augustine, that knowing what will happen is not the same as *making* things happen. Nonetheless, as Kane points out, "if God has foreknown what we will do, we *cannot now do otherwise* than we actually do" (151). This means that "if free will requires the power to do otherwise, then no one would have free will" (152).

One counterargument to the notion that divine omnipotence negates the existence of free will has been posited by Pizarro and Helzer in their paper "Stubborn Moralism and Freedom of the Will" (2010). They argue that God may in fact be "outside" the current time and space in which we, as humans, find ourselves. God does not know "in advance" the decisions that we carry out in our time because God exists simultaneously at all points in time; therefore, "he does not *fore*know anything" (Ganssle 2001). "He knows the future in the same timeless moment he knows the present and the past" because "God knows everything *as it occurs* and *because it occurs*, yet from an eternal, timeless perspective" (Boyd and Eddy 2009). Our actions, then, are free because God's beliefs are not written in our past (Fischer 1989). As Kramer himself says in *Saw IV*, "time is an illusion." This statement further implies a divine quality to Kramer's understanding and knowledge of those he targets, even while it seems to contradict this idea of a god whose simultaneous existence at all points in time would — potentially — place that same god outside of time and, therefore, negate the possibility of His directing human actions or other events (such as natural disasters).

It can be argued that Jigsaw is in no way linked to God by the narrative; he did not create his subjects, he cannot "predict the future" (according to the normal meaning of that phrase), and he is totally at ease in his role as an engineer with expert knowledge of human behaviors and attitudes. However, we must also accept that both Jigsaw's forecasts and his torture mechanisms work perfectly, without any failure, even after Jigsaw dies in *Saw III* (Bousman, 2006). Also, all of the parties involved — both his victims and his accomplices — act exactly as he had expected them to act. Even when it seems that his plans have been subverted, there is always a contingency plan to ensure the originally-intended final result. For example, during the climax of *Saw VI* (Kevin Greutert, 2009), Jill Tuck subjects police officer Mark Hoffman (Costas Mandylor) to one of her husband's classic traps, the reverse bear trap, with which Amanda Young (Shawnee Smith) was tortured in the original *Saw* (James Wan, 2004). Hoffman manages to save himself from the device. Jill has not achieved her purpose or that of her late husband, which was to ensnare Hoffman and make him pass through a trap to test his own "interest in life."[1] Jill seeks police protection to escape Hoffman's vengeance, but he eventually finds her and kills her using the same trap. However, another accomplice will emerge to subject Hoffman to the tests that he had hitherto avoided. Dr. Lawrence Gordon (Cary Elwes) has, unknown to the audience, been an accomplice to Kramer throughout the series, and is revealed as such in the finale of *Saw VII* (Kevin Greutert, 2010). He then works to ensure that Hoffman passes through the situations which Kramer had intended for him from the beginning. This contingency plan shows that Jigsaw seems to have every event under his control, leaving nothing to chance, even after his own death. One could argue that even Jill's death was part of Kramer's fatalistic plans, given the level of control he has exercised both throughout his lifetime and beyond.

In all seven of the films to date, Jigsaw punishes his subjects for their free actions of the past, even while his actions in the present seem to contradict the very idea of the possibility of free will. His foolproof schemes seem to force his subjects to live out their horrific fates as they follow out Jigsaw's plans as it was thought they would. But what is meant by free will? A person who is really free has the *power* or *ability* to do what s/he wants to do, which in turn entails an *absence of constraints* or impediments preventing that person from doing what s/he want (Kane 2005). Freedom of action will depend, then, upon freedom of will (Pink 2004), and depends upon the decision to perform a certain action. To have free will, there should be nothing in the past of the person who exercises it which can determine the course of the actions they take. This is the basic idea supported by the Incompatibilists, who agree that causal determinism is incompatible with free will (Martin Fischer 1989; Pink 2004, Kane 2005, Nahmias et al., 2008). However, many philosophers throughout history have argued that determinism is not exactly incompatible with free will; this is referred to as Compatibilism Theory (Pink 2004; Kane 2005, Keim Campbell 2011; Doyle 2011). An individual can reach a predestined certain situation, but once in that situation, that person is free to choose the option that s/he considers best. What makes the subject genuinely free is the fact that s/he can choose between two or more options in what is called the principle of Alternate Possibilities (Frankfurt 1969; Doyle 2011). This principle states that individuals are morally responsible for their choices and actions only if they could have acted otherwise.

Responsibility for one's actions is an important point in the *Saw* franchise. This is illustrated not only in the reasons *why* the subjects are tested, but also in the narrative and thematic unity which runs throughout all of the films as a body. The *Saw* films are notable for the relatively high degree of continuity in the series, particularly in the attention given to the various stories and subplots, many of which return in the films following their initial appearance. Events begin in one film (i.e., in *Saw V*, Jill receives from her lawyer a wooden box containing John Kramer's last will and testament) and are resolved in another (the contents of the box are open for the audience in *Saw VI*). Elements that make their appearance in certain chapters anticipate future events in subsequent films (the metallic coffin containing broken glass is shown for the first time in *Saw IV* and then is used in *Saw V*), while many characters reappear throughout the franchise, some as main protagonists and others in minor roles revealed through brief flashbacks. Thus, the actions are continuously connected from one film to another, while each new character who appears in the series reveals a connection to past events and to the lives of Kramer and Hoffman. Every action seems to have created a strong effect that resonates not only in the film where the action takes place (or, in some cases, is first mentioned), but also throughout the saga.

But John Kramer, as can be seen throughout the franchise, actually punishes those who play with human life—those who want to embody the role of an all-powerful God. Therefore, Kramer rejects the possible framing of himself in the role of a divine being, in fact punishing those who assume that role. In fact, *Saw* as a franchise contains an important contradiction: on the one hand, the series highlights the existence of free will; on the other hand, it depicts, in Jigsaw, the existence of an omniscient, omnipotent figure who can (and does) weave together all of the saga's narrative threads, leaving nothing outside his control. Kramer assumes in himself the panoptic condition of "voyeur–God" (Martin 2011) that Michel Foucault discusses in *Discipline & Punish: The Birth of the Prison* (1977). According to Foucault, those who wield true power are invisible to those being punished—an invisibility which enables someone like Jigsaw to function in a god-like way.[2] So, most of the interactions between Kramer and his subjects occur through cameras and microphones, never in person, in order to maintain Jigsaw's anonymity and panoptic power (indeed, even the fact that we know the killer initially only as "Jigsaw," and do not learn his real name until *Saw II*, adds to his intangibility). This is reinforced with Kramer using a variety of gadgets, and the figure of Billy the Puppet, to communicate with the hostages. Even the puppet speaks through a television set, thereby creating a double removal of Kramer's physical presence. Upon closer examination, however, it is actually Hoffman who runs a virtual relationship with his subjects. Kramer does not have too much trouble making actual contact with his victims, when it is required. Indeed, all of the action in *Saw II* is framed by a dialogue between Kramer and Detective Eric Matthews (Donnie Wahlberg), most of which happens face to face. Kramer has no compunctions against making himself known personally when he first introduces himself to Detective Hoffman in *Saw V* (David Hackl 2008). Nor does he have a problem in being operated on by Dr. Lynn Denlon (Bahar Soomekh) with the intention of being kept alive a little longer in *Saw III* (Darren Lynn Bousman 2006).

Because Kramer is willing to interact in person with his victims whenever he feels that it is necessary, it is possible to argue that, despite some themes within the franchise which would suggest otherwise, Kramer/Jigsaw *cannot* be linked conclusively to a god-like entity, at least in the Christian sense. The notion of God's presence in the Christian tradition is one which claims that it is impossible for a human being to look upon the true face of God; indeed, our mortal inability to withstand a physical manifestation of God is such that even looking upon Him could be fatal (Wiersbe 2007), rendering His direct intervention in our lives, in physical form at least, to be impossible. Therefore, God is invisible if we consider that the "mystical sight of God transcends any experience we might indentify as seeing" (Miller 1996). Clyde Lee Miller, following neo–Platonic thought, argues that looking directly at our own face (through a mirror, for example), or looking at the faces of our fellow human beings, means that we actually see imperfect imitations of God's real face, and assumes that all human faces can be linked — mime-like — back to the notion of God as a perfect original, in whose image we have all been made. In other words, looking right at God's face would imply seeing the real face hidden behind our imperfect facade. Therefore, if Jigsaw/Kramer believed himself to be acting as/assuming the role of God on Earth, then he would avoid any instances in which he might interact with his victims or his disciples, as this is impossible in the Christian conception of God. The fact that he *does* interact personally with others, however, demonstrates that he does *not* consider himself divine.

Phibes and Biblical Revenge

In order to contrast the complexities inherent in Jigsaw's construction in terms of his possible divinity, it is helpful to compare him with a character whose framing within the realm of the divine is much clearer: Dr. Phibes, the main character of *The Abominable Dr. Phibes* (Fuest, 1971). *The Abominable Dr. Phibes* follows a series of horrible murders committed by Anton Phibes (Vincent Price), who is avenging the surgical team (eight doctors and a nurse) who let his wife die on the operating table. The doctor uses his theological knowledge to subject his victims to murders that resemble the Ten Plagues of Egypt from the Old Testament, and thus the victims are murdered by recreating versions of, for example, the sixth plague (which Phibes recreates by inflicting boils caused by bee stings), the plagues of frogs (the second plague) and locusts (the eighth plague), and the first-born's death (the tenth and final plague).

A number of parallels can be seen between John Kramer and Anton Phibes: both use highly sophisticated instruments to commit their murders. For example, at one point Phibes decides to murder one of his victims by locking him in his own car and, using an ice-spraying machine, freezes him to death (the seventh plague, the Plague of Hail). In addition, both Phibes and Kramer use methods which ensure the slow deaths of their victims, such as the agonizing blood extraction to which Dr. Longstreet (Terry-Thomas) is subjected (recreating the first plague, the Plague of Blood). The more significant relationship between the two characters and their ways of killing, however, is shown when Phibes decides to reenact the "death of the firstborn (the tenth plague)." In this test, Dr. Vesalius (Joseph Cotten) must withdraw from the anesthetized body of his son a key that will open the halter around his son's neck, thereby saving his son from a device which will pour acid on the boy's face if Vesalius does not unlock the trap in time. In a scenario which has the most obvious parallels to Kramer's traps in the *Saw* franchise, Dr. Vesalius has only six minutes to retrieve a key lodged near the boy's heart. This idea may well have inspired several similar "tests" faced by characters in the *Saw* series, such as in *Saw II*, when Michael Marks (Noam Jenkins) is tested by having to extract a key lodged in his eye if he wants to escape, or when, in *Saw VI*, a key that would open a trap is hidden within William Easton's (Peter Outerbridge) body. Moreover, the conversion of Kramer and Phibes into ingenious psychopaths is related to the death of a loved one: in Kramer's case, the trigger was the death of his unborn child when a pregnant Jill miscarried the baby after being injured by a drug-addict, Cecil (Billy Otis); as already noted, Phibes acts to "revenge" his wife's death during surgery. It is because of a personal loss that both men decide to enact what they would consider to be divine justice, rather than simply revenge.

This, clearly, is the idea that underlies Phibes' actions. If scientists and doctors in horror films like to "play God" (Stone 2009), Phibes literally takes on this role when he unleashes the ten plagues of Egypt on his unsuspecting victims. Like Kramer, Phibes makes carefully-calculated plans (e.g., victims die following the exact order in which the Biblical plagues fell). Like Jigsaw, his plans are developed, despite their complexity, in such a way that they run very smoothly, no matter how improbable it is that their plans could ever come together. Victims get the correct mask; rats must attack a pilot, and he responds in such a way that it seems predestined; cars stop to help a damsel in distress, as was expected; and so on, completing a series of highly-calculated events. It is this infallibility in the realization of the plans that could be said to imply each killer's divine aspects.

The final plague in the film, the Plague of Absolute Darkness (the ninth plague), is reserved for Doctor Phibes himself. After completing his plans, Phibes prepares "to sleep the eternal dream" next to his wife's preserved body, locking himself forever in a black casket whose cover contains a representation of the cosmogony. According to the film's narrative, at the end of the film, Phibes lies as the creator of the cosmogony after having assumed the role of God in the world.

There are, however, two important differences between Phibes and John Kramer. The first one is that most of the victims of Phibes' reenactment of divine punishment never have the opportunity to see Phibes' actual face hidden beneath his mask. Neither Phibes' face nor his voice are depicted as being perceptible to humans. Phibes' face — the real one — is hidden behind a mask, and even the mask, we are told, does not resemble Phibes' actual face. If humans are an imperfect copy of a divine creator, Phibes takes refuge in human skin to hide the "true" face of humanity, the true face of God. His face is revealed, briefly, when Phibes momentarily removes his mask to show himself to Vesalius (and by extension, to the audience). The face behind the human mask, which according to the Neoplatonists would be the true face of God of which we are imperfect copy, is that of a corpse, a skeleton. Phibes reveals the true human essence by revealing what it is behind the flesh, muscles and blood. The horror of dehumanization is thereby revealed. This face is only glimpsed briefly before Phibes hides it again under his mask, thereby returning it to the shadows. Likewise, the voice that we hear is not supposed to be Phibes' true voice (even if, clearly, it is undeniably Vincent Price's distinctive — even iconic — voice): the character speaks through a little voice box on his neck. Thus, at least according to the internal narrative of the film, the true face and voice of the "divine" Dr. Phibes are hidden from the sight and hearing of mere mortals.

The second difference is even clearer: Phibes, as stated, acts as though he was a God. His coffin becomes the universe for him; likewise, as discussed above, his "true" face is invisible to men and punishes by divine means. John Kramer, however, invokes an aura of God-like power in the omniscience shown in his plans. As he sees it, he does not punish anyone; he gives "opportunities" to his subjects so they can "appreciate" their lives. Furthermore, both sit in judgment upon others. Even the name chosen for Kramer's unborn child, Gideon, is a biblical reference to being "chosen by God"[3] to be a judge on the actions of humans (Mather 114). But Kramer believes that he tests his subjects so that they can decide freely. He does not consider himself to be judge and executioner, as Phibes thinks of himself. Kramer gives his victims the possibility of choosing between two alternatives, however horrific or morally questionable those alternatives might be. Though certainly the audience can see the illogical nature of his thinking, Kramer nonetheless presents the choices with which tests his victims as reasonable, and he depicts their saving of their own lives — even if it means the death of someone else (such as when Amanda Young viciously kills a man in order to retrieve from his body the key that will release her from the reverse bear trap) — as a kind of "path to salvation," complete with the spiritual and ethical aspects usually implied by the phrase. As Kramer himself seems to see it, offering his victims a chance to save themselves is the same as Kramer "giving them life," and putting them (if they survive the test) on a better path in life, where they will appreciate each new day and every new opportunity (thereby implying that, before Kramer — B.K.? — they did not). However, does all of this — but in particular the notion that Kramer "gives" his victims (new) life by offering them the chance of "salvation" — mean that, therefore, Jigsaw possesses divine traits?

To answer this question, we must distinguish between Kramer and Hoffman. Both men have in common the fact that their highly-complicated plans are performed flawlessly, which would imply certain quality of divine foreknowledge. But Kramer discloses not only his physical presence, becoming humanized in the process (unlike Hoffman, who eliminates those who suspect his true identity), but also acts with absolute contempt for those who precisely want to take on the role of God.

It is *Saw VI* that best illustrates this idea. The film's main victim is William Easton, President of Health Umbrella, a large health insurance corporation. Kramer's request for an experimental cancer treatment is denied because the expectations for his recovery are very low; thus, he is denied the chance for a cure or, at the very least, an extension of his life. Easton explains to Kramer how his business operates, analyzing the possibilities of success (the possibility of actually being covered by insurance) for his customers. According to Easton, the formula is "pretty complicated, actually, but in essence it breaks down to monthly payments multiplied by lifespan, minus the probability of illness, and if its sum is positive, we consider coverage." Kramer's reply is telling: "So, in a sense ... you choose who lives or dies?" What disgusts Kramer is the arrogance inherent in Easton's words: Easton's attitudes and working mode imply that he has invested himself with certain traits of Divine Providence, since he — like God — decides, ultimately, who lives and who dies. Easton, however, notes that he and Kramer have important traits in common. As Easton points out to him, in reference to Kramer's work in his and Jill's clinic, "Well, you try to predict people's behavior. So do I."

Nonetheless, despite this similarity, there is an important difference between the two men: Easton, by deciding who will receive insurance coverage, inhabits a role that produces divine fatalism; John Kramer's aura of divine foreknowledge, by contrast, does not necessarily imply that his ability to foretell his subjects' actions makes him responsible for those actions. We know that if we hold up an object and then let it go, it will fall to the ground; it does not mean that we have control over the force of gravity. Instead, it is from his refined knowledge of his subjects' personalities that he can predict their actions and, thus, appears to assume a role of divine foreknowledge. However, the contradiction between free will and fatalism still exists: Easton, for example, judges others by their free actions. When a client complains about the lack of insurance coverage (which is denied because the client forgot to mention a small surgery), Easton reproaches him: "I'm sorry, but your own actions have caused this." The client responds: "You've just given me a death sentence." Easton acts solely in response to the free actions of those individuals under his power (the clients), but offers them no alternatives by which they might "redeem" themselves. It is the refusal to offer an alternative that Kramer condemns, not only in Easton but also in Hoffman when, at the beginning of *Saw IV*, Hoffman condemns Seth (Joris Jarsky), his sister's murderer, to a death sentence disguised as an exercise of free will: even if the sentenced man breaks his own hands, the chances of coming out alive are nil, because the trap will not open anyway. Thus, Hoffman does the same as Easton and Phibes: he assume a role in which he decides the fate of others. That is why Jigsaw proclaims repeatedly that he did not kill anyone ("I give people a chance"): the subjects themselves decided their fate.

Likewise, Lt. Daniel Rigg (Lyriq Bent) in *Saw IV* is punished for his decision to set his marriage aside in favor of an obsessive search for the missing Eric Matthews. Jigsaw puts Rigg in a position from which he must assume a role similar to Kramer, as an agent who will show people the possibilities before them and eventually let them make their own decisions. Trying to save them all would be assuming for himself the role of divine providence: "His Salvation is out of your hands," says Jigsaw from a cassette recorder when Rigg comes face to face with another victim. "Force him into position to face his demon. And let him make the decision." If Rigg does what Jigsaw asks, placing the chosen subjects into their test scenarios, he will achieved his mission: find Matthews alive. If, instead, he insists upon saving them, misfortune will fall upon all the people immersed in the "game."

Conclusion

We thus return to the question asked at the beginning of this chapter: why and how does everything go as Kramer planned it? Is there no place for chance in his plans? Regarding the latter question, in *Saw V*, Kramer explains to Hoffman his decision to include Amanda[4] in his plans:

> HOFFMAN: "You're assuming this is gonna play out the way you want it?
> KRAMER: I assume nothing. I anticipate the possibilities and I let the game play out.
> HOFFMAN: Then why do you need Amanda in the game?
> KRAMER: To ensure that the rules are followed. She won't make decisions for anyone. She will just ... offer choices. (...) If you're good at anticipating the human mind, it leaves nothing to chance.

This brief dialogue provides some answers, showing that, in several important ways, Kramer is no Phibes. Although both appear to inflict similar tortures upon their victims (that is, punish them for past actions), Phibes acts as if he has embarked upon a theological crusade, in the sense that his assumption of a divine role means that everything that follows is pre-determined. He decides who lives and who dies, and how, where and when they will die. Phibes reenacted the biblical plagues of Egypt upon the sinners without leaving any alternate possibilities open to his victims by which they might survive. Like Jigsaw, his elaborate plans come to perfection despite their excessive complexity. Unlike Jigsaw, there is no chance or option for Phibes' punished subjects. Kramer, however, rejects that divine role. He punishes, but he also perceives himself as giving his victims the chance to correct past choices. If at certain times it appears that Kramer is a divine figure, this is because he ensures in his plans the complete absence of free will's great enemy: chance. Of course, the inclusion of Amanda to act as a sort of guide to prevent anyone from doing something that can derail Jigsaw's plans (what would happen if the imprisoned people just do not find the hidden recorder?) could be seen as a "cheat" since, in fact, she would be a determining agent who guides the imprisoned people to some extent. The same thing happens in *Saw VII* when Dr. Gordon appears to ensure that Kramer's plans are posthumously completed after Jill's failure. But does the fact that Kramer has created a world with hidden rules — rules that have left nothing to chance — make John Kramer a divine creator?

One might argue that the contradictions inherent in John Kramer's rejection of a divine role when — clearly — his sitting in judgment upon others and his testing of them has obvious parallels with Judeo-Christian stories of the tests God has inflicted upon his people (the trials of Job, and Abraham's near sacrifice of his son, Isaac, are just two such examples). It is this constant dialectic that makes the *Saw* franchise a series of complex films, far more than simply concerned with gore and torture. While Phibes assumes a divine role as an agent of vengeance whose plans come out just as they were conceived, the narrative is clear and linear. He is the "King Sun," the center of the cosmic system. The *Saw* films reveal John Kramer's almost divine capacity to predict human behavior, but what stands out in the franchise is the capacity of humans to discern and perform morally in free actions; hence the narrative is constantly fragmented by flashbacks. This strategy prioritizes how each individual action reverberates throughout the saga. Every free action affects another person and, therefore, a domino effect is produced as inter-connected links unfold. This narrative strategy is in line with Kramer's views about the free will of his subjects. Therefore, one can find — easily — contradictions in Kramer's role; these contradictions are summarized and highlighted in the saga's fragmented *mise-en-scène*.

In a direct contrast between Phibes and Kramer, it is possible to observe that Phibes does not present contradictions: using the knowledge gained in earning a Ph.D. in theology, Phibes decides who should die, and works relentlessly to implement divine punishments (Divine Providence). So, all his plans turn out flawlessly, just as he intended. All of the people he targets behave as he already knew that they would behave (Divine Foreknowledge). Kramer/Jigsaw, however, does not decide on his own who lives or dies: the subjects themselves choose — albeit unknowingly — through their free actions. Kramer is depicted as someone whose superior knowledge of human behavior allows him to predict unerringly every action that his subjects will perform. This divine foreknowledge, potentially, places the possibility of free action in danger — foreknowledge defies free will. But Kramer hates those who, like Easton, assume a divine role. He rejects divinity because it contradicts free will. If Kramer *seems* to have the gift of divine foreknowledge, one wonders whether this is just because he has the uncanny ability to eliminate the possibility of chance from his plans, which he manages by keeping the rules deliberately vague. But it is these very contradictions between Jigsaw's godly and human aspects that imbue the *Saw* franchise with a complexity which allows it to rise above the label of "torture porn" and achieve a true cult status.

Notes

1. It is necessary not to forget that Hoffman can be said to pervert Kramer's legacy.
2. Surveillance and panoptic principles are embodied in Jeremy Bentham's model prison, with its central observation tower, occupied with an officer who remains unseen, invisible to the prisoners, watching every prisoner's behavior. From that tower, a single guard could watch an entire row of prisoners from a central position. In fact, he could see everything.

3. Judges, 6–8.
4. In *Saw II*, she is locked up with other people in spite of being one of Jigsaw's accomplice, and thus she knows all the strategies in advance.

References

Boyd, Gregory, and Paul Eddy. *Across the Spectrum: Understanding Issues in Evangelical Theology*, 2d ed. Grand Rapids: Baker Academic, 2009.
Doyle, Bob. *Free Will: The Scandal in Philosophy*. Cambridge: Phi, 2011.
Fischer, John Martin. "Introduction: God and Freedom," in *God, Foreknowledge, and Freedom*, edited by John Martin Fischer, 1–56. California: Stanford University Press, 1989.
Foucault, Michel. *Discipline and Punish. The Birth of the Prison*. Alan Sheridan (trans.). New York: Pantheon, 1977.
Frankfurt, Harry. "Alternate Possibilities and Moral Responsibility." *The Journal of Philosophy*, Vol. 66, No. 23 (Dec. 4, 1969), 829–839.
Ganssle, Gregory. "Introduction: Thinking About God and Time," in *God & Time: Four Views*, edited by Gregory Ganssle, 9–27. Downers Grove: InterVarsity, 2001.
Kane, Robert. *A Contemporary Introduction to Free Will*. New York: Oxford University Press, 2005.
Keim Campbell, Joseph. *Free Will*. Malden: Polity, 2011.
Martin, David. *Curious Visions of Modernity. Enchantment, Magic, and the Sacred*. Cambridge: MIT Press, 2011.
Martin Fischer, et al. *Four Views on Free Will*. Malden: Blackwell, 2007.
Mather, Tim. *Judges. Book of Heroes*. Port Colborne: Gospel Folio, 2010.
Miller, Clyde Lee. "God's Presence: Some Cusan Proposals." *Nicholas of Cusa on Christ and the Church*, edited by Gerald Christianson and Thomas Izbicki, 241–250. New York: Brill, 1996.
Nahmias, Eddy, et al. "Is Incompatibilism Intuitive?" in *Experimental Philosophy*, edited by Joshua Knobe and Shaun Nichols, 81–104. New York: Oxford University Press, 2008.
Pink, Thomas. *Free Will: A Very Short Introduction*. New York: Oxford University Press, 2004.
Pizarro, David, and Erick Helzer. "Stubborn Moralism and Freedom of the Will," in *Free Will and Consciousness*, edited by Roy Baumeister, Alfred Mele and Kathleen Vohs, 101–120. New York: Oxford University Press, 2010.
Stone, Bryan. "Evil on Film," in *The Continuum Companion to Religion and Film*, edited by William Blizek, 310–321. New York: Continuum, 2009.
Wiersbe, Warren. *The Wiersbe Bible Commentary*. Colorado Springs: David C. Cook, 2007.
Williams, Clifford. *Free Will and Determinism: A Dialogue*. Indianapolis: Hackett, 1980.
Zagzebski, Linda. "Recent Work on Divine Foreknowledge and Free Will," in *The Oxford Handbook of Free Will*, edited by Robert Kane, 45–64. New York: Oxford University Press, 2002.

A Voice and Something More: Jigsaw as Acousmêtre and Existential Guru
Brian H. Collins

Using the ideas of Jean-Paul Sartre, Søren Kierkegaard, film theorist Michel Chion and the contemporary Slovenian philosopher Mladen Dolar, this essay will examine the *Saw* franchise in light of its deep continuities with Christian and existential morality and the central idea of the *acousmêtre*, the disembodied voice, which according to Dolar, "is precisely at the unlocatable spot in the interior and exterior of the law at the same time, and hence a permanent threat of a state of emergency."[1] And it is precisely this state of emergency, in which the participants in Jigsaw's games can make the existential decision to live in a new authentic way, that makes *Saw* a different kind of horror film. While the other great horror franchise of the last decade, the *Final Destination* series, focuses on the violent intrusion of the uncanny into normal life and the irresistible power of the death drive, *Saw* is built around the idea that, in the absence of an existential ethics, human freedom is far more terrifying than the inevitability of extinction. And this fact is the key to understanding the films.

"Hell Is Other People"

In contemporary horror cinema, the nearest antecedent to *Saw* is the 1995 film *Se7en*. Like *Saw*, *Se7en* uses the template of the crime thriller or police procedural combined with elements of physical horror and an eerily omniscient, charismatic master criminal, reviving the subgenre exemplified by Jonathan Demme's *The Silence of the Lambs*. In *Se7en*, "John Doe" is a killer inspired by the writings of Thomas Aquinas and Dante's *Inferno*, torturing and murdering people who commit the seven deadly sins using their own sins against them in *contrapasso* fashion. In *Saw*, Jigsaw's death traps and victim selection follow much the same principles, with the difference that suffering is not portrayed as punishment, but redemption. While *Se7en*'s super villain John Doe sees himself creating some kind of grisly *tableau mort* to edify and perhaps redeem the sinful world, Jigsaw is ostensibly out to help his victims directly by offering them the hope of redeeming themselves.[2] But unlike *Se7en* and *The Silence of the Lambs*, which continue to belong more to mainstream filmgoers than the fanatical fandom of the horror community, *Saw* has taken its place among the ranks of the great slasher franchises, earning the distinction of being the go-to Halloween movie from 2004 to 2010.

Like *Se7en* and the traditional slasher film, *Saw* is preoccupied with human evil, or sin. But *Saw*'s way of dealing with sin is very different from that of *Friday the 13th* and its ilk. The morality of the traditional slasher film can be summed up by Romans 6:23, "For the wages of sin is death, but the free gift of God is eternal life in Jesus Christ our Lord."[3] As Carol Clover famously observed,[4] those who frolic and fornicate in the slasher film become victims, while the "final girl" who survives the ordeal by keeping her Christian virtue gets to live past the credits and often into the sequel, and in terms of narrative time, what could we call that but "eternal life"? And it is a "free gift" in that the final girl is often someone (like Laurie Strode in *Halloween*) whose special status derives from her relationship to the killer, which is a result of circumstance and thus an unearned gift.

The morality lesson in *Saw* is quite different and seems to be taken from Jesus' famous words from the Sermon on the Mount recorded in Matthew 5:30: "And if your right hand causes you to sin, cut it off and throw it away; it is better for you to lose one of your members than for your whole body to go into Hell." But what, in this context, is "Hell?" To answer that question, we turn to Jean-Paul Sartre.

Traditional slasher films punish sins of the flesh with swift and violent retribution. But *Saw* punishes something more like what Sartre calls *la mauvaise foi* or "bad faith," an inauthentic existence, exemplified by the dishonest self-help guru Bobby Dagen in *Saw 3-D*, who falsely claims to have survived one of Jigsaw's traps.[5] It is in its rejection of bad faith, a position that on the surface appears to be a kind of narcissism ("I've got to be me!"), that we can see what rescues Sartre's philosophy from being a facile bourgeois individualism best suited for disaffected teenagers and neoconservatives, like Ayn Rand's execrable "Objectivism." As the French term suggests, bad faith is above all a deception of oneself. As a human being, Sartre argues, I am an ego consciousness anchored in a physical body. My freedom derives from self-consciousness and my responsibility derives from my spatial-temporal physicality. Bad faith is when I conveniently think of myself *only* as free (arrogance) or *only* as responsible (despair).

Ultimately, Jigsaw is not a vigilante figure who punishes (or tests) the guilty based on some absolute transcendent morality. In *Saw II*, Eric Matthews is being tested precisely because he has used his power as a police detective to dispense vigilante justice, planting evidence on those he knew were guilty. The sins of Jigsaw's victims are almost always grounded not in lust, malice or greed, but in bad faith, an inability to bear up to the twin burdens of freedom and responsibility that makes them unworthy of or unable to appreciate the precious gift of life.

How do Jigsaw's games work to cure bad faith? In short, by introducing the victim into a situation or game in which he or she is forced to make a choice. Sometimes the choice is to take a life, as Jigsaw instructs Dr. Gordon to take Adam's life in *Saw*. Sometimes the choice is to save a life, as in *Saw III*, where Jigsaw gives Jeff Denlon the choice to spare the drunk driver who killed his son and escaped punishment. Sometimes the choice is to do nothing, as in *Saw II*, where we learn that if Detective Eric Matthews had stayed and talked with Jigsaw as he was asked to do, he would have found his son, who was unharmed in a time-release safe in the room the entire time. In his efforts to outline an existential psychoanalysis Sartre writes:

> The fact that the ultimate term of this existential inquiry must be a choice, distinguishes even better the psychoanalysis for which we have outlined the method and principal features. It thereby abandons the supposition that the environment acts mechanically on the subject under consideration. The environment can act on the subject only to the exact extent that he comprehends it; that is, transforms it into a situation.[6]

What Sartre is describing here could well be one of Jigsaw's traps. Another verse from the book of Matthew will illustrate the point. Immediately before advising his audience at the Sermon on the Mount to hack off their right hands, Jesus says in Matthew 5:29, "If your right eye causes you to sin, tear it out and throw it away; it is better for you to lose one of your members than for your whole body to be thrown into Hell." This metaphor is made flesh in the pre-credits sequence that begins *Saw II*, in which Michael Marks wakes up to find an iron maiden-style spiked helmet locked to his head. The helmet has a timer that will cause it to snap closed over Michael's skull if he does not use a scalpel to cut out his right eye and retrieve the key that has been surgically implanted behind it. His eye has been causing him to sin because Michael, we learn, is a police informant who makes his living spying on others. Like many of Jigsaw's traps, this one combines *contrapasso* with an opportunity for personal redemption. It also forces the existential choice in which the subject transforms his or her environment into a *situation*. The eye versus body metaphor is even starker in *Saw IV* with the game of the rapist Ivan, who must either blind himself with spikes, Oedipus-style, in 60 seconds or be torn limb from limb.[7] Ivan and Michael fail their tests, both being unable to face the terror of freedom.

The first film, the one in which the titular tool figures most prominently, begins with a scene that strongly recalls Sartre's 1944 play *Huis Clos,* often translated "No Exit" or "In Camera." The play is about a man and two women locked in a room together in what they soon surmise is Hell. While they wait for their torturers to come, the room's inhabitants begin talk to each other about their past lives. And as they do they gradually realize that they are each other's torturers. "There's no need for red hot pokers," exclaims the man, "Hell — is other people."[8] Jigsaw would agree with the second part, but probably not the first; there clearly *is* a need for red hot pokers.

In the opening scenes of *Saw,* we are introduced to two men (later revealed as Adam and Dr. Lawrence Gordon) who find themselves chained by the leg to steam pipes on opposite sides of a decrepit bathroom. Between them in a pool of blood lies the body of a man seemingly dead from a self-inflicted gunshot to the head, holding in his hand a mini-cassette player. Each man finds on his person a mini-cassette with the Lewis Carrollesque instructions, "Play me." Adam is able to reach the player with some effort and plays his tape. But when Dr. Gordon asks Adam to throw the player to him so that he can play his own tape, the latter is mistrustful and replies, "No, you throw me the tape." Their subsequent fight over the mini-cassette player introduces one of the recurring themes of the *Saw* movies, recalling a well-known and anonymous parable: A man is shown Hell in the form of a room where a group of starving people are sitting around a huge pot of stew, holding spoons with handles so much longer than their own arms that they can not be used to get the stew into their own mouths. Heaven is another room, identical to the first, but where everyone is happy and well fed because they have learned to feed each other.

For Sartre, Hell is other people in that our sense of self is made possible by the way we see and are seen by the Other. This relation to the Other can either be masochistic (being for the Other) or sadistic (making the Other for me), both of which demonstrate bad faith. In the former case, I deny the freedom in myself; in the latter case, I deny it in the Other. Or, as Alain Badiou puts it, "The Subject is freedom's never-ending flight from being, and man is hell to man."[9] In Sartre's philosophy, Hell may be other people (or perhaps "Other people") but in *Saw* other people are the only way out of the real Hell, which is the alienation of modernity. This is very much the situation when we initially meet Adam and Dr. Gordon. We first hear the voice of Jigsaw, the still faceless and nameless man behind the game, playing on the mini-cassette player in Adam's hand. His first words could come right out of the book of Genesis, but this is not the Garden of Eden: "Rise and shine, Adam.

You're probably wondering where you are. I'll tell you where you might be. You might be in the room that you die in.... So are you going to watch yourself die today, Adam? Or do something about it?"

Adam truly is the "First Man" in that he is the first one (in narrative order, not chronologically) that Jigsaw tries to awaken from his miserable pseudo-existence into real Sartrean *vie engagée*. But it soon becomes apparent that this Adam, like the Biblical Adam, will fail and die, giving up the life he could have had and choosing death. In *Saw 3D* we will finally see that Dr. Gordon, not Adam, is Jigsaw's true disciple, keeping his faith pure against those who would pervert or distort it. Dr. Gordon, after all, is the one who makes the existential choice to use the saw on his own leg. It is fitting that *Saw* becomes the title of the series, since this titular tool stands as an emblem of the human predicament that the films more or less consistently address.

Sartre's solution to bad faith is a complex one that is elucidated throughout the 500-plus pages of ontological argument in *Being and Nothingness* and in his subsequent attempt to politicize his thought, 1960's *The Critique of Dialectical Reason*. But *Saw* takes a simpler approach, ignoring politics and ontology and focusing on the body, specifically as it experienced through Sartre's three modes of pain (*doleur*), illness (*mal*) and disease (*maladie*). "The body," Sartre writes, "is the instrument which I am. It is my facticity of being 'in-the-midst-of-the-world' in so far as I surpass this facticity toward my being-in-the-world."[10] In *Saw*, intrusive and violent experiences of pain and illness force awareness of their bodies into the consciousnesses of the participants in Jigsaw's games through intrusive and violent experiences of pain and illness. Pain is a nearly universal element in Jigsaw's traps, where victims stab, electrocute, mutilate and burn themselves to survive. In *Saw II*, illness too becomes a major part of the game, as the victims in the "Nerve Gas House" grow steadily weaker and more disoriented under the influence of an unseen poison that permeates the air. But it is really only Jigsaw himself who experiences his rapidly deteriorating body through all three modes: the *pain* of the car wreck in which he attempts suicide, the *illness* that accompanies his cancer treatments and the *disease* of his fatal brain tumor. The motive behind Jigsaw's games is ostensibly the desire to recreate in others the spontaneous existential moment of decision that he came to on his own as he pulled himself free of the wreckage of his car (as we see in a flashback sequence in *Saw IV*). It makes sense then that the unfolding of Jigsaw's back-story is such an important part of the series. Jigsaw's biography is the key to understanding what he wants for and from others. In the next section, we will examine Jigsaw himself using the thought of another existential philosopher, Søren Kierkegaard.

The Sickness unto Death

Let us begin by examining parallels between some of the defining events and aspects of Kierkegaard's life and the events that lead to John Kramer's transformation into Jigsaw. Returning to Sartre's triad of pain, illness and disease as themes in Kramer's life, we recall that Jigsaw suffers from an inoperable brain tumor brought on by colon cancer, the knowledge of which drives him to attempt suicide by car. After the car wreck, Kramer experiences an awakening and embarks on his career as Jigsaw. He still, however, lives under a death sentence and is progressively weakened by his disease until he succumbs to it on the operating table in *Saw III*. Kierkegaard too believed himself to be living under a death sentence. Before he turned twenty-one, he watched his mother (who had been the maid to his father's deceased first wife), two brothers and three sisters die and became convinced that he would not live past the age of thirty-three. Although he lived to be forty-two, Kierkegaard's fixation on his mortality was a profound influence on his thought, prompting him to reflect on the transitory nature of the world. Writing as Anti-Climacus in *The Sickness unto Death,* he argues that in the modern situation, "[the] biggest danger, that of losing oneself, can pass off in the world as quietly as if it were nothing; every other loss, an arm, a leg, five dollars, a wife, etc., is sure to be noticed."[11] The logic of Jigsaw's traps reflects a similar concern. Take for example his early practice of cutting a puzzle piece out of the skin of those who did not survive his traps ("a symbol that that subject was missing something — a vital piece of the human puzzle — the survival instinct")[12] suggests that people should pay more attention to what they are losing.

Another parallel between Jigsaw and Kierkegaard is the presence in each man's life of a broken relationship that does not seem to be over, but somehow suspended, and whose failure leads each man to choose a life of asceticism. We learn in *Saw IV* that John Kramer was once a civil engineer happily married to Jill Kramer (née Tuck), a doctor who runs a clinic for drug addicts. But after Jill miscarries her and John's child seven months into her pregnancy as a result of one of her clients attempting to rob the clinic, their marriage deteriorates and ends in divorce. Kramer's depression after the miscarriage seems to have been the major contributing factor in the dissolution of the marriage. But after he becomes Jigsaw, he remains in contact with Jill, even involving her in his games. While he is undergoing brain surgery in *Saw III*, Jigsaw hallucinates that the surgeon is Jill and tells her that he loves her, provoking jealous tears from his protégé Amanda. And in a videotaped will seen in *Saw V*, he tells Jill she is "[his] heart."

Kierkegaard's famous broken engagement with Regine Olsen shares some important characteristics with Jigsaw's relationship with Jill. At the beginning of their courtship, Kierkegaard pursued Regine (who was ten year younger) for two years before they became engaged in 1840. Soon after the engagement Kierkegaard began writing his dissertation and grew increasingly depressed, largely cutting himself off from his fiancée except for written correspondence. And less than a year after he proposed, Kierkegaard broke off the engagement, plunging himself and Regine into heartbreak. Guilt-ridden, he tried to spare her the public humiliation by making it look as if it were she who had rejected him and he never pursued romance again. Regine eventually married another man and moved away to the Dutch West Indies, but in her absence she remained at the center of Kierkegaard's emotional, spiritual and intellectual life. In a dedication page (no longer extant) to the posthumously published *The Point of View of My Work as an Author*, he cites her as his direct inspiration, dedicating to Regine the book "which to some extent belongs to her, by one who belongs to her completely," despite the fact that the two almost never spoke after their engagement ended.[13]

Kierkegaard left Regine largely because he felt that he could not reconcile his religious vocation with the demands of married life, an idea he examined in one of his most famous works, 1843's *Either/Or*, which outlines two mutually exclusive realms of existence: the aesthetic and the ethical. In a subsequent work, *Stages on Life's Way*, Kierkegaard adds a third realm, the religious, which supercedes the ethical just as the ethical supercedes the aesthetic. In a strange way, John Kramer's transformation into Jigsaw roughly follows a progression through Kierkegaard's three realms, also presented as stages toward authentic religious experience. The first stage, the aesthetic, corresponds to Kramer's life helping to develop properties as a civil engineer. Admittedly, the dashing Don Juan figure that Kierkegaard describes as the exemplar of the aesthete in *Either/Or* bears little resemblance to the dour John Kramer, who seems to grimace and glower continually even in his most carefree days with Jill. But even if his prior life is not exactly the life of an aesthete, the crisis that destroys it is certainly the *crisis* of the aesthete. As John Caputo explains,

> The aesthete's life is volatilized into a series of discontinuous moments, governed by the rule of forgetting whatever is unpleasant about the past and recalling only its pleasures, and of reducing the future to a new supply of possible diversions. The aesthete lacks the unity of existence conferred upon life by assuming responsibility for the past and giving assurance that one's word will be kept in the future.[14]

In *Saw IV*, we see Jigsaw administering his first ever test (discounting his own) to Cecil Adams (another "Adam," or First Man), the drug addict responsible for Jill's miscarriage.

JIGSAW: I forgive you Cecil. I do, but addiction has ruined your life.
CECIL: I'm bleeding man. Please just let me go.

JIGSAW: I could let you go, but that wouldn't serve you. I'll tell you what I will do though. I will give you a tool to reclaim your life, and to discard the vices that have corrupted your soul.
CECIL: I don't have a fucking soul.
JIGSAW: Maybe you will in the next life. You see things aren't sequential. Good doesn't lead to good nor bad to bad. People steal, don't get caught. Live the good life. Others lie, cheat and get elected. Some people stop to help a stranded motorist and get taken out by a speeding semi. There's no accounting for it.

Jigsaw may not have lived as an aesthete himself (although there is something to be said for the fact that he spent his career designing for high-dollar construction projects), but as his conversation with Cecil Adams demonstrates, in the wake of his misfortunes he sees the world as one devoid of consequence or continuity. In many ways, his traps, especially the ones that target typically (and topically) 21st century villains like the predatory lenders and HMO executives in *Saw VI*, seek to deliver consequences to those powerful or influential enough to avoid them. Many of them also force people to make ethical choices, like the man who must save the drunk driver who killed his son in *Saw III* or the woman in *Saw 3D* who must set herself free of her abusive boyfriend.

The uniquely consequential world Jigsaw creates in his traps corresponds to Kierkegaard's second stage, the ethical, which really begins for John Kramer with his involvement in Jill's vaguely explained clinic for drug addicts. In *Either/Or*, Kierkegaard contrasts the seducer with the married man as paragons of the aesthetic and ethical modes, respectively. John Caputo, again, explains,

> The aesthete lacks a self because his life lacks the decisiveness of a choice, the most pointed example of which for Kierkegaard is the marital vow. The "moment" ... is not a slice of time frozen on the face of a Grecian urn but the moment of choice, or moment of truth, that is charged by the enduring commitment of the vow. In the moment, the dispersed flow of life is gathered into a unity. [The] self assumes responsibility for its past and its future, committing itself to a course of action and accepting responsibility for its consequences. A self then is a unity in which all that one has been and commits oneself to is gathered together in a moment of decision.[15]

It is not hard to see the parallels between Kierkegaard's existential self and the "soul" Jigsaw is offering Cecil. The self in Kierkegaard's thought is neither a substance nor an essence, but the result of a moment of decision. In the same way, when Jigsaw tells Cecil he may have a soul "in the next life," he is not talking about the afterlife but rather the life that will begin when Cecil makes the choice to save himself by pushing his face into a rack of knives.

It is difficult to pinpoint the moment when Jigsaw begins to enter the third stage, the religious, in which, Kierkegaard argues, true authenticity is possible. Kierkegaard's most sustained reflection on the religious suspension of the ethical comes in what is probably his best known work, *Fear and Trembling*, a meditation on the Binding of Isaac described in Genesis. The religious suspension of the ethical, for obvious reasons, is the point at which many readers see Kierkegaard's project taking an ominous turn. Over the course of the *Saw* series, we see Jigsaw's ethos—out of which he acts to kidnap, kill and torture so that participants in his games may save themselves and (sometimes each other)—being warped (or warped further, depending on one's point of view) by his less scrupulous disciples. One by one we see Amanda Young, Mark Hoffman and even Jill Tuck abandon Jigsaw's insistent requirement that every game have a way out.[16] In short, they no longer want to help, but simply to kill; they no longer have the properly religious love for humanity that allows Jigsaw to do his work. In Kierkegaard's analysis of the character of Abraham as the "knight of faith," he writes,

> The absolute duty can lead one to do what ethics would forbid, but it can never lead the knight of faith to stop loving. Abraham demonstrates this. In the moment he is about to sacrifice Isaac, the ethical expression for what he is doing is: he hates Isaac. But if he actually hates Isaac, he can rest assured that God does not demand this of him, for Cain and Abraham are not identical. He must love Isaac with his whole soul. Since God claims Isaac, he must, if possible, love him even more, and only then can he sacrifice him, for it is indeed this love for Isaac that makes his act a sacrifice by its paradoxical contrast to his love for God.[17]

While his disciples choose victims whom they hate or on whom they want revenge, Jigsaw (generally) chooses those whom he thinks need the most help, like the despicable insurance executive William Easton in *Saw VI*, modern day equivalent of the hated Roman tax collector in the Gospels. The audience is presumably ready to applaud the just punishment of business-suited men and women introduced as those who exploit the poor with predatory loans or cancel the health insurance of gravely ill patients, but in Jigsaw's game, they can be redeemed. In the end William Easton passes all his tests, but is killed in the end by the son of a man whose insurance he cut off, causing him to die for lack of treatment. This revenge is clearly the fulfillment of the audience's wish, not Jigsaw's.

But if we compare Jigsaw and his games with God's command to Abraham to sacrifice Isaac on Mount Moriah, it is clear that Jigsaw's analogue in the Bible is not Abraham, but God himself. Jigsaw does, it is true, act on a religious suspension of the ethical, brought on by his road-to-Damascus experience pulling himself out of his wrecked car following his failed suicide; he is justified by his faith and feels charged with spreading it. But Jigsaw does not act like an evangelist. To the majority of those who play his games, he is much more like the God of Abraham, a disembodied divine voice, demanding the faith of others — faith that if they do what he says, no matter how horrific it sounds, they will survive.

Finally, Jigsaw and Kierkegaard are also alike in their use of pseudonymity, the taking up of various identities. Kierkegaard wrote under a long list of pseudonyms, including Victor Eremita, Johannes de Silentio, Constantin Constantius, Johannes Climacus and Anti-Climacus. Jigsaw claims never to have encouraged the pseudonym the media gives him, but he does multiply himself through disguises to the point where it is impossible to tell whether it is him or one of his disciples acting in a given game. Jigsaw's avatars include Billy, the garish tricycle-riding mannequin; a robed figure whose face is covered in a pig mask; and of course a disembodied voice recorded on mini-cassettes, in which he is at his most Godlike. In the next section, we will treat this last avatar of Jigsaw in detail.

Ecce Corpus

Throughout the first film Jigsaw hides in plain sight like Poe's purloined letter, first as the ersatz corpse lying between Adam and Dr. Gordon, then as Dr. Gordon's unconscious patient. Every time we see him, John Kramer is outside the realm of the living, which makes all the more dramatic the film's closing scene in which he slowly stands up from the floor and reveals himself to have been waiting and listening with a terrible kind of patience to see the outcome of his game. Both men took him to be dead. Dr. Gordon in fact, took him to be dead (or as good as) when Jigsaw was his patient. But at the end of the film, there is a great reversal that can only be called religious in which those who appeared to be living are revealed to be (spiritually) dead and the one who is dead is revealed to be alive. Jigsaw is the man who has died to this world in order to be resurrected, Christ-like, into a new life. And like Kierkegaard's Christ he wants followers, not worshippers.[18]

But like God in the story of Abraham and Isaac[19] or the Wizard of Oz, Jigsaw is first (and most often throughout the franchise) represented as an acousmatic voice. The word "acousmatic" derives from the French *acousmêtre*, a term first used by early 20th century theorist and avant-garde composer Pierre Schaeffer to describe a sound heard from an unseen source via some kind of mediator like a radio or a record player or, in cinema, from off-screen like the unseen killer in Fritz Lang's *M*. The origin of the word is the Greek term used to designate the outer circle of Pythagoras' followers, the *akousmatikoi*, who only heard the teacher's voice from behind a curtain while the inner circle, the *mathematikoi*, received face-to-face instruction. According to Porphyry, the *akousmatikoi* received the summary version of his teachings, while the *mathemetikoi* learned the detailed version of the doctrine. After Pythagoras' death, his followers split along these same lines with the *akousmatikoi* embracing mysticism, religion and secrecy and the *mathematikoi* becoming, naturally, mathematicians.[20] Another explanation, this one from Diogenes Laertius, is that the *akousmatikoi* were not a sect of Pythagoreans but that the term referred to novices in the school who were required to take a vow of silence and listen to the master through a curtain before they were allowed to see his face during the teaching. Both of these understandings of the term bring to mind central elements in *Saw*. Porphyry's explanation recalls the schism that follows Jigsaw's death between those like Mark Hoffman and Amanda Young who made it impossible to survive the death traps and those like Dr. Lawrence Gordon who stayed true to Jigsaw's vision. The explanation of Diogenes Laertius fits the image of the players in Jigsaw's games, who only hear his acousmatic voice and never see his face.

Schaeffer, who, along with Jérôme Peignot, took the idea of the *akousmatikoi* from Pythagorean legend and applied it to modern sound technology was not only the originator of *musique concrète* and a music theorist, he was also a deeply Catholic thinker. He investigated sound through the framework of phenomenology as developed by Edmund Husserl, a man who saw the fundamental problem of philosophy as the problem of God, and who argued that the "great problem that can be solved only at the end of philosophy consists in the clarification of the symbolic process that takes place in religious symbols."[21] We must read Schaeffer as a devout man as well as a follower of Husserl, and therefore always in pursuit of "the problem of God," which, I argue, profoundly informs his writings on the *acousmêtre*.

True to his phenomenological roots, Schaeffer writes:

> [Acousmatics] corresponds to a reversal of the usual procedure.... It is no longer a question of knowing how a subjective listening interprets or deforms "reality," of studying reactions to stimuli. It is the listening itself that becomes the origin of the phenomenon to be studied. The concealment of the causes does not result from a technical imperfection, nor is it an occasional process of variation: it becomes a precondition, a deliberate placing-in-condition of the subject. It is *toward it*, then, that the question turns around: "What am I hearing?"[22]

In other words, when I am listening to someone who is present and speaking directly to me I am paying attention to a whole host of visual cues, some as subtle as eye movements and others as blatant as pointing a finger, to confirm that I am properly understanding what is being said; I am listening to the speaker. But with the acousmatic voice all those visual cues are absent and all my attention is focused on the sound of the voice; I am listening to sound. But at the same time, in the absence of the speaker, I begin to question the source of the voice and use my deepened awareness of the sound to make guesses about who is speaking. We see this in *Saw* when Adam and Dr. Gordon first listen to their respective tapes. Listening to his tape, Adam's gaze moves from the tape player in his hand to the top right corner of the screen before resting on the floor in the middle distance. Dr. Gordon, when listening to his tape, scans the room continually for clues, looking at Adam when the voice tells him that he must kill him, looking at the clock when the voice tells him he must do so by six o'clock and looking at the body of Jigsaw when the voice mentions the "man in the room." But, as Schaeffer predicts, he is also listening with a deepened awareness of the texture of the sound and this allows him to detect the faint background voice saying "follow your heart," which is heard first as an unidentifiable click or tape hiss before being deciphered by rewinding the tape and replaying it. This hidden message would have been, of course, impossible to convey in a live conversation.

In this episode and others, *Saw* also plays with the distinction between acousmatic voice and text. By nature acousmatic sound is public and heard by everyone within range, even if it is addressed only to one person, and so Jigsaw uses it to convey a message he wants everyone to know, for example, the fact that the game requires Dr. Gordon to kill Adam in order to save his family. He uses text, on the other hand, to convey a message to one person that he wants to be kept secret from the other, for example, the message found next to the cigarette in the box that reminds Dr. Gordon he "[doesn't] need a gun to kill Adam," the implication being that he can surreptitiously dip one end of the cigarette in the poisoned blood that surrounds the body on the floor and then give it to Adam, a smoker.

The connection of Schaeffer's phenomenology of listening to the esoteric speculations of the Pythagoreans speaks to the mystical, Catholic bent in his thought and his idea of acousmatics is inextricably linked to ritual initiation and the contemplation of the unseen and perhaps unseeable. In subsequent acousmatic theories developed by Schaeffer's student Michel Chion the phenomenology of listening becomes less significant and its role in film is seen as central. Chion writes,

> Fiction films tend to grant three powers and one gift to the acousmetre, to the voice that speaks over the image but is also forever on the verge of appearing in it. First, the acousmetre has the power of seeing all; second, the power of omniscience; and third, the omnipotence to act on the situation. Let us add that in many cases there is also a gift of ubiquity — the acousmetre seems to be able to be anywhere he or she wishes. These powers, however, often have limits we do not know about, and are thereby all the more disconcerting.[23]

We can read the plot development in *Saw* as an attempt to discover these limits. We should also notice that the powers and the gift Chion ascribes to the *acousmètre* are nothing less than Godlike.

In many ways, *Saw* combines the cinematic aspects of the *acousmètre* as explicated by Chion with the mystical and initiatory aspects of the Pythagorean acousmatic voice that inform Schaeffer's phenomenological investigations. Jigsaw's "movement" shares many characteristics with the community-philosophy-religion founded by Pythagoras. Both require an initiation of new members that centers on properly understanding the words spoken by the master's voice. Both rely on secret communication and the interpretation of symbols and codes. Both suffer a schism following the founder's death. Both deify their leader even before his death. One poster for *Saw VI* illustrates the Pythagorean aspects of Jigsaw's character. Under the tagline, "Jigsaw's scheme will finally be understood," the poster shows a large grayscale image of Jigsaw's face in profile, with a blood-spattered puzzle piece covering his mouth. What better way to illustrate the acousmatic voice of Jigsaw?

In cinema, disacousmatization occurs when the source is revealed, as when Dorothy pulls back the curtain to show the diminutive man behind the "Great and Powerful Oz" in *The Wizard of Oz*. In *Saw*, Billy the puppet, which is first seen by Amanda, represents a partial disacousmatization: we see a source for the sound, and since the puppet is built like a ventriloquist's dummy with a moving lower jaw, it even appears to be speaking in some way. There is even a false disacousmatization that precedes the film's final twist: After Adam has bludgeoned Zep to death, Adam, Dr. Gordon and the audience believe they have seen Jigsaw's death. Zep, after all, has been the one watching the two men through a hidden camera and since the voice on the tape is obviously disguised, it is reasonable to presume that it is his. But when Adam begins going through Zep's pockets looking for a key to his chain, he finds another tape recorder and it becomes clear to everyone that Zep is not Jigsaw. The real disacousmatization of Jigsaw comes at the end of the film when he is revealed to be the corpse on the floor and comes dramatically to life. At the denouement, the one who has been dead is alive and every living person we have seen turns out to be dead (at least in Jigsaw's judgment).

Building on the work of Chion and Schaeffer, Dolar argues that the Pythagorean practice of divorcing sound from vision is "a stroke of genius at the very origin of philosophy" whose point is "to separate the spirit from the body."[24] Hitchcock's *Psycho*, Dolar tells us, "revolves entirely around the question 'Where does the mother's voice come from? To which body can it be assigned?'"[25] *Saw* also addresses itself to this question of assigning the voice to a body. When Dr. Gordon finds the saw and begins to strongly suspect that they are in a game devised by the infamous Jigsaw, whom he knows from the television news, the problem of the voice and the body begins to move toward a solution. The script reads:

> LAWRENCE: (everything is becoming more clear now) He doesn't want us to cut through our chains. He wants us to cut through our feet. (Adam looks up at him, eyebrows raised.) I think I may know who's done this to us.

ADAM: What did you say? (he stands up; is Lawrence hiding something from him?)
LAWRENCE: It's not someone I know personally. It's ... just someone I know of.
ADAM: (getting slightly frantic again) Jesus Christ! Tell me, who is it?![26]

For Dolar, the use of recording devices to produce an acousmatic voice represents the banalization of the *acousmêtre*, depriving it of its uncanny properties by making the tape player or phonograph into "an un-problematic stand-in" for the real source of the voice.[27] But *Saw* restores the uncanniness of the acousmatic device by allowing multiple bodies to serve as sources for the recorded voice of Jigsaw, notably that of Mark Hoffman. Add to that the fact that Jigsaw, like Professor Brian O'Blivion in David Cronenberg's *Videodrome*, survives his own death and lives on by continuing to act in the world through the traps he has set up and the tapes he has recorded and planted for others to find. In this aspect, *Saw* owes much to Wes Craven's ingenious meta-slasher franchise *Scream*, where we also find the problem of connecting a voice to a body. Taking the famous "Babysitter and the Man Upstairs" motif used in 1979's *When a Stranger Calls* and updating it for the cellular age, each of the four *Scream* movies hinges on the question of whose disguised voice is making the mysterious phone calls to his or her victims before dispatching them. We know, of course that the Ghostface Killer is making the calls, but in each movie a different character (sometimes more than one) is using the identity. The Ghostface killer, like Jigsaw, achieves a non-supernatural immortality by virtue of being a disguised voice that can be replicated after the murderer's death[28] and used by others who continue to murder in his or her name, creating an illusion of continuity. The idea of Jigsaw as a role rather that an individual is suggested in the advertising art for *Saw V*, the film in which Mark Hoffman takes up Jigsaw's identity. The poster shows a dark haired, younger man with what appears to be the death mask of John Kramer strapped to his face. *Scream* also involves a partial disacousmatization in that when the Ghostface Killer appears on the screen, the body to which the voice belongs is revealed without revealing the identity of the speaker. The Ghostface Killer's face is covered by mask that closely resembles, perhaps by design, the figure in Edward Munch's 1893 painting "The Scream." Its eyes and mouth are elongated black ovals, making it a face that is no face. Connecting Munch's painting to the acousmatic voice, Dolar writes,

> The painted scream is by definition mute, stuck in the throat; the black opening is without the voice which would mollify it, fill it, endow it with sense, hence its resonance is all the greater. Not only are we unable to hear the scream, it is also the homunculus, the strange screaming creature, the alien, who cannot hear us; he/she/it has no ears, he/she/it cannot reach anybody by the scream, nor can he/she/it be reached. If disacousmatization posed the problem of pinning down the voice whose source is hidden, here we have the opposite problem: a source of voice

to which no voice can be assigned, but which for that very reason represents the voice all the more.[29]

The paradigm of the acousmatic voice is the Mother's voice, heard from within the womb. *Psycho* makes this connection by connecting the voice to the Spectral Mother, abject and decaying. This Spectral Mother, exemplified by the slowly decomposing, dried-out corpse of Mrs. Bates, takes center stage in Wan's two other horror films from the *Saw* period, 2007's *Dead Silence* and 2010's *Insidious*. In *Dead Silence*, she is the decaying corpse of Mary Shaw[30] and in *Insidious*, the Spectral Mother returns as the Old Woman portrayed by William Friedman. Both Mary Shaw and the Old Woman closely resemble each other as well as their archetype, Mrs. Bates, with desiccated skin covered in sores and black Victorian ankle-length dresses. Accompanying both these Spectral Mothers is the figure of the mannequin, a stand-in for the child. In *Dead Silence*, this latter figure takes the form of an evil ventriloquist's dummy, shown in the cover art with Mary Shaw's grotesquely gnarled index finger covering its mouth in a hushing gesture. In *Insidious*, the mannequin is subtly introduced as a drawing of Billy, the mannequin from *Saw*, which appears on the chalkboard over the shoulder of the film's main character, Josh Lambert; the mannequin that stands in for the child in *Dead Silence* is here being connected to the man who will eventually fall victim to the nightmares of his childhood when the Spectral Mother returns from the grave to possess him.

Dead Silence, more than *Insidious*, takes up the problem of the acousmatic voice: Mary Shaw steals her victim's voices by tearing out their tongues and leaving them with gaping, empty mouths, their jaws distended like a broken puppet's. In the form of Billy, the puppet, recalling both the ventriloquist's dummy in *Dead Silence* and the "homunculus" Dolar sees in "The Scream," is an important figure in the early *Saw* movies, while the Spectral Mother is completely absent from the series. Why does Wan rely so strongly on this figure in his other horror films and completely leave her out of *Saw*? One possibility suggests itself. In psychoanalytic terms, *Saw* takes place not in the realm of the Spectral Mother, but the Law-giving Father. More to the point, we are in the realm of God the Father, the one who commands Abraham to sacrifice his only son, the Pythagorean God of mystery, secrecy and fanatical devotion, the God whose acousmatic voice signals the threshold across which his followers can pass through death to life.[31]

Conclusion

The sickness that Jigsaw diagnoses in the world is what Sartre calls "bad faith," a flight from freedom that translates into a general lack of appreciation for the possibility inherent in human life. Passing through Kierkegaard's stages of the aesthetic and the ethical, he arrives at a religious suspension of the ethical in which he acts in the place of God, making terrible demands and offering the gift of life to those he calls into his games. But, as Matthew 22:14 has it, "Many are called, but few are chosen." As John Kramer, Jigsaw is a bounded individual entity, a deathly ill man who embodies First Corinthians 1:25, "For God's foolishness is wiser than human wisdom, and God's weakness is stronger than human strength." But in his other forms — the puppet, the pig-headed figure and the voice — he is merely a function. And we see many others step into this function throughout the franchise, including Jill Tuck, Mark Hoffman, Amanda Young and Lawrence Gordon, creating a kind of priesthood, an office to be passed on. But as Jigsaw survives death through his followers, he becomes something more than a mortal man. This idea is expressed in the poster art for *Saw VI*. Above the tagline, "His disease is spreading," (recalling Sartre's pain, illness and disease) we see what at first seems to be simply a minimalist rendering of Jigsaw's face, but which a closer inspection reveals is a bird's eye view of a vast crowd of figures, identically clad in Jigsaw's black-and-red cloak and pig's-head mask. This image recalls Slavoj Žižek's argument in *The Monstrosity of Christ*:

> What, then, is "sublated" in the case of Christianity? It is not the finite reality which is sublated (negated — maintained — elevated) into a moment of ideal totality; *it is, on the contrary, the divine Substance itself (God as a Thing-in-Itself) which is sublated: negated (what dies on the Cross is the substantial figure of the transcendent God), but simultaneously maintained in the transubstantiated form of the Holy Spirit, the community of believers which exists only as the virtual presupposition of the activity of finite individuals.*[32]

In Jigsaw's existential "religion" (complete with doctrinal squabbles, heretics, schisms, myths and of course, sacrifice), the role of the acousmatic voice, freed from Jigsaw's human body, transcendent and sacramental, serving as Paraclete to his "community of believers" and creating a ritualized state of emergency in which the participants in his games can pass from un-life to life (or, more often, death). With Jigsaw dead, disacousmatization becomes impossible and the always-already acousmatic nature of his voice illustrates that death has lost truly its sting — his commandment to "Cherish Your Life" does not mean to fear death, but rather to face up to freedom.

Notes

1. *A Voice and Nothing More* (Cambridge, MA: MIT Press, 2006), p. 120.
2. Another variation on this theme is Pascal Laugier's 2007 film *Martyrs*, in which a vaguely Catholic cult kidnaps and tortures young women to vicariously experience through them the kind of religious ecstasy experienced by martyrs like Joan of Arc.
3. Bible verses taken from *The HarperCollins Study Bible: New Revised Standard Version*

with the Apocryphal/Deuterocanonical Books, ed. by Wayne A. Meeks, et al. (New York: Harper-Collins, 1993).

4. "Her Body, Himself: Gender in the Slasher Film," *The Dread of Difference: Gender and the Horror Film*, ed. by Barry Keith Grant (Austin: University of Texas Press, 1996), p. 66–113.

5. This idea is not, of course, followed consistently throughout the series. In fact, *Saw 3D* itself opens with the death of a typical slasher victim when a sexually promiscuous and duplicitous female being eviscerated with a buzzsaw by the two men with whom she has been false.

6. *Being and Nothingness: A Phenomenological Essay on Ontology*, trans. Hazel E. Barnes (New York: Washington Square University Press, 1956), p. 572.

7. Jigsaw calls Ivan a "voyeur" because he videotapes his assaults, although that seems by far to be the least of his crimes. It would make far more sense for a rapist to castrate than to blind himself, but perhaps here we can follow Freud, who argued in a footnote he added in 1911 to *The Interpretation of Dreams* that, "The blinding in the legend of Oedipus, as well as elsewhere, stands for castration." *The Interpretation of Dreams: The Complete and Definitive Text*, trans. and ed. James Strachey (New York: Basic, 1955), p. 408, n. 1.

8. *No Exit and Three Other Plays*, trans. by Stuart Gilbert and I. Able (New York: Vintage International, 1989), p. 43.

9. A. Badiou, "Jean-Paul Sartre (1905–1980)," in *Pocket Pantheon: Figures of Postwar Philosophy*, trans. David Macey (London: Verso, 2009), p. 18.

10. Sartre, *Being and Nothingness*, p. 359.

11. *The Sickness unto Death: A Christian Psychological Exposition of Edification and Awakening* by Anti-Climacus (Søren Kierkegaard), Trans. with an Introduction and Notes by Alastair Hannay (London and New York: Penguin, 1989), pp. 62–63.

12. *Saw II*.

13. Steen Tullberg, "On the Genesis of *On My Work as an Author*," *Kierkegaard Studies Yearbook 2010: Kierkegaard's Late Writings*, ed. by Niels Jørgen Cappelørn, Herman Deuser and K. Brian Söderquist (Berlin and New York: Walter de Gruyter, 2011), p. 245.

14. *How to Read Kierkegaard* (London: Granta, 2007), p. 37.

15. Caputo, *How to Read Kierkegaard*, p. 37.

16. We must note, however, that only the game player gets a way out. There are often others, like the man whom Amanda is made to eviscerate in *Saw* to find the key that unlocks her reverse bear trap, that presumably never had a chance to survive. But we see the same thing in the Bible. The Binding of Isaac is a test for Abraham, not Isaac, and in God's testing of Job, Job's entire family is killed.

17. *Fear and Trembling/Repetition: Kierkegaard's Writings, VI*, ed. and trans. by Howard V. Hong and Edna H. Hong (Princeton, New Jersey: Princeton University Press, 1983), p. 74.

18. "O Lord Jesus Christ, Thou didst not come to the world to be served, but also surely not to be admired or in that sense to be worshipped. Thou wast the way and the truth — and it was followers only Thou didst demand." *The Prayers of Kierkegaard*, ed. by Perry D. LeFevre (Chicago: University of Chicago Press, 1956), p. 96.

19. Another example comes to us from Indian mythology. In the Sanskrit *Mahabharata*, an epic poem composed in India between 500 B.C.E. and 500 C.E., the five heroic brothers who are the protagonists of the story encounter an acousmatic voice at a pool in a famous episode that demonstrates the wisdom of the oldest brother, Yudhishthira. Wandering in exile, the brothers arrive in marching order, at a pond where a voice belonging to a concealed water sprite commands them not to drink without answering his questions. One by one each brother ignores the voice and drinks the water, then consequently drops dead in his tracks. When Yudhshthira finally arrives to find the bodies of his brothers strewn about the pond, he heeds the Yaksha and answers a long series of riddles. Satisfied, the voice gives him leave to drink and offers to raise one of his brothers from the dead. Surprisingly, Yudhishthira chooses one of his comparatively unimpressive brothers over two that are considered the mightiest warriors in the land. When the voice asks why, he explains that this younger (half-) brother is the son of his father's second wife and the law of non-cruelty dictates that he must make sure each woman has at least one

son alive. At this selfless act, the Yaksha identifies himself as the god Dharma, the embodiment of law and order and Yudhishthira's divine father, and raises all four brothers from the dead. Bhandarkar Oriental Research Institute, *The Mahabharata: Text as Constituted in Its Critical Edition Volume I* (Poona: Bhandarkar Oriental Research Institute, 1976), p. 797.

    20. Kirk and Raven suggest that Porphyry's story of the division in Pythagoras' lifetime may only be an attempt to account for the schism after his death. G.S. Kirk and J.E. Raven, *The Presocratic Philosophers: A Critical History with a Selection of Texts* (London and New York: Cambridge University Press, 1957), p. 227.

    21. Louis Dupré, "Husserl's Thought on God and Faith," *Philosophy and Phenomenological Research*, Vol. 29, No. 2 (December 1968), pp. 201–215.

    22. D. Schaeffer, "Acousmatics" in *Audio Culture: Readings in Modern Music*, ed. by Christoph Cox and Daniel Warner (London and New York: Continuum, 2004), p. 77.

    23. M. Chion, *Audio-Vision: Sound on Screen*, ed. and trans. by Claudia Gorbman (New York: Columbia University Press, 1994), pp. 129–130.

    24. Dolar, *A Voice and Nothing More*, p. 61.

    25. Ibid.

    26. http://www.imsdb.com/scripts/Saw.html.

    27. Dolar, *A Voice and Nothing More*, p. 63.

    28. In fact, the murders in the first *Scream* movie are already a repetition of previous murders from years before, as are the murders in *Halloween*, *Friday the 13th*, *A Nightmare on Elm Street* and the 2009 slasher-inspired television series *Harper's Island*.

    29. Dolar, *A Voice and Nothing More*, p. 69.

    30. The role is played by Judith Roberts, familiar to horror fans as the Mother Superior in the infamous 1984 holiday-themed slasher *Silent Night, Deadly Night*.

    31. If this idea of Jigsaw as a God-figure seems like an unsupported claim, examine the poster for *Saw 3D* that shows the construction of a skyscraper-sized statue of Jigsaw that does not look so much like a statue as like a flesh-and-blood giant.

    32. S. Žižek "The Fear of Four Words: A Modest Plea for the Hegelian Reading of Christianity," in *The Monstrosity of Christ: Paradox or Dialectic?*, Slavoj Žižek and John Milbank, ed. by Creston Davis (Cambridge, MA: MIT Press, 2009), p. 61, italics in original.

References

Badiou, A. *Pocket Pantheon: Figures of Postwar Philosophy*. Translated by David Macey. London: Verso, 2009.
Bhandarkar Oriental Research Institute. *The Mahabharata: Text as Constituted in Its Critical Edition*, vol. I. Poona: Bhandarkar Oriental Research Institute, 1976.
Caputo, J.D. *How to Read Kierkegaard*. London: Granta, 2007.
Chion, M. *Audio-Vision: Sound on Screen*. Edited and translated by Claudia Gorbman. New York: Columbia University Press, 1994.
Dolar, M. *A Voice and Nothing More*. Cambridge, MA: MIT Press, 2006.
Dupré, L. "Husserl's Thought on God and Faith." *Philosophy and Phenomenological Research* vol. 29, no. 2 (1968): 201–215.
Freud, S. *The Interpretation of Dreams: The Complete and Definitive Text*. Translated and edited by James Strachey. New York: Basic, 1955.
Glover, C. "Her Body, Himself: Gender in the Slasher Film," in The Dread of Difference: Gender and the Horror Film, 66–113. Edited by B.K. Grant. Austin: University of Texas Press.
Kierkegaard, S. *Fear and Trembling/Repetition: Kierkegaard's Writings*, VI. Edited and translated by Howard V. Hong and Edna H. Hong. Princeton, NJ: Princeton University Press, 1983.
_____. *The Sickness unto Death: A Christian Psychological Exposition of Edification and Awakening by Anti-Climacus*. Translated and with an Introduction and Notes by Alastair Hannay. London and New York: Penguin, 1989.

Kirk, G.S., and J.E. Raven. *The Presocratic Philosophers: A Critical History with a Selection of Texts*. London and New York: Cambridge University Press, 1957.

Lefevre, P.D., ed. *The Prayers of Kierkegaard*. Chicago: University of Chicago Press, 1956.

Satre, J-P. *Being and Nothingness: A Phenomenological Essay on Ontology*. Translated by Hazel E. Barnes. New York: Washington Square University Press, 1956.

_____. *No Exit and Three Other Plays*. Translated by Stuart Gilbert and I. Able. New York: Vintage, 1989.

Schaeffer, P. "Acousmatics," in *Audio Culture: Readings in Modern Music*, edited by C. Cox and D. Warner, 76–81. London and New York: Continuum, 2004.

Tullberg, S. "On the Genesis of On My Work as an Author," in *Kierkegaard Studies Yearbook 2010: Kierkegaard's Late Writings*, edited by N.J. Cappelørn, H. Deuser and B. Söderquist, 237–52. Berlin and New York: Walter de Gruyter, 2011.

Žižek, S. "The Fear of Four Words: A Modest Plea for the Hegelian Reading of Christianity," in *The Monstrosity of Christ: Paradox or Dialectic?*, edited by C. Davis, 24–109. Cambridge, MA: MIT Press, 2009.

Twisted Pictures: Morality, Nihilism and Symbolic Suicide

Steve Jones

Although numerous critics have complained that *Saw* is ethically confused,[1] little attention has actually been paid to how morality manifests in the series' rolling narrative. Rather than seeking to understand the films by exploring them in detail, critics have accused *Saw* of being potentially corrupting, making a leap in logic between the overt preaching of Jigsaw — *Saw*'s lead protagonist-cum-killer — and the films', filmmakers' or audience's moral intentions. This chapter seeks to redress that imbalance by examining Jigsaw's moral agenda in depth. To get to grips with *Saw*'s morality, I employ a theoretical model that has resurged in recent philosophy: Nietzschean nihilism (see Diken, 2009; Taskale, 2010; Pauley, 2011, for instance). This chapter is shaped by three interlinked nihilist paradigms, two found within Nietzsche's "European Nihilism" (*The Will to Power* [1967: 3 and 11]),[2] and a third related form coined by Hans Enzensberger (2005). I will apply each to the *Saw* series, testing whether Jigsaw is a Nietzschean passive nihilist, a Nietzschean radical nihilist, or an Enzensbergerian radical loser. My aim is not to categorize Jigsaw, but to better comprehend his moral mission. This is vital if we are to understand *Saw*, since Jigsaw's morality drives the series.

Nihilism illuminates how coherent Jigsaw's project is, and allows us to better grasp what critics have (vaguely and unspecifically) hinted at: that Jigsaw is a monster who reflects a problem with contemporary ethical attitudes. Jigsaw's commitment to his ideals — which he upholds by killing — contrasts starkly with the apathy he sees around him. In that sense, Jigsaw's genocidal campaign has been envisioned as uncannily mirroring the off-screen world contextualizing the *Saw* franchise, which is both post-political (relativistic, passive) and haunted by the looming specter of fundamentalist terrorism.[3] Rather than literally reading Jigsaw as a terrorist (or as an allegorical Dick

Cheney, as Kellner [2010: 6–8] does), I am more interested in the broader philosophical-political issues that undergird such a comparison. *Saw* does not need the War on Terror to make the series interesting: that is, *Saw* is not as "of the moment" as allegorical readings risk implying. The series articulates moral concerns that Nietzsche raised in 1887. Those moral issues may have become particularly urgent in the first decade of the twenty-first century, yet their significance is broader than critical discussion has yet accounted for.

When approached via nihilism, it becomes apparent that although Jigsaw's dialogue is hypocritical, the series' morality is not "confused" as its detractors have averred. Contrary to Jigsaw's declarations, his quest is not to save others and become immortal via legacy. Such a quest would privilege creation and longevity. Rather, Jigsaw's mission is destructive, seeking to inalterably change the world around him. The nihilist reading ultimately demonstrates that following the loss of his unborn son and a failed suicide attempt, Jigsaw seeks to eradicate himself, choosing victims that mirror his own obsessive traits. Illustrating that point will entail working through each type of nihilism, scrutinizing how they differ and how they interlink.

"Conundrum of Carnage"[4]*: Moral Confusion and Jigsaw's Nihilistic Project*

Even if lacking precision, critics' accusations regarding *Saw*'s moral confusion are understandable. As a starting point then, it is vital to detail these sources of contention in order to elucidate *Saw*'s ethical foundations. Foremost, Jigsaw's agenda is undermined by his poor phrasal choices. For example, in *Saw,* Jigsaw states that Amanda requires a key to escape from the reverse bear-trap, and that the key is located in the stomach of her "dead cellmate." Jigsaw underscores his instruction with the assertion "know that I am not lying." As it transpires, Amanda's cellmate is drugged rather than dead. Jigsaw *was* lying. Similarly, in *Saw III,* Jigsaw proclaims to be "the only person who knows where [Jeff's abducted] daughter is." This again is untrue: Hoffman, Jigsaw's co-conspirator, is also privy to that information. Jigsaw's calm, precise tone connotes that every word he utters is measured. Resultantly, it is unclear whether these errors are simply scripting mistakes, or intentional untruths. Regardless, these slips mean Jigsaw appears to be incoherent. That feeling is amplified by his oxymoronic instructions. In *Saw IV,* for example, Jigsaw instructs Rigg to "*force* [Ivan] into position ... and *let him*" decide his own fate. The caveat that "in 60 seconds the choice will be made for" Ivan further undercuts the test's purpose: teaching Rigg that people must decide to save themselves. Such inconsistencies have been interpreted as hypocrisy since the stakes could not be higher — they are literally life or death choices — and because Jigsaw's endeavors are coded as moralistic in intent.

Other ethical problems stem from Jigsaw's demands, which coerce his victims into committing immoral actions. In *Saw*, for example, Zepp is told to murder a mother and child in order to "save [him]self." Endorsing a self-orientated, sacrificial mind-set does not sit well with Jigsaw's proclaimed desire to force people into valuing life. Jigsaw's victim-selection process is equally perturbing. *Saw IV*'s Ivan and Brenda are both guilty of criminal wrongdoing (being a rapist and prostitute, respectively). However, the two crimes are punished in the same way (by death), despite being unequal and incomparable criminal offenses.

Moreover, these victims are little more than pawns in Rigg's game. Rigg is not given instructions on how to save Brenda. The test's aim is that Rigg should *not* save her, meaning she is meant to die. Similarly, Adam (*Saw*) is never given a game to play. He is only a sacrifice in Lawrence's game, and is also condemned. Pawn sacrifice occurs throughout the series. Unlike *Saw V*'s Mallick, who recognizes that he has done wrong and "deserve[s] to be" punished, Joyce (*Saw 3D*) is entirely innocent, and is burned alive only to punish her fiancé Bobby. Bobby explicitly points out that Joyce does not "deserve to be here." *Saw 3D* is notable for its ill-selected victim-base more broadly. There is little indication why numerous victims such as Dina or the racist gang are selected from the populace's sinners. The script offers no answer when the investigating officer (Mike) asks himself "Why them? Why now?," leaving the audience to ponder those very questions.

Ultimately, these flaws undermine Jigsaw's proposed aim: to make people value their lives. Being unrighteous — selecting victims whimsically or using them as sacrifices — is unconvincing as a position from which to preach about justice. Moreover, many of the victims are not guilty of failing to value their own lives. *Saw IV*'s Rigg distinctly prizes and seeks to preserve life. There is no evidence that Ivan in *Saw IV*, the five victims in *Saw V*, or William in *Saw VI* do not value their own lives. They flagrantly do not value *other people's* lives, but that is an entirely different issue. Bobby in *Saw 3D* does not even fall into that category: he simply lies about having undergone a Jigsaw test. While that may be disrespectful to genuine survivors, it does not evince that he does not value life.

Thus, confusion arises from the disparities between Jigsaw's desire to "save" people and his willingness to murder. Kerry proclaims that Troy's trap (*Saw III*) does not fit Jigsaw's modus operandi because Troy was welded into a room, and so could never escape. Kerry thereby confirms Jigsaw's repeated assertion that he allows victims to decide their fate ('Live or die. Make your choice'). However, the idea of choice is undermined in various ways throughout the series. The exchange between Hoffman and Jigsaw in *Saw V* negotiates that tension explicitly. Although Jigsaw declares that he "assume[s] nothing ... anticipat[ing] the possibilities and ... let[ting] the game play out," he requires Amanda's presence in the game to restrict the victim's choices ("to make sure the rules are followed"). His announcement that "if you're good at anticipating the human mind it leaves nothing to chance" undercuts the idea that victims can affect their fate. As Lawrence declares in *Saw*, the victims are given the impression that "every possible angle has been pre-thought out" (*Saw*). That is, resistance is impossible. The game-scenarios are so limited that they are likely to result in death before any change in world-view can occur.

Consequently, Jigsaw comes across as a murderer rather than an emancipator. Jigsaw's project amounts to selecting, then eliminating people. While he openly avers that he wants the subjects to change, he is far less vocal about their failure. This may be because he sees death as a by-product rather than the point. From the police perspective, the opposite is true. The viewer is offered both stances, and may read that balance as narrative ambivalence. This does not mean the narrative attitude to murder is pluralistic. The binary tension between these two parties illuminates Jigsaw's project, evoking several overlooked, yet vital questions that form the basis of my investigation here. What exactly is the aim of Jigsaw's mission? Is it to change or to terminate people? Are the two outcomes significantly different? Is change only possible via destruction?

These questions belong to the terrain of nihilism. Nietzsche, the founder of contemporary nihilist philosophy, envisages the nihilist as someone "who judges of the world as it is that it ought not to be and of the world as it ought to be that it does not exist" (1967: 318). That is, because teleological meaning is unknowable, the nihilist is unable to accept the world as it is. For Nietzsche, there are two intertwined forms of nihilism — radical and passive — that differ depending on the nihilist's response, or what exactly the nihilist apprehends as being the source of their dissatisfaction. Passive nihilists seek to change prevailing value-systems while preserving the world. The passive nihilist is disorientated because values have eroded, and sees potential for the world to become ideal if values change. Radical nihilists, on the other hand, live in despair. The radical nihilist adheres to supreme values that cannot exist in the world-as-it-is. On this view, this world cannot be ideal, and so must ultimately be destroyed. The passive nihilist thus lives in a "world without values" (Deleuze 1983: 148), while the radical nihilist has "values without a world" (Diken, 2009: 29; see also Heidegger 1977: 61, Pauley, 2011: 109, and Reginster 2006: 34). Both stances aim to incite change by moderating the present. As such, they are not opposed, even if they differ.

Working though those differences will help to elucidate Jigsaw's intentions, despite the disparities between his actions and his pronouncements. Jigsaw is clearly dissatisfied with the world, but it is not immediately apparent whether his aim is to change or to destroy the world since the former is suggested by his speech and the latter by his actions. Assessing Jigsaw's aims thus amounts to asking whether Jigsaw is a passive or radical nihilist. Verbally, he appears to be passive, angered by and seeking to change others' values (centrally, their attitudes towards life). In action, he seems to be radical inasmuch as his values are staid, and his obsessive attachment to principle leads him to destroy others that do not fit his standards (that is, everyone). The two might seem incompatible at first, but the following sections will demonstrate that these positions lead to the conclusion that Jigsaw's agenda is coherent. Although the double-standards outlined in this section remain, the nihilist approach permits an interpretation of *Saw* that encompasses and works with narrative and character motivations rather than dismissing the films — as numerous critics have — because they are ethically difficult.

Rebirth/Rhetoric: Passive Nihilism

Jigsaw may be considered a passive nihilist insofar as he is angered by the populace's attitude to fundamental values: their apathy towards their own existence. Nietzsche's term "passive" thus also appositely evokes the indifference Jigsaw perceives in his test-subjects. Jigsaw's anger stems from his belief that appreciating one's existence is what gives life purpose. To "take life for granted" is to be goalless. The games aim to force subjects into recognizing that survival is the only pertinent objective, and that endurance is always-already life's telos. The games render that goal present and possible in this world, resolving Jigsaw's nihilistic crisis.

The narratives validate Jigsaw's agenda by bearing out his assumptions about the test-subjects. The victims evince their apathy of their own accord. Alison, Lawrence's wife, complains that Lawrence pretends to be happy while actually being passionless, for example. Lawrence is thus characterized as "sleepwalking" rather than living. Lawrence's ordeal is juxtaposed with other trap-victims as *Saw* unfolds, implying that his lifestyle is comparable to Amanda's reality-evading drug-addiction, or even Paul's suicide attempt (that is, relinquishing life altogether). The same is true of Adam's desire to smoke a potentially poisoned cigarette during his incarceration. Adam declares that he wants "that sweet cancer. I don't care. I really don't." His passivity is evoked in the latter clauses. More poignantly however, Adam's statement is imbued with dramatic irony. Jigsaw himself is dying of the very disease Adam so carelessly brings upon himself. Adam's flippant remark therefore underlines Jigsaw's motivation.

Jigsaw's dissatisfaction with others arises from such disparities: that people have choices, but fail to choose; that people who have "every advantage in life ... refus[e] to advance" (*Saw III*); that people are "angry yet apathetic. But mostly just pathetic" (*Saw*). His test-subjects perceive themselves as unable to change the world that they inhabit. The victims thus corroborate Jigsaw's outlook that the world-state is unsatisfactory. Rigg is frustrated that he (as a cop) cannot save everyone, despite his compulsion to try. Jeff (*Saw III*) obsesses over the inadequate punishment bestowed on the man who killed his son. Both perceive the world as flawed, although they act as if they cannot change their conditions. *Saw*'s populace thus demonstrate that the dissatisfactions underpinning passive nihilism are normative and prevalent. For Taskale (2010: 82) such a state verifies Nietzsche's vision of passive nihilism, since it "impl[ies] that the experience of the loss of truth, value, and meaning no longer generates a crisis but is now accepted as matter of fact" (Taskale, 2010: 82).

Although Jigsaw's value-dissatisfactions are shared by the diegetic populace, the characters are more accurately passive ressentimentists rather than passive nihilists, because they remain inactive (see Deleuze 1983: 111 and Diken, 2009: 16). Indeed, the test-subjects are so inured in their powerlessness that they behave as if they have a priori submitted to their impotence and the resultant frustration. Rigg complains "how the hell are we supposed to [cherish our lives] when this [i.e., murder] is our life?" in *Saw IV*, articulating his exasperation regarding his inability to change the world. Hoffman's response— "we chose this" (*Saw IV*)— is equally telling, conveying their responsibility for entering into and constituting that world. This is a rare instance of self-recognition in *Saw*'s diegetic universe. The vast majority of the characters' statements blame external forces for immediate pressures, thereby negating responsibility for or their capacity to respond to their situation.

Jigsaw's games indicate that he, in contrast, purposefully takes nihilistic action. However, as is typical of his character, his dialogue is less consistent. His verbal rationalizations swing between nihilistic intentionality and ressentimentist liability-denial. When Cecil automatically projects responsibility for his suffering in *Saw IV* ("*you* did this to me")— thereby confirming the prevailing outlook — Jigsaw directly challenges him ("you did this to *yourself*"). However, in doing so, Jigsaw refutes his accountability, and thus denies his role as nihilistic agent. This renunciation does not sit well with statements of ownership he makes to his subjects elsewhere in the series, which include the proclamation that he has "given [their] life a purpose" (*Saw III*). Although Jigsaw avidly denies being a murderer throughout the series, other characters continually assert that Jigsaw is a (nihilistic) agent. Matthews (*Saw II*) reminds the audience that "[p]utting a gun to someone's head and forcing them to pull the trigger is still murder," for example. Such assertions flag that Jigsaw's actions mark the difference between passive nihilism and his victim's passive ressentiment. Indeed, Jigsaw evades answering Matthews' accusation by turning the focus back on Matthews' own faults, and explaining his philosophy. In doing so, Jigsaw retains agency in the conversation, driving it forward to his preferred ends and forcing Matthews to retreat, dialogically. Jigsaw continues to force change, despite being confronted with his hypocrisy. Jigsaw's evasion underscores how apt Matthews' accusation is.

Yet the conflicts between Jigsaw's words and his actions reveal much about how Jigsaw envisages his position. Jigsaw only claims responsibility for any positive (as he sees it) effect his traps have — giving lives purpose — and seeks to evade the messy violence that his method entails. The distinction Strahm makes between being "saved" (dictated to) and given "freedom" (choice) is thus pertinent. If the apathy Jigsaw critiques is defined by subjects' inability to see their choices as power to change the world, it is unclear how undermining victims' power to choose can result in overarching change. Jigsaw posits that the participants' goal is to survive, yet that does not tally with the games themselves. Not only are they a somewhat arbitrary valuation-gauge, they also only endanger the subjects' survival. Despite Jigsaw's rhetoric about being "reborn" (*Saw II*), which suggests that he seeks to make his idealist values exist in the world, Jigsaw denies that his method is destructive. In practice, Jigsaw's aim may be to change the world, but his method is genocidal, not rehabilitative. Jigsaw's failure to recognize this fracture undermines his "salvation" discourse. He desires the conceptual outcome (change), but repudiates the physical consequence (murder). This disturbs his role as nihilist. Jigsaw perceives himself as different to the apathetic masses because they do not take action and refute responsibility for their circumstances. Yet he cannot have it both ways. Either he too is not accountable for contributing to the dissatisfactory world-state, or he is a violent agent of change set apart from his subjects. The latter means taking ownership of the ensuing destruction.

The discrepancies inherent to Jigsaw's viewpoint problematize his method's foundation: his complaint over the subjects' attitudes. The films offer scant evidence to explain why Jigsaw is so self-assured that his values are correct while his victims' mind-sets are not. The disparity between Jigsaw's intentions (active) and his behavior (passive) thus renders his evaluation of the world-as-it-is questionable. The passive nihilist assesses that the values held in the world-as-it-is are erroneous. On their view, transformation is necessary, and the passive nihilist seeks to instigate that change to make the world ideal. They seek to modify prevailing value-systems while preserving the world. In Jigsaw's case, his desire for change is flawed because he does not perceive that his subjects share his evaluation that the world-as-it-is is unsatisfactory. If the victim's world-view needs to change, so does Jigsaw's, because they are founded on the same groundwork.

Hence, Jigsaw's inconsistencies expose a problem with passive nihilism more broadly. In order to distinguish between the nihilist's ideal values and the existent unsatisfactory values that plague the world-as-it-is, a stable axis must be maintained. The passive nihilist seeks change, yet contradictorily requires that their values be retained in order to instigate transformation, or to apprehend that change has occurred. The problem is that in order to be successful, the passive nihilist must completely alter all existent values, including their own. Jigsaw cannot alter his subjects' values without first modifying his. Consequently, they all must die. Jigsaw's agenda is problematized by the unyielding nature of the world he inhabits. Rather than modifying existent dominant values as he proclaims, Jigsaw's actions mean he actually alters the world itself. His actions are thus closer to radical nihilism.

Death/Action: Radical Nihilism

The central difference between Jigsaw and his subjects is that he seeks change (he is a nihilist), while they remain inactive (they are ressentimentists). Fundamentally then, Jigsaw cannot both repudiate responsibility and also be the agent of change. Radical nihilism embraces the kind of world-changing that results from Jigsaw's actions, while also permitting that he might cling to his ideal values. Since the radical nihilist's dissatisfaction arises from their recognition that their ideal values cannot exist in the world-as-it-is, the radical nihilist seeks to negate and ultimately destroy the world (see Diken, 2009: 3). Applying this paradigm to *Saw* involves examining Jigsaw's values, asking whether his ideal standards can exist in the world-as-it-is, and if his aim is to change others' values, or to alter the world by annihilating others.

Much of the apparent hypocrisy arising from Jigsaw's actions is overcome if he is understood as a radical nihilist. For instance, there is an apparent disparity in Jeff's game (*Saw III*): Jigsaw asks Jeff to see Danica and ultimately Timothy as people that made mistakes rather than "cipher[s]" responsible for Jeff's son's death. Jeff does not pass his test as he fails to rescue either Danica or Timothy. However, his failure is written into the game. When Danica pleads "I made a mistake ... I'm human," the test's premise is exposed. Jeff is only human too, and will a priori also make mistakes that lead to deaths. In fact, Jeff's choices entail almost everyone involved in the game — including Jigsaw and his protégé Amanda — being killed. Jeff is not Jigsaw's test-subject: *humanity* is. There was never any hope that Jeff's values would change, because he, like Jigsaw, is inherently flawed by belonging to the world-as-it-is.

Amanda herself further evidences that Jigsaw cannot sway others' values. As the first "survivor," Jigsaw declares that Amanda is the "proof that [his method] works" (*Saw VI*). As the plot continues however, it is clear that Amanda is not converted. Jigsaw retests her in *Saw III*, demonstrating the inadequacy of his method. She concurs, declaring that "nobody is reborn." Her assessment is consolidated by Jeff's willingness to kill Jigsaw moments later, in response to Jigsaw's question "you haven't learned anything tonight have you?" Survivor retesting is commonplace in the series, and is a continuing reminder that Jigsaw cannot change others' values. Art survives his mausoleum trap only to become the head of another game (where he is killed) in *Saw IV*. Eric fails his test in *Saw II*, but proves his willingness to live by escaping. Yet he is then used as bait in the same trap that kills Art. These events verify Amanda's claim that "[n]obody changes" (*Saw III*). In fact, nobody is permitted to survive, Jigsaw included. As he confesses in *Saw II*, Jigsaw too is "unfixable."

Jigsaw's admittance is indicative of the radical nihilist's despair. When Tapp accuses Jigsaw of being "sick" (*Saw*), Jigsaw's response — that he is "sick of" those who "don't appreciate their blessings" and "scoff at the suffering of others"— culminates in the declaration that he is "sick of it all" (that is, the world and/or existence). This utterance is transferred into a murderous will to destroy because Jigsaw slits Tapp's throat on making the final statement. Nihilistic despair resonates in the word "sick," since Jigsaw is also physically, terminally ill. Jigsaw's destructive nature is intertwined with his bodily decline. The only change Jigsaw issues is devastation. His actions are not capable of changing values, and instead aim to destroy the world itself.

Reading Jigsaw as a radical nihilist explains why Jigsaw adheres to his belief that "if the subject survives my method, he or she is instantly rehabilitated" (*Saw IV*), despite evidence to the contrary. Jigsaw's values remain staid despite the impossibility of those ideal values becoming existent in the world. It also explains Jigsaw's willingness to forsake the victims who survive. Obliteration is inherent to every game. William's first trap necessitates one of the participants dying since "the only escape is in the other's failure" according to Jigsaw's instructions. Similarly, Jigsaw blames Amanda for making Kerry's game impossible to win, but his instructions to Kerry imply that she is precondemned: "you have spent your life among the dead ... you, like them, are also dead." His method thrives on eradication, despite his frequent verbal proclamations to the contrary.

However, radical nihilism does not resolve all of *Saw*'s apparent contradictions. Being part of the world-as-it-is, the radical nihilist is among the factors that inhibit their ideal values from coming into existence. That is, the destruction of *everything* a priori necessitates the nihilist's extermination too.

The radical nihilist's despair is underpinned by that realization, and is amplified by a further problem. The radical nihilist's ideal values may also be obliterated along with them. Radical nihilism is futile then, insofar as it essentially involves destroying even the values that inspire annihilation. The result is hopelessness, and without faith in the possibility of change — the prospect of the world-as-it-ought-to-be — the radical nihilist's dissatisfaction with the-world-as-it-is can only lead to spiraling decay.

Radical nihilism therefore entails relinquishing to the impossibility of change. Radical and passive nihilism are thus intertwined. The nihilist comes to rely on the world-as-it-is being non-ideal in order to understand existence, since the nihilist is defined by their attitude towards that non-ideal world. The formulation "world-as-it-is" is founded on the imperfection of that state, which is diametrically opposed to the idealized world-as-it-ought-to-be. Jigsaw's world-view is one of destructive acquiescence. He resigns himself to the fact that people are "easily" anticipated and thereby slaughtered. He allows them to be human, and being human they inevitably doom themselves. Despite Jigsaw's destructive actions, he *relies* on the world-as-it-is continuing, despite also being the source of his dissatisfaction.

Hence, it is apt that the *Saw* series has no distinct beginnings or ends inasmuch as the earliest and latest points in the *Saw* timeline are continually revised as the narrative unfurls. Beyond *Saw III*, flashbacks uncover earlier and earlier points in the plot. The rolling narrative moves backwards as much as its diegetic present moves forwards. Nihilism stems from disorientation based on telotic uncertainty (Heidegger 1977: 61). That is, causal relations and aims are not assured. *Saw* reifies that irresolution via the narrative's continual revision of events, as well as Jigsaw's inexact attitudes towards his own role as causal agent. His inability to relinquish his values is induced by the series' flashback-laden narrative structure, which continually evokes the past as if it is recurring in the present. Despite his nihilistic actions then, Jigsaw is more akin to his ressentimentalist victims than he proclaims to be. In the language of nihilism, Jigsaw is a "man of ressentiment," who "does not, cannot, forget" (Diken, 2009: 16), and who is thus "never through with anything" (Deleuze 1983: 113).

Both in form and theme, *Saw* presents a state of flux where meaning is not final. Jigsaw's method consumes the unfolding narrative. His nihilism cannot ever become a stable replacement belief system since that implies a clear telos, and it is the loss of telos that instigates a nihilist outlook in the first instance. That is, if nihilism fulfils its goal (total destruction), the nihilist's life is given purpose. Having a reason to exist would undermine the nihilist's motive, which arises from their perceived purposelessness. Necessarily, the nihilist's campaign can have no end. Rigg's game — which is placed at the franchise's mid-point — revolves around the criticism offered to Rigg by several characters: "what you can't do is save everyone" (*Saw IV*). The opposite is equally true: what Jigsaw cannot do is *kill* everyone. Jigsaw fails to spot not only that Rigg's quest to "save everyone" is a form of action (meaning Rigg is not a man of ressentiment), but also how similar the flaws in Jigsaw's and Rigg's quests are.

The traps create an impression that Jigsaw is different to his victims because he is physically distanced from them. However, closer inspection of the victims' apparent flaws reveals how similar they are. Indeed, those physical distances connote Jigsaw's inaction, and ultimately his unwillingness to destroy everything. Centrally, Jigsaw's campaign can never result in total destruction as it would mean that he "would be deprived of his 'evil enemy,' the hostile world, which he can accuse for his impotence and failures" (Diken, 2009: 18). The victims are sacrificial pawns in Jigsaw's games because they do not matter as individuals, at least for Jigsaw's purposes. The beginning and end point of Jigsaw's nihilism is Jigsaw himself.

"I am still among you"[5]*: Auto-Nihilism*

Nihilism may initially appear to be egotistical insofar as it entails one individual's dissatisfaction with the world being forced onto everyone. However, the target of the nihilistic mind-set is not the world or values per se, but the nihilist's own self. Suicide is the most obvious means of resolving the nihilist's dissatisfaction with the world, and the hopeless futility of their hatred. This is the key aspect of *Saw* overlooked in complaints about Jigsaw's hypocrisy. The target of his campaign may appear to be other people since others are so graphically tested. However, as the nihilism paradigm highlights, Jigsaw's true target is himself. His victims are selected because they are involved in his personal history, and their destruction ultimately serves to erase aspects of Jigsaw himself from the world.

Jigsaw's proclamations misdirect because they are outwardly focused. He overtly blames others for his dissatisfaction with the world-as-it-is. Verbally, Jigsaw downplays his responsibility for murder, but this also seeks to mask his self-orientation. Lawrence (Kramer's oncologist) and William (Kramer's health insurer) are picked as targets specifically because Jigsaw holds personal grudges against them. Even if Jigsaw proposes that their mistreatment of him is indicative of their broader faults, the changes Jigsaw instigates are highly limited in scope, only affecting individuals in his immediate vicinity. This personal bias is confirmed by a news report in *Saw VI* that warns "victims have included anyone associated with the life of John Kramer, however remote." Despite Jigsaw's declaration that tests "can never be personal," the only way "all the pieces ... fit together" (*Saw V*) is via Jigsaw himself. This is typical inasmuch as nihilists internalize external factors that ruin their life. By "inflicting evil" (acting spitefully), nihilists thus fail to "comprehend the dimensions and meaning" of their actions (Pauley, 2011: 107).

Since Jigsaw is at the centre of his own destructive campaign, it is frequently self-oriented. For instance, he selects Bobby (*Saw 3D*) and Pamela (*Saw VI*) because they appropriate his "message," gaining fame from his "notoriety." These targets are not selected because they fail to value their own lives, but because they personally affront Jigsaw. Yet, Jigsaw is not properly egotistic inasmuch as his self-focused actions are futile. His proclaimed aim is to become immortal by "creating a legacy ... living a life worth remembering" according to Amanda (*Saw II*). Bobby and Pamela help Jigsaw in that regard by bolstering his reputation. Jigsaw over-invests in himself, but also eradicates his own legacy. His self-focus contributes to the eventual destruction of everything. This self-defeat is ultimately a form of self-mastery, rather than an exertion of power over others (Nietzsche 1996: 67–8; see also Taskale, 2010: 79).

Jigsaw is, in this sense, a "radical loser" who cannot reconcile his own responsibility for others' fates with his desire to blame others. As Enzensberger (2005: 10) theorizes, the radical loser resolves that tension by "fus[ing] destruction and self-destruction, aggression and auto-aggression." Refusing to passively accept the fate they themselves cause, the radical loser instead "radicaliz[es] ... resentment into spiteful acts" (Diken, 2009: 5; see also Taskale, 2010: 79). Jigsaw's motivating factor — dissatisfaction with the world-as-it-is — is really concerned with his relation to the world. Accordingly, change begins with himself. Kramer tries to commit suicide, intentionally crashing his car following an act of fate (Jill's miscarriage). Jigsaw internalizes that trigger-event, declaring the miscarriage to be his fault ("I find it difficult to forgive myself for what happened" [*Saw V*]). Auto-destruction is as close to gaining control as the radical loser comes, and here Kramer's suicide smacks of auto-abortion ("auto" both in the senses of "self" and "automobile"). The suicide attempt reverses Kramer's inability to control his unborn son's accidental death by targeting himself. Moreover, the suicide attempt underscores that *Kramer* is guilty of not valuing his own life ("[t]hose that do not appreciate life do not deserve life" [*Saw II*]). When he survives the crash, Jigsaw continues to reverse blame by externalizing punishment rather than internalizing further. Hence, killing others is an expression of Jigsaw's own self-punishment and blameworthiness.

Jigsaw's nihilism, which "paradoxically, turns back against itself" and annihilates the nihilist, is thus "perfect nihilism" (Diken, 2009: 6; see also Taskale, 2010: 84) precisely because it results in total destruction. His attempted suicide is pivotal since Jigsaw posits that "it was the moment ... that started me in my work and brought meaning to it" (*Saw II*). While a fleeting incident in *Saw*'s narrative-whole, its centrality is highlighted by the suicide motifs that resonate across the series. Jigsaw's victims choose whether to "live or die," meaning that "technically speaking, he's not really a murderer ... he finds ways for his victims to *kill themselves*" (*Saw*, emphasis added). Paul (*Saw*) is selected because he attempts suicide. Jeff's test (*Saw III*) is focused on his inability to overcome the death of his son, reflecting Jigsaw's own motivation. The message that Jigsaw presents to Jeff—"one bullet will end it all"—is permeated by that interconnection. Even Kramer's proposed cancer treatment carries auto-destructive connotations, since it involves injecting "suicide genes" (*Saw VI*). Given this running theme, it is unsurprising that the series' very first shot of Jigsaw depicts him lying on the bathroom floor as if he has recently shot himself in the head.[6]

This opening disguise is apt inasmuch as it presents Jigsaw as "dead" from the outset. Jigsaw is like a ghost haunting the series' events. He is uncannily both involved in and yet distanced from each trap. Even the test-subjects' various dialogic claims hint towards Jigsaw's spectral qualities. Cecil declares "you're fucking dead" to Jigsaw in *Saw IV*. Lyn refers to Jigsaw as "a deadman walking" when discussing Jigsaw's cancer in *Saw III*. Indeed, Jigsaw's plans and presence continue beyond his death in *Saw III*. That is, Jigsaw is literally dead for the majority of the series. *Saw IV*'s refrain—Jigsaw's beyond-the-grave "promise that [his] work will continue"—could not be more apt to signal that auto-eradication defines his character.

In this light, it becomes clear why the games involve coerced suicide rather than murder. Jigsaw projects his destructive desire outward, killing himself via his victims. Jigsaw's targets are more than just people who personally affronted him. In keeping with the series' emphasis on auto-nihilism, the victims commonly mirror Jigsaw's own obsessive traits. Jigsaw's motivation is not to punish others' wrongs, but to erase problematic aspects of himself that he sees reflected in external ciphers. Jigsaw abducts people to gain control over his own fears: his inability to protect his "loved ones" (Jill and his unborn son), which led Kramer to feel "powerless" (*Saw V*). In the individual cases, the correspondence becomes much more specific. *Saw VI*'s central victim (William), is paralleled to Jigsaw. On refusing to give a client (Harold) health insurance, Harold refers to William as "a criminal," declaring that the decision is a "death sentence." William's response—"those are the rules ... your actions have caused this"—recalls Jigsaw's dialogic motifs, which are well-established by that point in the series. Moreover, William's disciple Josh is said to want "to be" William by another colleague. Before Josh is executed, he states that

William's calculations are "bullshit." These strains uncannily echo Jigsaw's disciple Amanda denouncing Jigsaw's "bullshit" campaign moments before her death (*Saw III*). The parallel between William and Jigsaw is corroborated by a conversation they have when they first meet, before Kramer becomes Jigsaw. William observes that it "sounds like we're in a similar business ... you try to predict people's behavior. So do I." Kramer's reaction — "you choose who lives or dies" — expresses Kramer's aversion to William's comparison, yet it only underlines the aptness of William's appraisal. William is targeted to quell Jigsaw's distaste over his own murderous project. That is, erasing William is a means of denying that Jigsaw makes cold calculations about who will live or die, and who is worthy of salvation.

Rigg's game (*Saw IV*) evokes the opposite side of the equation. Jigsaw critiques Rigg's "obsession" with saving others, requesting that Rigg allow people to save themselves. However, this criticism should also be allayed at Jigsaw's own coercive-salvation method. Rigg's test — training Rigg to "see what [Jigsaw] see[s]," and "save as [Jigsaw] save[s]" — implies that there is a difference between their perspectives. However, that proclaimed contrast misdirects away from their intrinsic similarities. Rigg already does "see as [Jigsaw] see[s]" inasmuch as Rigg stands in for Jigsaw's own obsession with others. Rigg's death manifests how futile Jigsaw's agenda is, insofar as the test fails to save Rigg, and also because Jigsaw's homicidal method cannot save anyone, period. Elsewhere, Jeff is punished for his inability to forgive those who hurt him. Jeff absolves Timothy and Jigsaw, but kills both (*Saw III*). Jeff's decisions parallel Jigsaw's own act of forgiving then slaughtering Cecil (*Saw IV*). Jigsaw's critiques of Kerry's solipsistic, obsessive character (*Saw III*), Adam's voyeurism (*Saw*), Eric's willingness to take the law into his own hands, condemn people and use violence as justice (*Saw II*) are all flaws that Jigsaw exhibits. Each of these victims reifies attributes of Jigsaw's persona that he rejects and erases.

Jigsaw's nihilism is not concerned with a disparity between ideal values and the world per se, but with the self that decides that what ought-to-be is not. In short, Jigsaw is the problem. The solution is his mission to expunge his own history. He systematically punishes every person that led to his suicide, including the drug-addict responsible for his unborn son's death (Cecil, *Saw IV*); the oncologist who failed to cure him (Lawrence, *Saw*); and the health insurer that prevented him seeking treatment (William, *Saw VI*). This purging also involves obliterating his legacy by massacring all the detectives that investigate the Jigsaw murders, as well as those who propagate his infamy via public discourse (Bobby [*Saw 3D*] and Pamela ([*Saw VI*]). Jigsaw even tries to defer the "Jigsaw" infamy onto his disciple, Hoffman, before seeking to extinguish Hoffman (*Saw VI-Saw 3D*).[7]

The same process of erasing himself via others applies to Jigsaw's disciples as much as it does Jigsaw's other victims then. As signaled by Jeff's test (that also tests Lyn, Amanda and Jigsaw [*Saw III*]) or William's test (that equally tests Harold's family and Hoffman [*Saw VI*]), the killers' "fates are linked" to their victims'. Hoffman superficially appears to be different to Jigsaw, especially since Hoffman is so physically strong and enters the narrative when Jigsaw is physically incapacitated (*Saw III*). However, Hoffman perfectly reflects Jigsaw's arrogance. Hoffman echoes Jigsaw's callousness, brutality and desire to control others. Although Jigsaw punishes Hoffman for exhibiting these traits in the close of *Saw 3D*, Jigsaw is just as guilty of exhibiting those characteristics. The traps expose that parallel. In *Saw V*, it is revealed that Hoffman illegally avenged his sister's murder by executing her killer (Seth). Hoffman mimicked Jigsaw's modus operandi to cover up his personal grudge. Jigsaw decries Hoffman's actions, proffering that Hoffman's behavior highlights the differences between them. In fact, it more pertinently reveals their similarities.

Amanda too is criticized by Jigsaw for being jealous of Lyn (*Saw III*), although Amanda's personalization of the issue, her self-harm, her cowardice, her anger, and her reactionary nature reflect Jigsaw's own worst characteristics. Fundamentally, Jigsaw disapproves of Amanda making her games "unwinnable" (*Saw III*), yet that futility equally beleaguers Jigsaw's games. Amanda herself is proof that his method is ineffective. Amanda angers Jigsaw not because her traps are unfair, but because Amanda's games expose how unjust the method itself is. Amanda was originally tested because she was "a fucking junkie," but she only became a drug-addict after Eric framed her for a drug-related crime she did not commit. That injustice is paralleled by how unfair Jigsaw's path is. Kramer did not choose to survive his suicide attempt or to contract cancer. *Saw*'s imposed order — the method — lays bare that the world is structured by injustice and chance. People do not have a choice to live, or to enter into existence. People only have the choice to survive or to die. Sometimes, as in the case for Kramer's unborn son, events conspire to make that decision on their behalf.

Game Over: Conclusion

Early in *Saw*, Lawrence makes a suggestion that has greater significance than is first apparent: "what we need to do is start thinking about why we're here." While Lawrence intends "here" to mean the bathroom in which they are imprisoned, his suggestion also conveys "in existence." The games are undergirded by that very question. Yet Lawrence's subsequent inference — that "whoever brought us here ... must want something from us" — attests to his bewilderment and commitment to the telos implied by the game's cause-effect, puzzle-solving, time-driven surface. Jigsaw's aim is not as productive as Lawrence implies, and this initial misdirection muddies Jigsaw's destructive intentions. The series' denouements are characterized by narrative twists that undermine present immediate aims. What appear to be concrete, knowable goals are revealed to be falsities. Adam could have escaped by using the key floating in his bathtub, yet simply by regaining consciousness, moving, and inadvertently removing the plug attached to his person, the key vanished before he was conscious of his imprisonment. All other goals are rendered meaningless for Adam because of this initial hopelessness. The franchise's opening incident is indicative of the nihilism that follows across the seven films.

Teleological ambiguity — that the solution is present yet unattainable — is paralleled by ontological uncertainty. Deaths ensue that are not technically murder despite looking like they are. Roles that traditionally signal a difference between "good" and "bad" (victim/killer/police) are problematized by victims who are also criminals, Hoffman's and Eric's presences as corrupt police-detectives, and so forth. *Saw*'s moral values are not "confused" as critics have asserted. These narratives just refuse to finally demarcate "good" and "evil." That is precisely a Nietzschean conception of morality (see Nietzsche 1996: 37). This is not hypocrisy. *Saw* defies unrealistic narrative conventions for distinguishing between "good" and "bad."

The self-destructive and apparently contradictory nature of Jigsaw's stance makes it difficult to relate to him, despite the lengthy access to him the franchise's seven films provide. That remoteness — which parallels the distances between Jigsaw and his victims — offers an opportunity to engage with the moral implications of Jigsaw's agenda. Critics who disregard the series as "muddled" miss its fundamental richnesses. As Pauley (2011: 103) notes (following Hegel), the idea that "all sorts of horrendous evils are 'necessary' for the full development of self-consciousness and freedom" causes "philosophical and moral offence." *Saw* openly, overtly and productively explores those forms of offence. The problems — being linked to Jigsaw's self-focused/projected nihilism — scrutinize the nature of existence itself. Jigsaw fits the Niezschean paradigm of a "paradoxical subject," to whom "pain and suffering are necessary" since they "construct his subjectivity" (Diken, 2009: 28). The series' violence — which provokes visceral reactions — connects these theoretical-existential notions to the characters' flesh and the viewer's bodily reality. This imbues the images with urgency. These are not abstract questions, but foundational conundrums about the lines between life and death, and the pertinence of what occurs in-between those states.

As Diken (2009: 6) argues, the "paradoxical, contradictory character [of nihilism] is the strength, not weakness, of the concept." The same is true for the *Saw* series' moral complexity, which implicitly critiques banal "good triumphs over evil" conventionality. The series offers an enquiry into the nature of justice itself, which could not be more Nietzschean in tone. The rolling narrative calls the value of all values into question, beginning with the presumption that "morality is a non-optional, in-eliminable part of civilized humanity" (Robertson, 2011: 563–4). Jigsaw's nihilistic reinvestigation of himself and his world is the franchise's driving force. The drama form allows the audience to perceive the tensions from numerous stances, and to frequently re-examine the same events from multiple perspectives. Horror narratives distance audiences from personal endangerment, but retain enough emotive engagement to curb apathy, prompting philosophical contemplation, even if audiences' responses do not immediately appear to fall into that category. This, I contend, is what makes *Saw* so rich, and why horror fiction more generally is so culturally valuable.

Notes

1. Graham (2009: 6), for instance, posits that "the general view among grown-up commentators is that the *Saw* movies represent an artistic and moral black hole"; Neumaier and Weitzman (2009: 37) refer to Jigsaw's "moral code" as "oblique"; Walsh (2006) berates *Saw*'s "smug moral hypocrisy"; and Thompson (2008) mockingly dismisses attempts to explicate *Saw*'s moral messages as "creative rationalisation." None of these critics engage with the series' content or morality in any detail or depth, pointing to a shortcoming with their analytical skills more than with the series itself. For a detailed examination of *Saw*'s ethical complications, see Aston and Walliss, 2012.
2. While Nietzsche is concerned with monotheism, I will not address religion per se. It would be rather insipid to suggest that Jigsaw is an ubermensch, a god-like adjudicator deciding who deserves to live, for example.
3. On nihilism and its relation to post-politics/terrorism, see Taskale, 2010: 90–92 and Diken, 2009: 75–83.
4. Hoffman quotes the title of Pamela Jenkins' "sensationalist" article in *Saw VI*.
5. Jigsaw in *Saw IV*.
6. The revelation that Amanda's apparently "dead cellmate" is actually alive hints that Jigsaw's disguise is a falsehood early on in *Saw*.
7. The futility of Jigsaw's strategy (which parallels the futility of his nihilism) is that each new murder only sustains his infamy.

Bibliography

Aston, James, and Walliss, John. (2012). "'I've never murdered anyone in my life. The decisions are up to them': Ethical guidance and cultural pessimism in the *Saw* Series." *Journal of Religion and Popular Culture* 24, no. 3.
Deleuze, Gilles. (1983). *Nietzsche and Philosophy*. New York: Columbia University Press.
Diken, Bulent. (2009). *Nihilism*. New York: Routledge.

Enzensberger, Hans M. (2005). "The Radical Loser." http://www.signandsight.com/features/493.html. Original German language version: Enzensberger, Hans M. (2005) *Der Spiegel* November 7.
Graham, Jane. (2009). "Caught in a Trap, and I Can't Back Out." *The Guardian*, October 16.
Heidegger, Martin. *The Question Concerning Technology and Other Essays*. New York: Harper, 1977.
Kellner, Douglas. (2010). *Cinema Wars: Hollywood Film and Politics in the Bush-Cheney Era*. Oxford: Wiley-Blackwell.
Neumaier, Joe, and Elizabeth Weitzman. (2009). "Fresh Blood at the Cinema Lifts the Lid on a Haunting Halloween." New York: *Daily News*, October 30.
Nietzsche, Friedrich. (1996). *On the Genealogy of Morals*. Oxford: Oxford University Press.
_____. (1967). *The Will to Power*. New York: Vintage.
Nishitani, Keiji. (1990). *The Self-Overcoming of Nihilism*. Trans. Graham Parkes and Setsuko Aihara. Albany: State University of New York Press.
Pauley, John. (2011). "The Problem of Evil and the Possibility of Nihilism." *International Journal of Philosophical Studies* 19.1.
Reginster, Barnard. (2006). *The Affirmation of Life: Nietzsche on Overcoming Nihilism*. Cambridge: Harvard University Press.
Robertson, Simon. (2011). "A Nietzschean Critique of Obligation-Centred Moral Theory." *International Journal of Philosophical Studies* 19.4: 563–591.
_____. (2009). "Nietzsche's Ethical Revaluation." *The Journal of Nietzsche Studies* 37.1: 66–90.
Taskale, Ali Riza. (2010). "Clash of Nihilisms." *Domination of Fear*. Ed. Mikko Canini. New York: Rodopi.
Thomson, Desson. (2008). "Hollywood and Indie Offerings." *The Washington Post*, February 15.
Walsh, John. (2006). "I Saw *Saw III* and Survived." *The Independent* November 4.

The Jigsaw Assemblage
Jacob Huntley

A rejected tagline for the "final" chapter of the *Saw* franchise, *Saw 3D* (aka *Saw: The Final Chapter*), was "His disease is spreading." It seems surprising that the legend wasn't used, given that it crystallizes various inferences pertinent to the *Saw* films, and instead the "growth" of Jigsaw was conveyed in the theatrical release poster through the visual metaphor of a towering Jigsaw construction bracketed by scaffolding, gantries and workmen. Both the tagline and the movie poster emphasize the extension of Jigsaw's program, developing the story of a sole serial killer into that of a narrative where a wider social body is party to a virulent strain or lethal franchise. As the paratextual material indicates, Jigsaw is no longer really a nickname that neatly applies to one person and instead it would be better to talk of the Jigsaw effect or the Jigsaw assemblage. The term "assemblage" here refers not just to the gathering of individuals working under that name but all that can be associated with this "trademark"; everything which goes to make up the picture of this Jigsaw from the people involved, the industrial aesthetic of the traps to the rules explained by the Billy doll or via various taped messages. In this wider conceptual sense it is borrowed directly from the work of Deleuze and Guattari and can, at this stage, be defined as the accumulating process of things that Deleuze and Guattari call a *machinic assemblage*, brought into particular relations alongside the discourses, meanings and forms of expression that are associated with these "things" (this latter dimension of the assemblage Deleuze and Guattari call a *collective assemblage of enunciation*) (Deleuze, Guattari: 1991: 88). The assemblage is, importantly, not a fixed structure but a process of relations and its composition is, in Jean Jacques Lecercle's phrase, an "ontological mixture" (Lecercle: 2002: 189). Whilst the trappings of the Jigsaw assemblage can be identified, what is less clear is the purpose of these enunciations and relations: Jigsaw's games are meant to reinvigorate an appreciation of life yet he chooses to achieve this through subjugation and bodily pain. The project's philosophical underpinnings and its realization seem to be fundamentally mismatched as enjoyment of life is gruelingly and proscriptively enforced; as odd an ontological mixture as commanding someone "Have fun!" and punching them to encourage compliance. Given that the ideological position appears to be at variance with the methodology, it indicates that either bodies have lost their majoritarian signification — the markers of hegemonically imposed and socially recognizable being — and signify differently through their incorporation within the machinic assemblage of a trap, or subjectivity is being taught afresh, to be read via these textual bodies. Either way, this isn't a dialectical maneuver. The following argument aims to explore the tensions and consequences of the project by considering the various aspects of the Jigsaw assemblage and perhaps, at this stage, the central concerns can be resolved into two related questions. Firstly, what exactly is at stake for those involved in the games? Secondly, what are the demands made by those enacting this project of revitalization and rehabilitation?

Learning Outcomes

Often the *Saw* films are dismissed as "torture-porn," implying that there is no more at stake here than the infliction of pain for kicks.[1] This misreads the varying desires operating within the Jigsaw assemblage (revenge does not equate with pornographic desire, for instance) and it ignores the lack of appetite Jigsaw himself displays throughout. He is no Freddy Kreuger, salaciously and lasciviously enjoying the suffering of his victims. There are several instances in the *Saw* films where John Kramer, the Jigsaw Killer, or just Jigsaw, refers to his project and his personal philosophy but there are two occasions where he most fully and most explicitly outlines his thinking in a way that could be called systematic and gives an insight into the conceptual element of his work. What he reveals is a desire to re-awaken (or in some cases, simply awaken) that appreciation of *being* to which he has come. In fact, this provides a provisional answer to the questions outlined above: he is trying to teach people a lesson he himself has learned. Jigsaw's motivation and method are therefore crucial to understanding how this particular assemblage works, as well as containing the seeds of what arguably goes wrong with his project and its legacy, through the contradictions within his thought.

The first occasion on which Jigsaw explains himself is in *Saw II*, during Jigsaw's testing of Detective Matthews (Donnie Wahlberg). Requiring Matthews to listen, rather than to act, Jigsaw recounts how the diagnosis of terminal cancer revitalized his perception of life, teaching him to "savor" everyday life, such as a glass of water or a walk in the park, and subsequent to this his surviving a suicide attempt motivated him to "test the fabric of human nature." As we know from the later films, Jigsaw is being characteristically careful in what he says and most pointedly in what he doesn't say (including the non-linguistic detail that he is drinking water in front of the inattentive Matthews whilst they converse), nevertheless it is plain that Jigsaw's notion of life is that of life lived positively. One may live a life of vice, usury or deceit yet this is the "wrong" way to exist, just as not appreciating or valuing one's life requires a corrective to bring one back on the right track. So the positive life doesn't just mean "not being a bad person," but "loving" everyday existence (savoring it). Jigsaw's thinking is not really concerned with morality, or even ethics but with individual's realizing the haecceity of this being. Of course, the paradox, if not outright contradiction, here is Jigsaw's role in staging these moments of "self-help." As Jigsaw tersely tells Jill (Betsy Russell), while she lies hospitalized after being injured by Cecil (Billy Otis), "You can't help them, they have to help themselves" and yet he will go to extraordinary lengths to make sure this happens. In the case of Matthews, if he can listen positively, or even just positively listen, then his son Daniel will be returned to him "safe and well." He has to help himself by learning to be an interlocutor, instead of the hot-headed action hero. Jigsaw's tutorial is essentially about relearning behavior.

The second explanation occurs in *Saw V* when Hoffman (Costas Mandylor) is kidnapped by Jigsaw. "Everybody deserves a second chance," Jigsaw shouts at Hoffman, when the detective tries to justify his killing of Seth in the pendulum trap. As he does during his talk with Matthews, Jigsaw expresses his "distaste" at killing, and refuses to acknowledge himself as a killer.[2] As far as Jigsaw is concerned, instead of being acts of revenge, the games and the traps are tests that through a process of painful revitalizing and reawakening offer redemption — in short, what Jigsaw deems life. As he outlines it to Hoffman, "there is a better, more efficient way ... [i]t's a different method I'm talking about. If a subject survives my method, he or she is instantly rehabilitated." This different method, for Jigsaw at least, is not simply punishment or execution but a chance for the subject to show their "fitness" to survive, as the etymology of "rehabilitate" — that is, "making fit" — indicates. Jigsaw's choice of word is typically precise, if a little oblique, yet it is corroborated through his apparently off-hand comment about the blade Hoffman used on the pendulum trap being inferior. "Tempering's better for the long haul. Are you in this for the long haul, detective?" Tempering, the process of taking the hardness and brittleness out of metal leaving it tougher is the appropriate metaphor for what Jigsaw is doing to Hoffman, and indeed to all his subjects it would seem, although Hoffman does not appear to understand the metaphorical import of Jigsaw's words, given that he merely answers, "I've been a cop for twenty years. Is that long enough for you?" What he misunderstands, and what we see played out in his subsequent actions, is that Jigsaw is attempting to make

Hoffman fit for the role of Jigsaw's associate; experience has little or nothing to do with it, this is about how one reacts to the potential of a "new" life, adapting to the rules of Jigsaw's game.

Fit In Theory

Making fit is crucial. For Jigsaw, the whole purpose of the games and the traps, the machinery of this different method, is to make his subjects fit for living (that is, a survival of the fittest in the Darwinian sense). During a flashback sequence in *Saw VI*, he uses Amanda (Shawnee Smith) as proof of this in talking with Jill. "You once told me she was a lost soul. But here she stands. She's clean and whole. And she has a new appreciation for her life." Standing in the office of the clinic, the medical establishment's inadequacies are implicit in Amanda's confirmation, "It works. It's real. He helped me." Unlike drug treatment or therapy, Jigsaw's rehabilitation is enacted upon the body in an almost Procrustean fashion, but the effects are meant to be holistic, extending beyond physical pain to affect and influence the subject's perception and approach to life. It is in this regard that Jigsaw can be read in a Deleuzian fashion, as his method is concerned with new thought, albeit violently and bloodily arrived at. As Ian Buchanan explains:

> Deleuze's most utopian idea, but not his only one, is that we can think differently — not merely new thoughts, but an entirely fresh way of thinking. It is neither the point of origin of thought (whether from the outside or not) nor the content of thought (thoughts of war and the steppes or the city and the streets) that is decisive, rather it is the manner or mode that can be new and distinct, though it may have been around for quite a while [Buchanan: 2000: 117].

Certainly, rehabilitation with a something of a jolt is no new idea (one recalls the "short, sharp shock" enthusiastically promoted by the first Thatcher government) yet what is new and distinct is the specific manner in which Jigsaw's subjects are rendered "fit." Whilst it may seem perverse to associate Jigsaw's methodology with "utopian" philosophy dedicated to new ways of thinking, as the two scenes above demonstrate Jigsaw ultimately explains his aims as being precisely this. Throughout the series he is pursuing a strategy of effecting in his subjects a fresh way of thinking, through his radical interventions, in order for them to lead their life in the best (i.e., most positive) way. It is Jigsaw's route to utopia in that the method's ultimate goal is a better-functioning society — and the philosophical underpinnings that stand revealed are close to Hegel's notion of *sittlichkeit* (ethical life) whereby action for which one could be decried is legitimated when it is for the good of the ethical unit of society or the universal. Now, as will no doubt be apparent, it is something of a philosophical solecism to draw in Hegel and Deleuze, two names that do not sit comfortably together. (Deleuze notoriously "detests" Hegel and Hegelian dialectics.) The reason for doing so is, hopefully, a simple one, and that is because there is a tension within Jigsaw's thinking and its reception, which can be figured in the enmity Deleuze expresses for dialectics. To explain the Deleuzian position: despite all the "authenticity" that might be attached to this conception of social good, there is still something of the woolliest of self-help thinking that pervades Jigsaw's method (which is precisely what Bobby Dagen [Sean Patrick Flanery] exploits with his Jigsaw survivors group in *Saw 3D*) and it reduces itself not so much to the "be-your-best-you" type of slogan as that clenched cliché "no pain, no gain." For all of Jigsaw's subjects, pain is the catalyst for change, so this rehabilitation is about hurting as part of the healing process and pain's influence upon thought is the manner or mode for new thinking. As David B. Morris says of how one makes meaning of pain, "Sometimes pain can reveal to us beliefs and values we did not know we held.... Pain can reorder priorities in a hurry. It can show us what truly matters" (Morris: 1993: 45). Deleuze, who repeatedly considers thought as a form of violence, something forced upon a thinker, links this to the notion of the disjunctive synthesis. This is one of his rewritten syntheses taken from Kant's formulation for how a subject makes sense of, or synthesizes, impressions and for Deleuze the disjunctive synthesis refers to separate terms or things that can be conjoined whilst maintaining non-relation and thus resist sublation. In *Anti-Oedipus* Deleuze and Guattari employ the figure of "the schizophrenic" to illustrate this.

> He does not reduce to contraries to an identity of the same; he affirms their distance as that which relates the two as different. He does not confine himself inside contradictions; on the contrary, he opens out and, like a spore case inflated with spores, releases them as so many singularities that he had improperly shut off, some of which he intended to exclude, while retaining others ... all affirmed by their new distance [Deleuze, Guattari: 1984: 77].

The "closed" system of the Hegelian dialectic, resulting in a new synthesis (*aufhebung*), is effectively burst open by Deleuze's maneuver. The disjunctive synthesis is open-ended in its production of series, be that thought and territory, desire and body-part, or language and things. In the world of *Saw*, Jigsaw's planned social engineering might look as though it is designed dialectically but even a limited familiarity with Jigsaw's traps should leave one thinking otherwise; these machines break apart, recompose and move in new ways. In what leaves Jigsaw's workshop, the proliferation of series emerges immanently through the mixing of the literal and the figural. Put bluntly, it often isn't clear what these machines *do*, as complex mechanisms mesh and crank, yet even their given function affirms that ontological mixture. The reverse bear trap, for example, can literally cleave apart a subject's head whilst figuratively it may be the very thing to open the survivor's mind to the positives of life. Jigsaw's subjects enact their singular pain game, coming into contact with machines of aleatoric potential; this can result in the subjects extending into further series (which one might term *becoming* or, as Sidney (Oluniké Adeliyi) puts it in *Saw 3D*, "I chose life. It was the best thing that ever happened to me") or this can turn to an "illegitimate" disjunctive synthesis (alive or ... game over).

An Ordeal for Living

From Jigsaw's first game, that which he designed for Cecil, traps are designated as "tools" and the game is presumed to "serve" the subject. However, as Cecil all too quickly discovers, it is evident that the subject is subjected to a game in which incorporeal change is figured through somatic challenge. Whether this challenge is closer to punishment is a detail of definition Jigsaw persistently overlooks or ignores (although the etymological root of the word pain, the Latin *poena,* means punishment or penalty), and that is significant. The subject is left to play with pain, testing their limits, in a manner that could be deemed torture, yet it could equally be defined as closer to the older judicial practice of the ordeal. Inevitably, resolving this terminological distinction between torture and ordeal requires an answer to the question of who, or what, constitutes the higher or transcendent power claiming the authority? At this stage that answer is unclear: Jigsaw is teaching a lesson, yet, as Cecil discovers, what that lesson is can only be reached indirectly. He is faced with the challenge and the tool with which he can "reclaim his life"; a set of knives into which he must push his face in order to operate a release mechanism. The subject's body is symbolically marked as a way of signifying the "transformative" process they undergo. Vice may start written on the soul, but sin can be brought to the surface, much as in that other kind of ordeal, a suspected witch would float. As Jigsaw tells Cecil, "Today, we're bringing the ugliness inside you out into the open. In order for you to stay alive, we have to match your face with the ugliness of your soul." Obviously, there is no logical match here as to why Cecil's thievery and addiction, the turpitude that lies at his heart (in both senses of the verb), need to be faced truthfully in an act of self-scarification other than this being part of his learning process. Ugliness seems to be reductively equated with the face one presents to the world in a similar presumption of symbolic marking as that which Bobby Dagen deems as a "badge of courage" when he addresses the Jigsaw survival group. In short, the rudimentary movements of the assemblage can be identified here in the "ontological mixing" in which Jigsaw indulges, which suggests that there is something (at least) of the concept of disjunctive synthesis going on after all.

Assembling

The assemblage is the concept Deleuze and Guattari elaborate upon throughout their collaborative writings, and they take the idea in part from their earlier notion of the machine, of which the best example is the execution device the Harrow featured in Kafka's story "In The Penal Colony." The assemblage develops this concept into something that combines things, states and utterances and through which desire flows (Deleuze, Guattari: 1991: 88). The canonical example (not least because Deleuze and Guattari provide so few illustrations) is the feudal assemblage.

> Taking the feudal assemblage as an example, we would have to consider the interminglings of bodies defining feudalism: the body of the earth and the social body; the body of the overlord, vassal, and serf; the body of the knight and the horse and their new relation to the stirrup; the weapons and tools assuring a symbiosis of bodies — a whole machinic assemblage. We would also have to consider statements, expressions, the juridical regime of heraldry, all the incorporeal transformations, in particular, oaths and their variables (the oath of obedience, but also the oath of love, etc.): the collective assemblage of enunciation. On the other axis, we would have to consider the feudal territorialities and reterritorialisations, and at the same time the line of deterritorialisation that carries away both the knight and his mount, statements and acts. We would have to consider how all this combines in the Crusades [Deleuze, Guattari: 1991: 89].

The value of the assemblage lies in the way the machinic assemblage relates to the collective assemblage of enunciation and therefore collects together all the variables of a historical conjuncture on whatever scale. Its very openness is what makes it such a valuable hermeneutic, as much as philosophical, concept. "Assemblages may group themselves into extremely vast constellations constituting 'cultures,' or even 'ages'" (Deleuze, Guattari: 1991: 406) yet assemblages can also be far smaller, more localized or "briefer." Deleuze returns to the above example in *Dialogues II* where he explains how the tools relate to the wider social whole.

> In the case of the stirrup, it was the grant of land, linked to the beneficiary's obligation to serve on horseback, which was to impose the new cavalry and harness the tool in the complex assemblage of feudalism.... There is indeed a historical question of the assemblage: particular heterogeneous elements caught in the function, the circumstances in which they are caught up, the set of relationships which at a particular moment unites man, animal, tools and environment [Deleuze: 2006: 52-54].

A further important detail of the assemblage, and something to which Deleuze and Guattari keep referring, is the relationship of the assemblage to environment, which is not simply the ground of the assemblage. Deleuze goes so far as to state, "There is no assemblage without territory, without territoriality and reterritorialisation" (Deleuze: 2006: 53–54) which emphasizes that the assemblage is composed of place in as much as that is designated or expressed. Lecercle discusses this as "a space, in other words territories on which desire circulates; and movements within this space, of deterritorialisation and reterritorialisation" (Lecercle: 186). On this point, Lecercle suggests, it is worth recalling the original French term, *agencement*, which is "a territorial organisation, an array of elements" so that ultimately "an assemblage is an unholy mixture of events and territory. An assemblage begins by extracting a territory out of the environment" [*ibid*]. In the case of the feudal assemblage, the territorialization refers to land but also to the effects of wealth (taxes and Crusades) and even the knight's "territory" of his horse. Overall, then, the assemblage's multiplicity of co-functioning elements also allows change between modes of thought to be acknowledged neither through negation (Deleuze is as resistant to the negative as he is to dialectics) nor sublation but through disjunctive synthesis. That is, assemblages are not fixed structures but proliferating processes, so assemblages are always leading to other assemblages as relations produce further relations.

To speak of the Jigsaw assemblage is not to cite John Kramer/Jigsaw *as* the assemblage: the assemblage never names or refers to *a subject*. In the world of *Saw*, the Jigsaw assemblage is composed of various elements (on the one hand bodies; states; materials; events, and on the other, utterances). The assemblage is variously distributed: the specific sites where games occur, the derelict, post-industrial milieus, deterritorialized such as the abandoned zoo, Jigsaw's workshop and police institutions; the various people involved in implementing the games (John, Amanda, Hoffman, Jill, Gordon); the event of the games themselves and those who are forced to play. And it has to include such small features as the serrated and smooth blades used to cut the jigsaw pieces from victims by Hoffman and Jigsaw respectively, which becomes a clue, in *Saw VI*, to Hoffman's complicity. All of these elements constitute the machinic assemblage, which Deleuze and Guattari tirelessly reiterate is a *machinic assemblage of desire*. Throughout their works, Deleuze and Guattari observe a correlation between desire and production in a proliferation of intermingling flows that function as the circulatory system for their thought. "Desire constantly couples continuous flows and partial objects that are by nature fragmentary and fragmented. Desire causes the current to flow, itself flows in turn, and breaks the flows" (Deleuze, Guattari: 1984: 5). It is probably worth remarking that desire as Deleuze and Guattari understand it is unlimited. In *Dialogues II* Deleuze speaks of the simplicity of desire, with sleeping, walking, writing, seasons, old age and even death being designated as desires (Deleuze: 2006: 71). Where this is most apparent in the *Saw* films is in the event of the game, which is the active fitting together of the elements on a literally mechanized plane. Jigsaw's elaborate traps are distinctive in that the engineering and machinery are always fore-grounded in the *mise en scene*; it takes the working of gears to grind someone to death, yet this is always powered by immaterial forces. Deleuze comments that, "every assemblage expresses and creates a desire by constructing the plane which makes it possible and, by making it possible, brings it about" (Deleuze: 2006: 71). The game is where Jigsaw's desire (his method of rehabilitation) enters into an assemblage with the desire of the subject (to save themselves) even as it breaks the flow of their life heretofore. The machinic aspect of each trap, however, is also composed of non-corporeal social relations.

To take the example of William Easton (Peter Outerbridge) in *Saw VI*, the open totality here involves as a flow the system of American health insurance, since it is Easton's own formula and his treatment of Jigsaw and Harold Abbot (George Newbern) that leads to his being targeted as a subject. Easton's impersonal policy condemns Jigsaw and leads to the final claim on Easton's own soul, yet it enacts an American "truth" (which Jigsaw calls "ass-backwards" when he comments upon an alternative cultural practice where people pay for health, not illness) so the flows of capitalism itself are thus implicated. Capitalism (one of the targets of Deleuze and Guattari's critique) has what they deem an originality in "the fact that the social machine has for its parts technical machines as constant capital attached to the full body of the socius, and no longer men, the latter having become adjacent to the technical machines — whence the fact that inscription no longer bears directly, or at least in theory has no need of bearing directly, on men" (Deleuze, Guattari: 1984: 251). Jigsaw's schizz, or break (*coupure*), is to replace the technical machine of the abstract formula with the men (and women) from Easton's staff at Umbrella Health; the inscription again bears directly on material bodies, extracting premiums of pain as incorporeal relations are re-inscribed as rules pertaining to human beings.

There is, though, more to consider as part of this concept. Combined with the machinic assemblage there is the collective assemblage of enunciation, the regime of utterances speaking through institutions and individuals. This is constituted by the recorded messages introducing and outlining each game; the "sensationalising" of Jigsaw carried out by the likes of Pamela Jenkins (Samantha Lemole); Jigsaw's "philosophy" and its revision by others involved in the project; the letters and notes; codes or hidden meanings within language. Lecercle identifies a difficulty here in deciding how these two assemblages are integrated into one assemblage. He notes how in *A Thousand Plateaus* we are told that the "assemblage of enunciation does not speak "of" things; it speaks *on the same level as* states and things and states of content" (Deleuze, Guattari: 1991: 87). Lecercle adds, "The French phrase is '*à même les choses*,' which does not mean simply 'on the same level as' but also 'in the midst of'" (Lecercle: 189). The distinction between states and utterances cannot therefore be insisted upon, since things and utterances are inseparable. In terms of discourse this is achieved by the ongoing reporting of the Jigsaw killings: the media of press and television collect up the individual deaths into a serialized and narrativized set of enunciations. That is, the Jigsaw killings become a news story. Just as the films fill in and embellish on what the audience knows previously, the textual world of *Saw* sees an increasing publicity of the games through the coverage of deaths and those who've survived. By *Saw 3D*, the predicament of Ryan (Jon Cor), Brad (Sebastian Piggott) and the woman between them, Dina (Anne Lee Greene), is familiar enough to be staged as a shop window display, with the crowd filming it on mobile phones for further dissemination. "The puzzle unfolds," says part of the news report that Easton watches in *Saw VI*. So Jigsaw's actions become part of the story, as it were, with others collectively contributing. This plane of expression is complemented by the police presence throughout the films, even though the attenuated manner of this suggests that the Jigsaw killings are something of a recondite investigation. In this regard, the *Saw* films are kept distinct from the police procedural, despite the markers of this mode that do occur, so a further institutional discourse helps to frame the narrative.

The Sentence and the Body

However, this still doesn't quite account for the specificity of the collective assemblage of enunciation within the *Saw* films. There are numerous films that deal with sensationalized serial killers, after all. In order to identify the specific features of these specific films it is Lecercle's observation — the assemblage of enunciation speaks in the midst of the machinic assemblage — that is of particular use here; the Jigsaw assemblage "speaks" in its own deterritorialized way. When characters wake to find themselves variously restrained in a trap it is only through the starting of Jigsaw's recorded message that their circumstances become a game and the ensuing rules serve to establish the territory. The assemblage of enunciation is an assemblage of words, and Deleuze gives an example of this when he formulates the assemblage of enunciation for a vampire: "A – VAMPIRE – TO SLEEP – DAY – AND – TO WAKE UP – NIGHT" (Deleuze: 2006: 71). Quite simply, in reducing the "flow" of the vampire into this grammatical arrangement, the "basic chain of expression, correlative to the least formalised contents" (Deleuze, Guattari: 1991: 263), it is apparent that this assemblage is not utterance but sentence. Something equivalent can be posited for the *Saw* films, although it is not quite reducible to such a basic semantic chain; perhaps, "Hello — to play — a game — to live or die — make a choice" would be a reasonable approximation to employ. However it is rendered, the plane of expression in the *Saw* films can be inscribed in a specific kind of sentence (correlates of instructions or order-words) and in keeping with the sorts of enunciation we are dealing with (where codes and hidden meanings abound) the variable meanings of "sentence" are drawn to the surface in correlation. The Jigsaw assemblage is inscribed in that very ontological mixture of the sentence enunciated in the midst of the game and pronounced upon the body. It is just such a relation that Elaine Scarry identifies in *The Body in Pain* as part of the structure of torture, where the disembodied voice of the torturer is placed in opposition to the unheard or unspoken body of the victim, so that there is "interaction between the ultimate source of each — the body, the locus of pain, and the voice, the locus of power" (Scarry: 1985: 51), yet this "colossal voice" imposing on the body can be the judgment of God or the edicts of a capitalist class. Order words are therefore not spoken by an individual, but are produced through collective enunciation: they are also terminal in what they transmit — or as Deleuze and Guattari put it: "the order-word is a death sentence; it always implies a death sentence, even if it has been considerably softened, becoming symbolic, initiatory, temporary, etc. Order-words bring immediate death to those who receive the order, or potential death if they do not obey, or a death they must inflict, take elsewhere" (Deleuze, Guattari: 1991: 107). When Jigsaw passes sentence, the body of the victim — or subject, to return to Jigsaw's preferred term — is where this becomes inscribed (again, it is worth recalling the machinic assemblage's of Kafka's Harrow, which similarly organizes a disjunctive synthesis between word and flesh) and this is regardless of from where, or whom, the enunciation has flowed. This *sentencing* is what the Jigsaw assemblage processes. The fitting together, as part of the method of making fit, is an active process and follows Deleuze's very frequent strategy of literalizing, or actualizing, the figurative. To provide two examples, there is Art Blank (Justin Louis), a lawyer who speaks for his clients and is therefore kept quiet by the thread sewing his mouth shut, or Eddie (Marty Moreau) and Simone (Tanedra Howard) who have to give up their pound (or more) of flesh following their predatory usury. In both, the sentencing contains earlier echoes. Blank speaks no evil whilst Eddie and Simone are faced with a reiteration of Shakespeare's own mixing of the literal and the figurative (Shylock is sanctioned to cut a pound of flesh, but prohibited from spilling Christian blood). These are, in short, less radical actions than enactments of cliché.

Given what has been said about how this comes down to the sentence and the body, it is now clear how one can read the Jigsaw assemblage and to suggest that in answer to the question left unresolved above, what Jigsaw is doing can best be called torture. And this is not a vague, imprecise and merely descriptive turn, as in the appellation "torture-porn." There are consequences to suggesting that Jigsaw is engaged in torture. In part his actions can be defined as such because it is a regulated process (Foucault explains how judicial torture was always a "well-defined procedure" of interrogation [Foucault: 1977: 40]) but perhaps more importantly because, as Scarry says, torture confers legitimacy, authority and power that would be otherwise debatable: "The physical pain is so incontestably real that it seems to confer its quality of 'incontestable reality' on that power that has brought it into being" (Scarry: 27). Certainly by the latter films, subjects know that they are being subjected to the extra-judicial authority of Jigsaw and the only way out is to obey the rules of the game. So rather than the ordeal, where will is sublimated to divine proof of innocence as a way of reaching truth, pain resulting from a process of torture becomes an "essential condition for permitting the truth to emerge" (Morris: 185). The pain experienced in a Jigsaw trap is "denied as pain and read as power" (Scarry: 45). The language of the torturer, as Deleuze discusses in "Coldness and Cruelty," is the language of an established authority (however dubious), rather than the personal, descriptive and individual language of the sadist (Deleuze: 1989: 19) and it is crucial not to mistake Jigsaw's actions as sadistic. He is not doing any of this for personal gratification — consider his equanimity in both allowing Hoffman access to a razor with which Hoffman might kill him and in revealing the shotgun cartridge that could have decapitated Hoffman (*Saw V*). Moreover, Jigsaw specifically tells Hoffman as they prepare Paul Leahy (Mike Butters) for his razor wire maze trap (*Saw V*), "The heart cannot be involved. Emotionally, there can be nothing there. It can never be personal." This is impersonal, collective, "conceptual" violence, that is, torture — designed to educate rather than instruct, as Deleuze puts it. As a result of this it is Jigsaw's very neutrality — the expression or performance of his personal and emotional distance — that confers his authority and his scrupulousness in allowing subjects to make choice is what "identifies the impersonal violence with an Idea of pure reason" (Deleuze: 1989: 20). Vitality is what speaks through the machinery of the traps and Jigsaw is only part of this mechanism, through which others will learn to speak — or utter a terminal scream. Jigsaw is indiscernible, a point of relative stability rather than a person, because he has been through an assemblage of his own. He has already been tested and whereas he was once the body, he is now the voice, or rather, a *collective assemblage of enunciation* flows through from this point. Deleuze and Guattari reject the notion of a fixed and stable subject and instead see subjects as being formed through syntheses, or flows, or the processes of assemblage. For those that survive the game, that are revitalized or rehabilitated through the process of being tested, they will help to produce further assemblages in turn, either as apprentices or assistants or by spreading these sentences.

Yet, as becomes apparent, what Jigsaw believes will result from his rehabilitative method is rather different from what actually emerges. Whilst one survivor might say "I'm better for enduring it. I'm stronger and, I must admit, I'm grateful to it" (*Saw 3D*), Simone indicates the stump of her arm and berates Hoffman saying, "What the fuck am I supposed to learn from this?" The reason for the inconsistency in Jigsaw's method is because, as Buchanan puts it, "Composed of its own relations, the assemblage is not, however, reducible to them, it has its own vitality. It also has its illnesses" (Buchanan: 120). The vitality of the assemblage cannot always be counted on and the illness of the assemblage is stratification: that is, anything that blocks the process of the assemblage. Deleuze and Guattari identify the "three great strata" as "the organism, significance, and subjectification" (Deleuze, Guattari: 1991: 159), which means "dismantling" the obstructions to the assemblage posed by psychoanalysis, structuralist semiotics and Marxism, respectively. Stratification is not limited to these three problems, however, and within the Jigsaw assemblage the illness is two-fold.

Stratification: The Jigsaw "Disease"

Firstly and most clearly, the process of rehabilitation is blocked by a different flow of desire entering the assemblage. This is the case in the traps set by Amanda and Hoffman that are designed as revenge against the subjects involved. Jigsaw dismisses these as *executions,* rather than games offering a legitimate choice, since they skew the sentence, re-constituting is as a nothing but a death-sentence through the specificity of the order that is carried. The angel-trap that kills Detective Kerry (Dana Meyer) and the pendulum trap that dispatches Seth (Joris Jarsky) are not designed to "make fit" and the flow of desire, acting as a current, is the desire for revenge. Whilst the machinic assemblage looks like the stuff of the Jigsaw assemblage, the assemblage of enunciation is inscribed with no choice, only death: a "block" on the content and expression as the "two variables of a function of stratification" (Deleuze, Guattari: 1991: 44) so that the assemblage tips towards the molar and the potential of disjunctive synthesis is lost. In short, the vitality and potential that can result from the process of the Jigsaw assemblage is not able to take place — the process cannot function — because this assemblage simply carries out the lethality of the order-word: it is a killing machine. Importantly, this still bears a strong relation to the Jigsaw assemblage since Amanda and Hoffman are operating in a paradigm of "judicial" killing — albeit one deriving authority from vigilante activity and the "common good" of the always-silent majority — rather than converting this to sadistic enactment. That is, they are not indulging in killings for *sexual* desire or as a way of recovering ego, given that the sadist's desire is concerned with ameliorating the overwhelming presence of the superego. For Deleuze, the sadist is effectively reducible to superego, which is why he goes on to make the claim "*The sadist has no other ego than that of his victims*; he is thus monstrously reduced to a pure superego which exercises its cruelty to the fullest extent and instantaneously recovers its full sexuality as soon as it diverts its power outward" (Deleuze: 1989: 124). Even where the Jigsaw assemblage "goes wrong" one cannot accurately identify sadism because it still retains the strong features of the Jigsaw assemblage — the language of the torturer in the collective assemblage of enunciation and the individual-as-torturer is only a representative of the (feigned) authority and, speaking more broadly, the trappings of these other traps are indistinguishable from a "real" Jigsaw game. Scarry argues that the torture victim has their world unmade in the face of objectified pain, so that ultimately everything — torturer, apparatus, environment, regime — stands in opposition to the tortured prisoner (Scarry: 45) and it would be right to see Amanda and Hoffman as being swept up in the machinic assemblage in this way. Their killings are not sufficiently deterritorialized, however much they misspeak or fix the rules, compromising the method even whilst they retain the means, so that the angel trap and the pendulum trap might be thought of as the negative of the Jigsaw assemblage or perhaps a *dark assemblage*.

The contamination or pollution that shuts down the rehabilitative potential of the Jigsaw assemblage uncovers the malady to which the Jigsaw assemblage is susceptible. It can also present in a way that is related to the former although through somewhat different symptoms and this second problem or weakness in the Jigsaw assemblage is not so much to do with the various flows incorporated and ensuing from the assemblage as with the process itself. When Jigsaw explains his vitalist approach to life, in conversation with Matthews, and outlines his different method to Hoffman he reveals the extent to which he has "become" the language of the torturer, having come though his own test of the failed suicide bid. During the course of the films he enlists others to assist in the work, to continue his project as his cancer debilitates him, and subsequently to pursue his legacy posthumously. So we witness declining health and ultimately death within one of the revitalized elements of the assemblage, namely John Kramer himself, which indicates that being made fit for a "good" life is not about bodily well-being but is only to do with the appreciation of life as an intensity rather than as an ontological category.

Rehabilitating "Life" and the body-without-organs is Jigsaw's deterritorializing line of flight, and a truly utopian one. The others who assist with the plans in accordance with what Jigsaw wants to achieve — such as Jill and Dr Gordon — are helping to stage a series of rehabilitative events yet, despite the variety of traps and their increasingly elaborate nature, this is always already a *repetition of a singular flow*. Just as Amanda and Hoffman constrict the potential of the assemblage through their misplaced desires, the Jigsaw assemblage is always in danger of being limited to making fit in the same way. The lesson Jigsaw wants to teach others is his lesson, rather than a design for life. For this reason, subjects like Simone can win their game but take no revitalizing appreciation of life from it since this is merely copying, not de-stratifying. Deleuze's resistance to Platonism (any form of Platonism) is in evidence throughout his corpus but *Difference and Repetition* explicates the difficulties he sees with the hierarchical separation between original and copy, signified and signifier when he considers how this might *work*: "We learn nothing from those who say: 'Do as I do.' Our only teachers are those who tell us to 'do with me,' and are able to emit signs to be developed in heterogeneity rather than propose gestures for us to reproduce" (Deleuze: 1994: 23). The malady of the Jigsaw assemblage, and the mistake that constantly endangers the "different method," is something that has haunted the edges of the collective assemblage of enunciation all along; the "educational" utterance has all too often been lost to pedagogical imperative and the tone of instruction, command or order. In deciding upon bodily pain and the language of the torturer as the method of rehabilitation Jigsaw proscribes choice unless subjects are willing to learn what he has, in the way he has. Enforced free will is a paradox that Deleuze sees as meeting the possibility of desire with lack. "If you tie someone up and say to him "Express yourself, friend," the most he will be able to say is that he doesn't want to be tied up. The only spontaneity in desire is doubtless of that kind: to not want to be oppressed, exploited, enslaved, subjugated" (Deleuze: 2006: 71). There can be rejuvenating successes, as Dr Gordon and some members of the Jigsaw survival group demonstrate, but this second chance is something of an imitative, second-hand chance since Jigsaw's aim of deterritorialized, utopian thought is not what he spreads. As his claims about neutrality make apparent — "Emotionally, there can be nothing there. This can never be personal" — Jigsaw always already reterritorializes his apparently-radical agenda in classically Enlightenment thinking, hooking emotion in the subject. This is an ideological glaucoma that circulates throughout the Jigsaw assemblage: Jigsaw has purportedly found a way for himself and others to reach enlightenment but in truth he's simply found the Enlightenment. The disease that spreads, for all the utopian impulse behind it, is nothing new, just the "mechanical" thought of re-learning extant ideological propositions by rote — and through the most punitive of pedagogical tactics. The liberating and creative vitality of a deterritorializing line of flight and the social engineering the Jigsaw assemblage desires seemingly requires the construction of a subtler machine to bring it about than any of Jigsaw's traps so far.

Notes

1. The term, applied to the *Saw* franchise and films deemed "similar," has a contested usage varying from pejorative and hyperbolic journalese to provocative marketing tag and even critical description. Whatever the inflection, the compound "torture-porn" tends to designate a hyper-realism that serves to collapse the distance between viewer and text so that textual effects become "real" or at least become valorized with referents beyond the textual world. It shares this with the earlier term "snuff-movie." "Torture-porn" is, of course, an example of disjunctive synthesis, as elaborated upon below.

2. Jigsaw has an aversion to being labeled a killer and is consistent in correcting this perception of his activities whenever it arises. It's a characteristic he shares with the Marquis de Sade, who was also at pains to differentiate between his violence of thought and the propriety of his deeds. The insistence upon such a distinction is arguably Jigsaw's most Sadean trait.

References

Buchanan, Ian. *Deleuzism: A Metacommentary*, Edinburgh: Edinburgh University Press, 2000.
Deleuze, Gilles. *Difference and Repetition*. Trans. Paul Patton. London: Athlone, 1994.
_____. *Masochism*, New York: Zone, 1989.
Deleuze, Gilles, and Felix Guattari. *Anti-Oedipus*. Trans. Robert Hurley, Mark Seem and Helen R. Lane. London: Athlone, 1984.
_____, and _____. *A Thousand Plateaus*. Trans. Brian Massumi. Minnesota: University of Minnesota Press, 1991.
Deleuze, Gilles, and Claire Parnet. *Dialogues II*. Trans. Hugh Tomlinson and Barbara Habberjam. London: Continuum, 2006.
Foucault, Michel. *Discipline and Punish: The Birth of the Prison*. Trans. Alan Sheridan. New York: Pantheon Books, 1977.
Kafka, Franz. "In the Penal Colony," in *The Transformation and Other Stories*. Trans. Malcolm Pasley, 127–153. London: Penguin, 1992.
Lecercle, Jean Jacques. *Deleuze and Language*. Basingstoke: Palgrave Macmillan, 2002.
Morris, David B. *The Culture of Pain*. London: University of California Press, 1993.
Scarry, Elaine. *The Body in Pain: The Making and Unmaking of the World*. New York: Oxford University Press, 1985.

Work Is Hell: Life in the Mannequin Factory
Dean Lockwood

A light is switched on. A small figure slowly emerges from darkness in the corner of a room, pedaling a child's tricycle and throwing alarming shadows against the wall. The figure stops, presenting itself to a terrified young woman, Amanda, who has, moments before, narrowly escaped death by removing a horrendous helmet-like device — a "reverse bear trap" — just as it was about to spring open and dismantle her head. In a close-up on the figure's face we see that it is a particularly unsettling male doll, reminiscent of an old-fashioned ventriloquist's dummy in a three-piece suit and bow tie, with white face, black hair, and garish red eyes and mouth. Appearing to pause in consideration of Amanda's achievement, its hinged lower jaw then moves, so that the doll shakes slightly, and somehow it speaks: "Congratulations, you are still alive. Most people are so ungrateful to be alive. But not you, not any more." The doll is a striking occasional presence in *Saw*, wheeled out here in the aftermath of one of the "games" around which the narrative is structured — ordeals in which victims race against the clock to follow instructions necessary to survive a variety of spectacular traps — designed by Jigsaw, the (presumably) psychopathic genius whose motives are one of the central enigmas of the film and its sequels.

"He helped me," says Amanda of Jigsaw, when later questioned by police detectives hunting him. Terminally ill, Jigsaw's last days are driven by a terrible purpose. His game campaign addresses what he perceives as the sickening bad faith of the people around him — parasites, malingerers, addicts, grubbing a miserable and unfeeling existence. His games teach a twisted kind of love, forcing those he takes as victims to confront their self-deception and make a decision — will they remain passive or will they become alive to the moment, present and engaged, prepared to do something drastic, to choose to survive?

Many academic critics have preferred to dismiss or sideline the explanation Jigsaw himself offers for his cruel and violent scenarios, rejecting these life lessons as an unconvincing alibi for the film's real focus, which is (as it is for many of those films which have been, like *Saw*, dubbed "torture porn") the amoral spectacle of unredeemed, meaningless suffering. Citing Jonathan Crane's analysis of contemporary slasher films, Brigid Cherry's interpretation, for example, is that *Saw*'s various assaults on the body testify to the monstrousness humans are capable of in the "nihilistic context" of our postmodern condition (2009, 201). However, an opposing view is taken by Matt Hills, who suggests that Jigsaw's way of seeing is the "crucial problematic of the franchise" (2012, 116). He considers that Jigsaw's monstrosity should be understood in terms of his "fantastic psychology" (115). Specifically, the moral rectitude claimed by Jigsaw for his designs can be related to the War on Terror's disjunctive synthesis of terror and security, in which these are not true antagonists but could be said to actually constitute twin faces of the same logic. The paradoxical nature of Jigsaw's fantastic psychology — *in extremis*, the cancer-riddled Jigsaw is inspired to liberate through victimization, acting out a psychopathological scheme he translates as an authentic response to a mad, perhaps diseased, world but which only really seems to ultimately collude with, and plunge him deeper into, the sickness — echoes the collapsing of terrorized and terrorist in the post–9/11 context: "Jigsaw can stand in both for the Bush administration's defence of 'righteous torture' and for terroristic radicalization" (118). Such an analysis has a great deal going for it, but my feeling is that *Saw* also resonates more widely with the world forged in the late twentieth-century networking of capital and the inception of what Gilles Deleuze has described as new "societies of control" (1995). What we seem to be dealing with here is not so much fantastic psychology itself as the way fantastic psychologies are produced or conscripted to abet a new, monstrous form of fantastic *power*.

In this vein, Catherine Zimmer argues that *Saw* is symptomatic of an entire ideological paradigm. She draws on Giorgio Agamben's work on the suspensive condition pertaining to contemporary states of exception — when sovereign power declares an emergency, such as Bush's 2001 order enabling terror suspects to be indefinitely detained. In this condition those banned from political participation, cast out from the protection of the law into what Agamben calls "bare life," continue, paradoxically, to be held in the grip of power, creating a strange "zone of indistinction" in which the outcast is actually neither properly included nor excluded (Agamben, 1998). Zimmer foregrounds the phenomenon of surveillance as key to *Saw*'s narrative logic and its collapse of watchers and watched in a zone of indistinction similar to the paradoxical spaces of power discussed by Agamben (ostensibly anomalous, but, for Agamben, in fact generalized in many contemporary societies). For Zimmer, every character in *Saw* is "both guilty and innocent" (2011, 85) and it is precisely surveillance "that blurs the distinction between who is the subject or object of torture, and which establishes the victims of the torture as somehow guilty in their own way" (89). Here, torture victims themselves are typically complicit with the practice of surveillance in various ways. So, as Zimmer formulates it: "'someone is being videotaped, and we don't quite know what it means, who is operating the technology, and what the association with that technology implies'" (90). The unstable space configured in *Saw* begs for resolution: "the ambiguous narrative formation around surveillance *asks* for torture, *hailing* it in order to turn the zones of indistinction into resolved deployments of power" (92). My argument here will be similar in some respects — it seems to me that plugging the concept of the zone of indistinction into the analysis of *Saw* is particularly useful — but in others somewhat different. Specifically, I place less emphasis on surveillance than Zimmer and others, and much more on *affective* control. I see *Saw*'s violence, not in terms of a disambiguating, resolution-fixated narrative function, as does Zimmer, but rather as a form of affective attunement with what the new tyranny feels like, how it feels to be made flexible; to be, as it were, ripped inside out and entrained into the rhythms of a new regime (Shaviro, 2010, 2). My argument situates *Saw* in the context of mutations of capital and ensuing transformations of labor, specifically, the affective dimension of labor. As industrial production has declined and the service sector grown, the nature of labor has been transformed. Labor, in the production of services, is more intellectual and informational but an important aspect of its transformation is that it has also come increasingly to involve the affective, vital powers underpinning interaction between people, whether contact is virtual or actual (Hardt and Negri, 2000, 292). Affective labor foregrounds corporeality and bodily states which, of course, also impinge upon thinking and mood, the creation of joy or sadness. As Hardt and Negri spell out, we are here dealing with "biopower," or the visceral "productive capacities of life" (364). Simply put, being a "people person," skilled in the manipulation of others' feelings and moods, is now high on the agenda of many employers. We could cite workers in fast food outlets, transport, hotels, education, media and journalism, etc., as examples of affective laborers, dedicated to the production of "a feeling of ease, well-being, satisfaction, excitement, or passion" (293). The argument here turns on the significance of an increasingly prevalent form of power which parasitizes the vitality of the affective life of living labor, instituting new modes of enclosure in a bid to extract value from affect. What if we take Jigsaw seriously and consider the film's violence and threat less as torture — a twisting to breaking point, exhausting the person's usefulness at the point of confession or bodily collapse — and more as *innervation*, as a kind of galvanism and harvesting of the affective potentials of the human body? Jigsaw's aim is to provoke affect, not simply to tear apart. The game revolves precisely around the stimulation and channeling of intense surges of affect, of life force.

As we learn in the course of the film, the troubling doll featured in *Saw* is an avatar of Jigsaw, one of the ways he communicates his intentions and instructions to players of the game scenarios. The voice with which it speaks is Jigsaw's. When, in the scene with which we opened, the camera closes on the doll's face, designs prominent on its cheeks become visible. They consist of red spirals. The spiral is, of course, an ancient device, suggesting the generative, dynamic powers of life and the universe, a vortex or rhythmic force of creation and growth, but it also frequently symbolizes the spinning of webs and wanderings in a labyrinth. The spiral, in its various and conflicting meanings, is the perfect symbol for the exploitation and capture of affective labor and life's creative powers. It makes sense to connect *Saw* up with the wholesale transformation, today, of living laborers into affective puppets. Ultimately, perhaps, Jigsaw is only another such puppet, borrowing his influence from a sovereign evil which acts and speaks through him. As Agamben notes: "It is the invisible sovereign that stares at us behind the dull-witted masks of the powerful who, whether or not they realize it, govern us in its name" (cited in Noys, 2005, 65).

We are not entitled to expect coherence or clarity with respect to *Saw*'s connection with the contemporary. Hills, refuting allegations that the *Saw* films are apolitical, suggests that even if they do not directly reflect political controversies, they do act at a certain remove and "circle thematically around" them. The relationship between text and context is not fixed, simple and univocal. It is a multiple and relative point of view (Hills, 2012, 110–1). *Saw* is political, but incoherently so precisely because it "codes" the incoherence and ambiguities of its contexts (121). In fact, I would suggest that the film can be understood in terms of an aesthetic of "affective mapping" such as we find theorized in the work of Flatley (2008) and Shaviro (2010) rather than reflectionism, however qualified. Reflectionism, and the representational paradigm, is not well suited to capturing vital, visceral affects and moods which characterize human experience. Deleuze and Guattari make a useful distinction between "tracing" and "mapping" (2004, 13). Representation involves "tracing" what already exists in actuality. But the real involves more than what is actual, it involves the virtual power of life to differ from itself. Here we are in the realm of affect, of corporeal potential, rather than meaning. To construct affective maps is not to represent or signify. It is to express life in a way which captures the changefulness, the processual character of life — its virtuality — regardless of how inflexible and fixed current forms of life may seem. This necessitates a certain detachment from actuality, an immersion in the virtual *potentials* of forms of life (see also Langer, 1953, on the concept of "semblance"). Affective mapping frees us from habitual, familiar ways of perceiving and attempts to disclose possibilities, propensities which have hitherto remained unknown, unperceived. In this way, cinema, "both symptomatic and productive," does not simply reflect actuality, but rather maps and generates virtual, affective flows (Shaviro, 2010, 2). Thought and feeling are affectively organized in terms of moods which shape our "bare activity," our worlding (to borrow a Heideggerian term), our finding ourselves just "going on" in the middle of doing (Massumi, 2011, 1). Cinema can critically map our affective worlding and the possibilities that this either precludes or allows to emerge, resonating with it in such a way as to foster in us an interrogatory, experimental attitude.

Lazzarato argues that contemporary capitalism "is not only a mode of production but a *production of worlds*" (2004, 187). The production of services, for example, is also a worlding process and this process is "inscribed in the souls and bodies of consumers and workers" (188). We here see a shift beyond Foucauldian disciplinary techniques of the body which are applied to consumers and workers from outside (through the various institutional moulds that Foucault describes). Now, the "reality" of business "merges with the relationships enterprises, workers and consumers have with each other" (188). Business captures pre-individual, affective life, captures and produces the possibilities of our bodies and the possibilities of our very "belonging to a world" (189). Contemporary capitalism is "no longer only based on the exploitation of labour in the industrial sense" (205), but moves to encompass and mobilize the creative, inventive capacities of living bodies. In a world in which "the company does not exist outside the producers or consumers who express it," in which capitalism merges with the reality of our relationships, creating the very world within which we exist as a lived semblance, an aesthetic of affective mapping might prove crucial. If we have shifted "from Capital-Labour to Capital-Life," as Maurizio Lazzarato insists, critically engaging with this situation must mean developing strategies for deployment in an affective and aesthetic struggle as much as an economic struggle (188). Perhaps we can approach the import of *Saw* in terms of mapping, creating a semblance, of the sense life comes to acquire in conditions of "Capital-Life"? In *Saw*, Jigsaw's game plan maps out the transformation, under conditions of Capital-Life, of individuals, workers — always defined by their occupation as much as their "sin"— into affective puppets. Every ordeal is an operation within the mannequin factory, every ordeal expresses "the company."

Down the Shit-hole

Saw begins with three men in a room. We're introduced to this room in a scene which resembles a kind of birth, as if there has never been any other room. The film's title swims, as if beneath dark water, and then we see a man's submerged face, eyes closed. It is the face of the first man (who we will discover is aptly named Adam), lit only by the blue light on a key ring that immediately disappears down the plughole of the bath in which he is immersed. He wakes, struggles from the bath. He cries for help, he wonders whether he is dead. What's that smell? A voice responds — calming — no, he isn't dead. Then there is sudden and blinding illumination as strip lights come on. Vision settling, the two men contemplate each other from opposite ends of what is apparently a disused industrial bathroom. It is a dismal, befouled room. Then — shock — they register what lies at the centre of the tiled floor. The camera spins upwards from the spectacle of a third man's corpse, hands clutching a gun and a tape machine. The corpse's head is ruined — suicide by gunshot? — and lies at the centre of a great pool of blood. The two living men make their introductions ("My name is very fucking confused, what's your name?"). Deepening the mystery, both Adam, initially of undisclosed occupation, and the second man, an oncologist, Dr Lawrence Gordon, are chained to sturdy pipes. Neither can remember how they wound up here. "I went to bed in my shit-hole apartment, and woke up in an actual shit-hole," Adam declares. It's as if here, in this abominable non-place of defilement and abjection, they wake to their true lives.

The sewer lines, one of *Saw*'s characters points out, run beneath the entire neighborhood. John Clute notes that the portal by which protagonists move between their primary world and the secondary world of fantasyland is a crucial element of much fantasy narrative architecture, but that in horror, characterized precisely by the impossibility of exit, we find only parodies of portals: "[The] term Cloaca is applied here to semblances of Portal when such are uncovered. If entering a Portal can be likened to swimming with the tide as upon a quest, then entering a Cloaca can be likened to swimming upstream like a gaffed fish ... the world is surely diseased, and we are all up shit creek without a Portal" (2006, 38). This image of the Cloacal mire impeding progress is particularly apposite in the case of *Saw*. "Bondage is stasis," Clute tells us, but, in fantasy, "stories move. They tell bondage away" (126). In *Alice in Wonderland*, for example, Alice falls down the rabbit-hole into the vestibule of Wonderland. She is hindered from further investigation by locked doors, but only momentarily, for she will discover food and drink to magically afford her access (the "Eat Me" and "Drink Me" of which are parodied in the "Play Me" of *Saw*'s tapes). Wonderland is a rule-generated world, operating "according to precepts which represent a rigorous working-out of various propositions carried to a point of absurdity" (Clute, 1997, 1030). Absurd rules, perhaps, but identifiable all the same, and it is in identifying them that Alice makes her escape. Not so down the shit-hole in *Saw*. Here, Jigsaw's victims are reborn into a hellish game world where, crucially, the rules themselves are in play. Story stalls as the game metastasizes, virally proliferating new traps, new levels, new challenges, ruling out escape.

Antonin Artaud wrote, inspired by Van Gogh, that "[no] one has ever written, painted, sculpted, modelled, built or invented except literally to get out of hell" (1988, 497). In popular culture, it is the horror genre that most clearly resonates with this declaration. In *Saw*, Lawrence, the oncologist, remarks that to overcome a condition such as cancer — a "perfect engine" — one must seek to understand it perfectly. Indeed, horror fiction posits the true nature of the world as malicious and sets out precisely to divine the ways in which it binds us. Clute characterizes the major current within horror literature — which I would wish to extend to encompass the horror genre considered more broadly — as the "Bound Fantastic" (2006, 33). The genres of the fantastic, Clute notes, emerged in the eighteenth century with the first clear apprehension of the planet as such, of Earth as a "mortal engine." Fantastic "grammars," further, have been erected upon "two underlying matrices ... bound-to-the-planet or ticket-to-leave" (34). Where the matrix of fantasy — or the "Free Fantastic" — licenses optimistic narratives of escape from imprisonment or of the healing of an injured land, the matrix of horror — the Bound Fantastic — generates tales of exitless prisons and endless hells. Horror subverts a great illusion. It exposes the lie of human dominion, mastery over the world. The world we thought we knew, laid out before us, charted and inventoried, is merely a cover-up, or "rind." The horror rests with our "unmapping," hooked by visions of reigning chaos which gather substance, becoming the primary reality as stories develop (142). All avenues back to the "known" world prove false or are pre-emptively blocked. Horror tales culminate in carnivalesque inversion and the revelation of terminal incoherence. As the rind of the world is peeled back, we are witness to the revelation that everybody wears a mask. Nothing and no-one can be trusted.

Horror posits a general imposture, rubbing our faces in the insecurity of our identities. The Gothic tradition is exemplary in this respect, as Patrick McGrath explains:

> The idea of the "real man" — or the "true self," or the "essential identity" — has no validity in the Gothic. The Gothic recognizes the fluidity, the multiplicity, the contingency of identity. It shies away from absolutes and essences, it understands that any figure — including the self — will change its appearance according to the perspective of the observer and the context against which it is observed. Both Dr. Jekyll and Dorian Gray, for example, become entirely different entities according to the time of day.... Many of the dominant themes and motifs of the Gothic — masks, monsters, grotesques, doubles, ghosts, madness, intoxication, dreams — speak to this *instability of identity*, and in the broadest sense make a question of our central assumption within identity, and ask: *what is the human?* [1997, 156–5].

The Gothic — of which the *Saw* franchise, with its dungeons and devices, its robed and hooded villains, its masks and its madness, is redolent — is a modern version of an ancient anxiety about the porosity of the human subject (Bruns, 2011, np). In its paranoid visions of a diseased world in which the boundary of the human cannot remain intact as we are both invaded by and lose our minds to the outside, the rind of subjective intentions is peeled back to expose the operation of a fantastic power, a demonism. How else are we to make sense of the tapes, videos, mobile phones (which only receive), the ventriloquism with which *Saw* is replete? Cast out in the Gothic's zone of indistinction, subjectivity mediatized and exposed to a wild and unwholesome traffic, we are no longer subjects of experience, actors or transmitters, but rather subject *to* experience, passive receivers, hollowed-out channels (Bruns, 2011, np).

As the two men begin to realize that their Cloacal prison is merely a node in a wider network, a web upon which the spider is yet to appear but is certainly watching and listening, Lawrence remarks to Adam that the game they are bound to play is entirely "pre-thought" (indeed, in a later scene, we will see a miniature model of the bathroom and its occupants in Jigsaw's lair). I want to go on, in the next section, to contend that the locus of horror in *Saw*'s Bound Fantastic is the "perfect engine" of work, which is an engine of living death. In Capital-Life, work is endless hell. It is work that makes us puppets, suspends us in its zone of indistinction.

Engine of Living Death

Saw ends with the entrance of a fourth man into the room. Having established some of the terms of their imprisonment by means of playing found tapes in the machine clutched by the corpse, Adam and Lawrence have overcome mutual distrust to collaborate on escaping their plight. Lawrence, whose challenge is to kill Adam in the set time in order to prevent the deaths of his wife and daughter, is prompted by a secret message to dip the end of a cigarette into the corpse's blood (which, we gather, is suffused by a deadly poison) and to offer the cigarette to Adam. Unwilling to connive in Adam's murder, he contrives to alert him to the set-up. Adam acts out his death so as to trigger the end of the game. No such luck … he is electrocuted through the chain which secures him and the fact of his still being alive becomes evident. Shortly thereafter the time allotted comes to an end. In desperation, Lawrence takes up one of two hacksaws discovered earlier and frees himself by sawing off his foot. Shooting Adam with the corpse's gun, he appeals once again to Jigsaw to call a halt and free his family. It is at this point that a fourth man, Zep —

whom we recognize, from an earlier flashback, as one of the orderlies at Lawrence's hospital — enters the room and, on the point of shooting Lawrence, informs him he is too late. Fortunately, it transpires that Lawrence has merely fired into Adam's shoulder. Adam attacks and kills Zep. Lawrence crawls away to seek help and Adam searches Zep's body. We have been led, hitherto, to suspect that Zep is, in fact, Jigsaw. He is the one who has held Lawrence's family hostage and has been monitoring the game's progress at Lawrence's apartment via a computer link to surveillance equipment secreted around the prison-room. However, Adam finds another tape which discloses that Zep has been merely another player of the game, compelled to participate to save his own life. As Adam ponders the implications of this discovery, we are startled by the spectacle, behind him, of the anonymous corpse slowly rising, sighing heavily and ripping off what is revealed to be a prosthetic head injury. With a voice we recognize from the tapes and the dummy — this, finally, must be Jigsaw — Adam is told that the key to his chain is now irretrievable. Adam threatens Jigsaw — revealed, at last, through flashback to have been "John," one of Lawrence's inoperable patients — with Zep's gun, but Jigsaw, who it seems has been all along controlling the supply of electricity into Lawrence and Adam's chains, incapacitates him with a final jolt. "Game over," Jigsaw declares, in shadow against swirling miasmic green fog, as he exits the room and slides closed the door on Adam's futile screams.

This climactic "reveal" of Jigsaw's identity has become celebrated as one of the most effective twist endings in genre cinema of recent years. In fact, playing dead, or living as if dead, is a recurring motif in the film. Jigsaw's death act is foreshadowed earlier in the film as he is ostensibly surprised in his lair in a mannequin factory — at 213 Stygian Street, in a rather contrived reference to one of the rivers running through Hades — by two police detectives, Tapp and Sing. On that occasion, he has clearly planned for the eventuality and, shot at by Sing, feigns death in order to lure the detective into a lethal booby trap. Adam also exaggeratedly acts out his death in the final scenes, as described above, and a previous victim — as shown in flashback — whose guts contain a key which the woman, Amanda, must bloodily retrieve in order to escape her "reverse bear trap," is only apparently dead, and is in fact, paralyzed by the action of an opiate. This ambiguity between life and death — indeed, this zone of indistinction, a zone of "bare life" into which victims are thrown — is central to the film and is writ large in Jigsaw's terminal condition. When we first see Jigsaw — as John — lying in a hospital bed as Lawrence discusses his condition with a group of trainee doctors, he is inert and ignored, a mere object rather than a person. In fact, what has attracted Jigsaw's enmity is precisely the disconnected, callous lack of empathy that he witnesses all around him. Each of his victims has turned their back on life in some way. Adam survives by being paid to watch others from the shadows, snooping and taking photographs. Lawrence, evidently distanced from both his family and his patients, considers adultery. Other victims shown at various points are suicidal, addicted to drugs, malingering or living out a purposeless existence. Again, it is Jigsaw's self-ordained mission to compel his victims to choose life, to reconnect with vital energies and recover their passion. He traps them to free them.

What presides over the game for much of its length is apparently a corpse, ignored but simultaneously impossible to completely overlook. William Bogard, inspired by the Foucauldian paradigm of modern disciplinary power, has argued that the corpse "represents an ideal of the modern subject, and indeed has its own unique 'subjectivity,' perfectly obedient, ready to serve as a model and means of instruction, to work for any purpose, and set an example to others" (2008, 189). The corpse is the ultimate in docility, a perfect model for processes of normalization. However, that *Saw*'s corpse is not a corpse — the dead man yet lives — chimes with the emergence of a new, monstrous postmodern form of power which is characterized precisely by *living death*. "In the late twentieth century," Bogard suggests, "a fundamental shift occurred in the biopolitical strategy of technical societies, in the direction of controlling life from its inception rather than from its end" (188). Power's imperative, once bound up with the decision to end life or to grant continuing life, now revolves around the pre-screening or premediation of life, "pre-empting the form of birth itself" (193). The figure of the corpse, bound up with "notions of the body's integrity and unity," is superseded by the postmodern figure of the *zombie* native, "product of a will that has no qualms about dividing the body into its tiniest parts in order to recombine and re-sequence them" (188). In this zombie scenario, no-one is infected by being bitten because, in contemporary capitalism, we are all zombies, engineered from our Cloacal birth.

Jigsaw's corpse that is not a corpse, the game master lurching zombie-like into ponderous animation in the closing scenes of *Saw*, presides over the transition from the Foucauldian carceral society of the disciplinary "mold" to the new Deleuzian "society of control" governed by the principle of "modulation": "like a self-transmuting molding continually changing from one moment to the next" (Deleuze, 1995, 178–9). Discipline is focused upon shaping discrete individuals as they are channeled through a series of institutions, from family to school to factory, armed forces, etc., squeezing them into an externally derived mold, molding them and making them efficient, fit for purpose, according to specific techniques of the body and self (what to do, how, when and where). Modulation, however, is not concerned with shaping behaviors in this way. Instead, it seeks to monitor, to detect emergent behavioral patterns in order that they may be pre-empted: "The moment when a person's weaknesses and strengths, likely diseases and resistances, likely failures and desires can be predicted, is effectively the moment one can order those persons in advance" (Savat, 2009, 49). Modulatory control involves the adjustment — modulation — of affective and behavioral patterns as they emerge rather than molding and organizing individuals in a serial, linear manner (50). Where corpses are proper to a phase of capital which places the emphasis upon individuation, the zombie is more befitting of a late, networked capital which works, as Deleuze argues, by "dividuation," the "continuous modulation of multiple forms" (Bogard, 2008, 191). The agenda for the production of subjectivity in networked capital's societies of control is flexibilization, the inception of "dividuated, informed, modular man" (192). Subjects must be rendered manipulable, programmable, held in the sway of affective flows of the network. In *Saw*, crudely, if participants are to progress in the game they must be willing to undergo a certain dismantling, or deterritorialization, of body and soul. There is no way anyone escapes intact, without having undergone a transformation. Just so, the worker in contemporary capitalism is infiltrated and fragmented, power moving to operate from within. Labor becomes recombinant, broken into omni-compatible cells, activity "fractalized," as what Marx once called "general intellect" is converted into "an infinite brain-sprawl, an ever-changing mosaic of fractal cells of available nervous energy" (Berardi, 2011, 130; see also 2009). We are desingularized, dividuated, affective puppets become "carriers of abstract fractal ability to connect, devoid of sensitive empathy" (Berardi, 2011, 132). What Jigsaw condemns in those around him he re-stages in his game installations, creating a semblance of Capital-Life. In this vision, our existence under networked capital constitutes an inescapable compulsion to flexibilize and fit with the protocological and algorithmic architecture of the network — we play and are played as in the logic of the video game. In the Empire of living death, as Bogard comments, life is informated, its control released "from the material constraints of place, and this includes the constraints of the material body. There is no 'place' of sovereign power today" (2008, 196). In the zone of indistinction, governed by conditions of affective control, the body has become "waves subject to modulated control, turn a knob and, at the molecular level, adjust the body's velocity, rates of compression and decompression, volume, rhythm, all in real time" (198). Wherever you are, you are at the mercy of a power of electrocution, as it were, or waves of control-modulation. Jigsaw sends a shock of electricity through the chains binding his victims, but even should they "escape" to move and wander freely, they will not pass from the system's clutches, which are rhizomatically extensible. There is no outside to this game. Everyone dragged unwittingly into the magic circle of the game is pinned there, even those who, like Detective

Tapp, investigate and hunt down Jigsaw, or those like the junkie, Amanda, who survive their immediate ordeal (only to become the psychopath's accomplice in later films). All are players and played, become fractal, modular. In other words, it is not really "us" the game is interested in — personal dilemmas are merely an alibi. The "life lesson" is rather the generalized enclosure and entrainment of affect, which is impersonal and nonconscious.

In interview, Leigh Whannel (Adam in the film and also screenwriter and key to the story's conception) has revealed that much of the inspiration for the film derived from a tremendously stressful and negative experience of work (Fallon, 2004). Whannel's unsatisfactory job eventually gave rise to physical symptoms, including migraines, and a hypochondriac conviction that he had a brain tumor, which drove him to seek an MRI scan. This event provided the seed for the character of Jigsaw and his motivation — to compel others to confront the inevitability and potential immediacy of death and thereby to be compelled to live more intensely. Rooted, in this way, in the maladies of work, Jigsaw's methods indeed would appear to offer a radical, cleansing nihilism, the catalytic potential of an extreme predicament. In this sense, Saw can be considered, as I have argued elsewhere, both as allegory of "becoming"— an intense, revitalized engagement with life and its power of difference and alteration — in addition, along the lines suggested above, to an allegory of (affective) control (Lockwood, 2009).

I have already noted, with Hills and Zimmer, that there is good reason for critics to take Jigsaw's game plan more seriously than has generally been the case. But this is ambiguous because it means recognizing Jigsaw as both jailor and liberator. Once again, we can frame this in terms of the world of work and the zombies it makes of us from our very birth. This world, for Carl Cederström and Peter Fleming, is a "dead world" in which work has virally penetrated all aspects of our existence (2012, 1). The worker is now "a person who exists between life and death, a figure whose only hope is that it soon might be all over" (5). The dominant affect might be described as an all-pervasive dread, a feeling of life at a "dead end," cut off from its vital wellsprings (2). What sustains us are fantasies of escape, but such fantasies become increasingly distorted, manifesting as addiction of various kinds, suicidal tendencies, quests for oblivion, all of which "tie us closer to the nightmare" and permit us to turn up for work again in the morning (52). In fact, more insidiously, the very notion of work's other, of an escape route, is harnessed and put to work in the contemporary corporate workplace. There is no effective retreat when what seems to offer a palliative — indulgence, in whatever way, in our "unruly and natural side" (39)— is now precisely what we are compelled to bring in and present at work. Cederström and Fleming draw our attention to the rise of the "fun-sultant," carrier of the ideology of "liberation management," whose job it is to transform our jobs into a life-affirmative game (4). Jigsaw's tapes, which castigate his victims for their zombie existences, announcing games designed to foster a more intensive engagement with the world, can be seen as liberation management techniques. We could consider this as symptomatic of the way fantastic power prods its workforce, shocks it into engagement. Jigsaw is in the business of inserting his influence inside another's affective state, to alter it, retune and entrain it. A kind of artist, he organizes elements to create a semblance of life — a "mannequin factory" — mapping felt life in the contemporary. In his injunction to be authentic, to confront the fact of existence, Jigsaw is revealed as a parasitic, coercive fun-sultant, a management man who refuses to permit us to zone out, extracting value from the play he enforces. Jigsaw wants his victims buzzing, wants to whip the zombies into a stir.

"Although dead," Cederström and Fleming say, "we are nevertheless compelled to wear the exterior signs of life" (4). More radically, I would say that contemporary capital, itself metamorphic and infective, seeks to take the future in hand as Capital-Life, to breach the future, as it were, by means of exerting command over life's excess, life's virtuality and power of difference. A crucial element of the capture of affect in the indistinct, placeless space of power, concerns what Brian Massumi has dubbed the "gaming paradigm." The participatory imperative dramatized in *Saw*'s gamespace comprises a compulsion to "become who you are," eliciting a visceral response. As Jigsaw's tape for Adam suggests, in such a situation one can no longer "sit in the shadows" voyeuristically spectating the lives of others. In the game, Massumi remarks, "you are viscerally exposed, like a prodded sea cucumber that spits its guts. You are exposed down to your inmost sensitive folds, down to the very peristaltic rhythms that make you what you are. This is generative power, a power that reaches down into the soft tissue of your life, where it is just stirring, and interactively draws it out for it to become what it will be, and what it suits the system that it be" (2011, 48). Not merely a matter of the "exterior signs" of life, Massumi's assessment suggests that the "gamification" of the world, to borrow a recent buzzword, encloses our very power of life. This gaming paradigm names the experimentalism of networked capital. For its part, *Saw*, as affective map, diagrams a laboratory-like game experience in which the potentiality of events — crudely, what the (fractal) body can do — is similarly locked onto, resonating with power's biopolitical migration inside the tissue of life to seek out value in the virtual. Moreover, the life it predates and mobilizes is not merely individual, but is rather a matter of the creative, dividuated power of the multitude, the fractalized and recombinant workforce. As Lawrence insists Adam understands, "we're gonna have to work together if we want to get out of here."

The Art of Crisis

The gaming paradigm in the specific case of cinema might be explored in terms of Thomas Elsaesser's concept of the "mind-game film" (2009). Elsaesser points out the tendency in much recent cinema for films to play games with characters, but perhaps more importantly, to also play games with viewers. *Saw* would seem to perfectly fit the bill of this posited tendency. The movies in question spring traps for their viewers just as they victimize their characters. Victims struggle to divine the rules of the games in which they find themselves. We, the audience, are conscripted to negotiate intricate flashback-strewn plots in order to complete a puzzle. The "mind" in mind-game film refers to an encouragement to viewers to fall in with a particular take on reality as perceived from the viewpoint of a pathological character — in other words, to be drawn into a fantastic psychology. The mind-game film invites the viewer to inhabit such a point of view as normal, offering no distance on the pathological condition *as* condition, no clear-eyed perspective against which distortions in perception might be measured (30). The result is disorientation. The mind-game film is part of a new complexity in twenty-first century storytelling which "suspends the common contract between the film and its viewers" (19), casting viewers out into a zone of indistinction. The tearing up of contracts constitutes a kind of cinematic state of exception, a withdrawal of sovereign protection. Until the mainstreaming of the mind-game film, we paid the ticket price and sat quietly, and for its part, we could expect narrative cinema to make sense, to be consistent and give it to us straight, running on straight rails, as it were, telling us where to look and who to identify with, who to love and who to hate. Now, however, not to put too fine a point on it, the mind-game film fucks with us, derails the narrative train and stirs up a big headache where characters, time lines and spaces are prone to mix up and fork off at the drop of a hat. Watching these films (Elsaesser lists a great many examples, although, strangely, *Saw* is not one of them) we are compelled to interact, engaging in "constant retroactive revision, new reality checks, displacements and reorganization, not only of temporal sequence, but of mental space" (21). We have to intuit the new rules of the game.

As a mind-game film, *Saw* is exemplary, both symptomatic and productive of new forms of audience engagement and new, corresponding forms of mediatized subjectivity. As the old contract is torn up or suspended, as old rules are flagrantly broken, *Saw* both articulates and provokes a "crisis" which will ostensibly give rise to new rules (16). That is, once again, it does not merely reflect the contexts and concerns of contemporary society, it participates in the emergence of an affective map, what, after Gilles Deleuze and Felix Guattari, we might refer to as a "diagram," of the social. A map or diagram in this sense does not signify or represent that which already exists in actuality. Rather, it actualizes, it produces something new. It "cannot be divorced from the thing that it describes, and more importantly, cannot be divorced from the action of creating the thing" (Elliott, 2012, 61). The mind-game film understood diagrammatically, or cartographically, thinks through and performs, teaches and learns new rules in interaction with the viewer (Elsaesser, 2009, 40), constituting what we might describe as an immanent transcendence of the common contract.

As Elsaesser comments, to consume media can be considered as an affective labor (34). Despite his "mind-game" label, what is at stake here is perhaps best thought of in terms of fantastic, affective politics. The mind is not in control in this situation. It is much more a matter of affective tuning, entrainment, the modulation of internal rhythms to synchronize with the rhythms and cycles of the system. Thus, in this tendency, affect is "directly addressed, stimulated, and appealed to, and thus 'organized' and 'controlled,' in order to fit the subject into the contemporary world and the social matrix of 'affective labour'" (32). Once again, we are dummies for affect, bodies and sensoria fractalized and made ready for insertion where required in the society of control, obliged to submit to incessant testing, subjected to this experience. The imperative is "to remain flexible, adaptive, and interactive, and above all, to know the 'rules of the game'" (34).

The soft tyranny that exploits our visceral stirring in the gaming paradigm equates with what Elsaesser describes, in the case of mind-game cinema, as generative powers of paranoia and other psychopathologies. In this cinema, pathology is seized for its productivity. In the case of *Saw*, Jigsaw is eminently capable of making new kinds of connection, provoking and responding to turbulence in the social field — the catastrophe of our living death — in innovative ways. Such ability constitutes an asset in the new zones of indistinction in which we (fail to) find ourselves (26). The trauma that triggers Jigsaw's psychopathy empowers him to connect up to the world differently, experimentally, puts him in "a different kind of relation to the man-made, routinized or automated surroundings" than would otherwise be afforded (31). However, the possibilities raised are, in the same breath, contained and paranoia harvested for powers of pre-emption which "potentially short-circuit the very connections they seek to establish" (29–30). Pre-emptive power is not simply to do with the amelioration of risk. It deliberately strives to *generate* risks, tapping into the mutative potential of the virtual, "multiple futures which are alive in the present, which always exist as not quite fully formed potentialities or possibilities" (Grusin, 2010, 8), whilst simultaneously containing this potential. This is controlled inception of the future, pre-empted birth. The new and the critical are stimulated into actuality in order to act upon and secure them.

Pre-emption is a fantastic power which promotes wildness, riot, break-out and psycho-social unrest. (see Coley and Lockwood, 2012, for a treatment of "fantastic" pre-emptive power).

Jan Simons, pursuing Elsaesser's concept of the mind-game film, associates it with a paradigm of "management-by-crisis" (as opposed to the more usual notion of management *of* crisis) (2008, 113), which is akin to the liberation management discussed above. This is a management strategy which seeks to profit by exploiting sources of its own jeopardy. It surrenders a degree of control, overtly initiating crisis and unleashing anomaly. It ludically dismantles the actual in order to liberate virtuals, new affects. The "critical crisis manager"—and I would suggest that we could place Jigsaw under this heading—manages to outpace the logic of gamification to some extent, precisely because he knows he is a doll blown about by forces he cannot fully gauge. His paranoia affords him the luxury of knowing he's making moves "in a game other players are often not aware that they are playing" (121). This is a powerful advantage. The critical crisis manager is alert to general propensities of the situation, alert enough to make the necessary adjustments to extract value on the wing. Ultimately, however, it is difficult to distinguish where the difference lies between Simons' critical crisis manager and the "invisible sovereign" of which Agamben speaks, the true genius behind the dummy's eyes. *Saw*'s efficacy lies precisely in creating a semblance of—without pretending coherence—this torturous problem today.

Elsaesser remarks that whether mind-game films are "part of the problem" or "part of the solution" is undecidable (2009, 39). Is *Saw* merely part of the cinematic schooling for the empire of living death or does it constitute an artful take on the "critical" possibilities of crisis management? As the fate of its characters suggests, once you're caught in the web, once you've been dragged into the magic circle, it seems to make no difference knowing who Jigsaw is, divining his motives. Despite what Lawrence claims about the importance of understanding the perfect engine, it still has the power to electrocute, to jerk your strings, no matter how well apprised you are of its mechanism. Nevertheless, as Michael Hardt and Antonio Negri, writing on our new mediatized and securitized forms of subjectivity in the grip of societies of control say, "Look for an escape door. One is always there ... sometimes flight takes unusual forms" (2012, np). They remind us that power needs its subjects, power is always relational. What is key is changing our relationship to power and our relationship to media. It is in this spirit we might plug into Jigsaw's pathology as into a strange art, a game plan the import of which is to present a semblance of the gaming paradigm *tout court*. These games provide a canvas animated to express a sense of life in the grip of capital, a grip more tenacious than ever before. *Saw*, exemplar of the Bound Fantastic, maps the coming of the Control society, drawing out the fantastic, Cloacal form taken by power. A Cloaca is a sewer, a place where the toxic wastes of a population wash through and are expelled from the city. It is also, in some animals, a bodily cavity, site of a confluence of ducts. As much as the red spiral mentioned earlier, these are apposite images for a power which grips life viscerally, moving in us as much as it creates the world in which we move. Is there no outside to the Cloacal labyrinth, no way we cannot play? Can critical games within tyrannical games be escape doors?

References

Agamben, G. (1998). *Homo Sacer: Sovereign Power and Bare Life*. Stanford: Stanford University Press.
Artaud, A. (1988). *Selected Writings*. Berkeley and Los Angeles: University of California Press.
Berardi, F. (2009). *The Soul at Work*. Los Angeles: Semiotext(e).
_____. (2011). *After the Future*. Edinburgh: AK Press.
Bogard, W. (2008). "Empire of the Living Dead." *Morality*, 13:2, 187–200.
Bruns, G.L. (2011). *On Ceasing to Be Human*. Stanford: Stanford University Press.
Cederström, C., and P. Fleming (2012). *Dead Man Working*. Winchester: Zero.
Cherry, B. (2009). *Horror*. London and New York: Routledge.
Clute, J. (1997). "Wonderland," in J. Clute and J. Grant (Eds.). *The Encyclopedia of Fantasy*, London: Orbit. 1030.
_____ (2006). *The Darkening Garden: A Short Lexicon of Horror*. Cauheegan: Payseur and Schmidt.
Coley, R. and D. Lockwood (2012). *Cloud Time: The Inception of the Future*, Winchester: Zero.
Deleuze, G. (1995). *Negotiations*. New York: Columbia University Press.
_____, and F. Guattari (2004). *A Thousand Plateaus*. London: Continuum.
Elliott, P. (2012). *Guattari Reframed*. London: I.B. Tauris.
Elsaesser, T. (2009). "The Mind-Game Film," in W. Buckland (Ed.), *Puzzle Films: Complex Storytelling in Contemporary Cinema*, 13–41. Chichester: Wiley-Blackwell.
Flatley, J. (2008). *Affective Mapping: Melancholia and the Politics of Modernism*. Cambridge: Harvard University Press.
Grusin, R. (2010). *Premediation: Affect and Mediality After 9/11*. Houndmills: Palgrave Macmillan.
Hardt, M., and A. Negri (2000). *Empire*. Cambridge: Harvard University Press.
_____, and _____ (2012). *Declaration*. Argo Navis.
Hills, M. (2011). "Cutting into Concepts of 'Reflectionist' Cinema? The *Saw* Franchise and Puzzles of Post-9/11 Horror," in A. Briefel and S.J. Miller (Eds.), *Horror After 9/11*, 107–23 Austin: University of Texas Press.
Langer, S. (1953). *Feeling and Form*. New York: Charles Scribner's Sons.
Lazzarato, M. (2004). "From Capital-Labor to Capital-Life." *Ephemera* 4:3, 187–208.
Lockwood, D. (2009). "All Stripped Down: The Spectacle of 'Torture Porn.'" *Popular Communication* 7:1, 40–48.
Massumi, B. (2011). *Semblance and Event: Activist Philosophy and the Occurrent Arts*. Cambridge: MIT Press.
McGrath, P. (1997). "Transgression and Decay," in C. Grunenberg (Ed.), *Gothic: Transmutations of Horror in Late Twentieth-Century Art*, 159–3. Cambridge, MA: MIT Press.
Noys, B. (2005). *The Culture of Death*. Oxford: Berg.
Savat, D. (2009). "Deleuze's Objectile: From Discipline to Modulation," in M. Poster and D. Savat (Eds.), *Deleuze and New Technology*, 45–62. Edinburgh: Edinburgh University Press.
Shaviro, S. (2010). *Post-Cinematic Affect*. Winchester: Zero.

Simons, J. (2008). "A Critical Mind: The Game of Permanent Crisis Management," in J. Kooijman, P. Pisters and W. Strauven (Eds.), *Mind Screen: Media Concepts According to Thomas Elsaesser*, 112–24. Amsterdam: Amsterdam University Press.

Fallon, J. (2004). "The Arrow Interviews Leigh Whannell." http://www.joblo.com/arrow/interview131.htm. Accessed 2 July 2012.

Zimmer, C. (2012). "Caught on Tape? The Politics of Video in the New Torture Film," in A. Briefel and S.J. Miller (Eds.), *Horror After 9/11*, 83–106. Austin: University of Texas Press.

Monstrous Bodies and Gendered Abjection
Madeleine Smith

When one thinks of the *Saw* (2004–2010) films, one thinks of blood, guts, bodily violation, unbearable torture and unthinkable pain. One is repulsed or intrigued at the sight, sometimes both. Scenes of mutilated and bleeding bodies are abundant throughout the franchise as each of serial killer John Kramer AKA Jigsaw's (Tobin Bell) victims must attempt to survive tortuous tasks wherein they must face or cause extreme bodily harm and pain to themselves or others. Barbara Creed (1993) describes such images of bodily secretions like blood and excrement, wounds, dead and decaying bodies in the horror film as "abject" displays or "abjection." Her theory is central to contemporary discussions of the abject because she is the key theorist on the subject. This is supported by writers such as Adam Knee (1996: p. 214) and Elizabeth Young (1996: p. 334), who both discuss the importance of Creed's analysis to interpreting gender relations in the modern horror film. Creed uses abjection to discuss the gendered presentation of women in the genre, arguing that the presentation of bodily secretions and unstable bodily displays in the genre are associated with female monstrosity and "Otherness" and are often rooted in a patriarchal fear of female sexual difference (1993: p. 62). She also aligns the mixed reactions one feels when encountering the abject with the taboo nature of the mother-child dyadic in patriarchal society (p. 7). Creed discusses these aspects of her theory in relation to films like *Alien* (Ridley Scott, Twentieth-Century–Fox, 1979, UK and U.S.), *Carrie* (Brian De Palma, Redbank Films, 1976, U.S.) and *The Exorcist* (William Friedkin, Hoya Productions, 1973, U.S.), in which abjection and the female form as a threat to patriarchy is examined extensively. As such, gender can be viewed as fundamental to analyses of the abject in the modern horror film.

Creed develops her abjection theory from Julia Kristeva's definition of the abject in literary theory as "A wound with blood or pus, or the sickly, acrid smell of sweat, of decay [...] such wastes drop so that I might live," with the corpse symbolizing "the utmost abjection" (1982: pp. 3–4). The need to expel such items from the body to maintain life, and the revulsion caused in a subject when faced with abject displays, suggests that abjection can threaten the integrity of the body from internally and externally. The notion that abject expulsions are necessary so that the subject can continue to live aligns heavily with the central thrust of the *Saw* franchise, wherein Jigsaw's victims must confront and survive abjection in various forms in order to re-enter patriarchal society. Kristeva discusses abjection and its significance in relation to patriarchy, arguing that "Excrement and its equivalents (decay, infection, disease, corpse, etc.) stand for the danger to identity that comes from without: the ego threatened by the non-ego, society threatened by its outside, life by death. Menstrual blood, on the contrary, stands for the danger issuing from within the identity (social or sexual); it threatens the relationship between the sexes within the social aggregate and, through internalization, the identity of each sex in the face of sexual difference" (p. 71). As such, abject displays signify the "Otherness" of female sexual difference, suggesting that femininity is threatening to patriarchal society.

Exploring this further, Creed situates the representation of abject displays in the horror film with the feminine figure, arguing that blood and bodily secretions signify both sexual difference and the mothering and reproductive functions of women (1993: p. 7). The abject also signifies unity between mother and child, or a time in which the subject was at one with the mother and took pleasure in its own abject displays before entering the phallocentric symbolic and disavowing the primacy of the maternal figure (pp. 12–13). As such, bodily wastes and secretions become a taboo signifier of the desire for the subject to reunite with the mother. Creed states that "The modern horror film often 'plays' with its audience, saturating it with scenes of blood and gore, deliberately pointing to the fragility of the symbolic order in the domain of the body where the body never ceases to signal the repressed world of the mother" (p. 13). With this in mind, the appearance of bodily wastes, blood and decay in the horror genre suggest the capability of abjection to destabilize and undermine patriarchal culture.

Creed outlines three main sites through which abjection is illustrated in the modern horror film that will be engaged with herein. The first focuses on images of abjection, "foremost of which is the corpse, whole and mutilated, followed by an array of bodily wastes such as blood, vomit, saliva, sweat, tears and putrefying flesh" (p. 10). Second, Creed points out the need of a "border" in order for abject displays to be viewed as horrifying both on- and off-screen. She argues that the horror film constructs a border between "'the clean and proper body' and the abject body, or the body which has lost its form and integrity." (p. 11). Finally, Creed argues that the horror film primarily constructs "the maternal figure as abject," widely in relation to the mothering and reproductive role of women in patriarchal society (p. 11). With the above in mind, the prevalence of scenes of graphic torture and body horror in the *Saw* films means that abject displays are very abundant throughout the series. Similarly, the notion of border violation is central to the franchise, as the skin is frequently depicted as vulnerable, penetrable and unstable; external dangers threaten to bring forth abject displays, exposing the internal abject state of the subject in question. Suggesting how Creed's theory will be challenged herein, there is a high volume of male victims as compared to females in the franchise, shifting the association of abject displays from the feminine to the masculine. Similarly, the depiction of bodily violation is always violent, bloody and destructive, firmly situating abject displays with males and masculine attributes. Such scenes are constructed by male Jigsaw, a punishing and instructive patriarch who forces his victims into a confrontation with the abject so that they can re-enter the symbolic. This suggests a reworking of the maternal role, effectively displacing the primacy of the feminine by aligning abjection firmly with a dominant masculine figure.

Confrontation with the abject and bodily violation is evident in the *Saw* franchise through the many images of mutilated, bleeding and unstable bodies present in each film, making them ideal texts through which to examine abjection. Creed states that "the presence of the monstrous-feminine in the popular horror film speaks to us more about male fears than about female desire or female subjectivity" (p. 7). As such, the overwhelming propensity to display males as abject in the *Saw* films suggests male fears of male vulnerability and bodily instability, challenging the centrality of women to Creed's theory. Rather than dismissing Creed's work, however, an analysis of the abject in the *Saw* films will illustrate the nuanced fashion in which her arguments can be engaged with, positioning a critique of Creed's theory as pertinent to interpreting contemporary attitudes to gender.

Therefore, this essay will argue that the series prominently portrays both males as abject and abjection as a patriarchal construct, challenging several key aspects of Creed's theories surrounding the monstrous-feminine. For instance, the feminine relationship with and displays of abjection are no longer depicted as "monstrous" but natural, suggesting a diminished portrayal of women as "Other" to patriarchal society. Similarly, the masculine body is not only positioned alongside the female body as abject, but is foregrounded as *the* primary site of abjection throughout the *Saw* franchise, displacing the prominence of females in Creed's discussions. Related to this and contrary to the assertion that male abjection is rooted in femininity, male abject displays are shown to be rooted in patriarchy. Several female and male characters in the *Saw* films will be discussed herein to illustrate how Creed's theory breaks apart when looking at contemporary horror, presenting the American male as the monstrous-masculine; threatened, vulnerable and indelibly linked to abjection post 9/11.

Gender Displacement and the Monstrous Feminine

The character of Brit (Julie Benz) in *Saw V* (David Hackl, 2008, Lionsgate and Twisted Pictures, Canada and U.S.) illustrates how the primacy of traditional female gender attributes associated with the monstrous-feminine are challenged by the inclusion of females in the franchise that possess masculine attributes. Brit is one of five self-absorbed captives that must learn to work together to survive tortuous tasks or face death. The tasks primarily involve external threats to the body such as a guillotine and nail bombs, heightening the notion that the skin is vulnerable and penetrable, and can easily give way to abjection. Brit is presented as at ease with abject displays, challenging the feminine trait of emotional instability that is generally attributed to the figure of the monstrous-feminine. Suggesting the mutable nature of gender roles in the franchise, surviving male Mallick (Greg Bryk) is repulsed by abjection when confronted with the bloody remains of two victims. He is sick, sweats and cries in fear, aligning the passive and unstable nature of Mallick's identity with traditional notions of femininity. However, Brit appears unaffected by the spectacle, instead appearing relaxed and authoritative with abject displays as she rolls her eyes impatiently at Mallick's behavior and demands they move on. This aligns Brit with rigid and assertive masculine attributes rather than the instability of the monstrous-feminine.

Creed asserts that, "women's blood, which symbolizes birth and life, reminds man of his capacity, even willingness, to shed blood, to murder." (1993: p. 62). This aligns the act of murder with aggressive masculinity. Brit's murderous actions challenge this assumption, suggesting gender mutability. For instance, Mallick watches in shock as Brit emotionlessly stabs a hook into fellow captive Luba's (Meagan Good) body to ensure her own survival. Brit displaces gender assumptions through her aggressive, penetrative and destructive act, characteristics associated with masculinity. Her ability to murder and cause the abject displays of others subverts Creed's assertion that males shed blood whilst women create life (p. 63). Brit's calm attitude to murder, blood and penetration suggests once again that she is comfortable with abject displays. Such a prominence of masculine characteristics in Brit undermines the prominence of the monstrous-feminine as a fearful symbol of female "Otherness."

In a macabre reworking of the mother-child relationship, Brit orders Mallick to assist her in stabbing more hooks into Luba's body. She excitedly cries, "Do it!" forcing Mallick to stab Luba as she does, encouraging his actions as if she were an instructive mother. Creed writes that the mother instructs the child in the ways of the "clean and proper body" (p. 11). This is undermined by Brit's instructions that Mallick must violate bodily borders. In *Saw V*, the abject must be confronted and expelled to ensure Brit and Mallick's survival. This presents a reworking the mother-child dyadic, displacing the gender rigidity of the maternal role in child rearing by aligning it instead with the overtly masculine acts of dominance, penetration and murder. Traditional gender roles are briefly restated as Brit assumes a more traditionally nurturing maternal role as she prepares Mallick's arm for the next task, attempting to soothe his fears by telling him, "It's okay."

Gender equality and abject unity between males and females is presented as possible and as a product of confrontation with abjection in *Saw V*, challenging the eminence of the monstrous feminine in abject displays as outlined by Creed (p. 62). For example, Brit and Mallick have to push their hands onto a saw that will sever open their arms to release blood. Both must experience bloodletting, linking to menstruation, and both must provide equal amounts of blood to survive, presenting gender equality through the act of bleeding. Reversed gender traits and a comfortable relationship between women and the abject are again illustrated as the two prepare for the task. Mallick panics and cries, "I can't do this alone, I can't!" suggesting a fear of penetration and of his own menstrual capabilities, reinforcing his association with feminine attributes. However, Brit is rational and calm as she explains that bloodletting is required. Her relaxed attitude to bleeding suggests a close and normalized relationship between women and the abject. Brit and Mallick push their hands onto the saw, their skin fragile as it disintegrates and gives way to blood, presenting the notion of border violation. As such, the pair are equally abject as they encounter penetration, loss and renewal. The possibility of gender equality in abject displays is further suggested by dialogue as Mallick cries that Brit is "a monster!" to which she replies indignantly, "So are you!" With this in mind, Brit is an example of how females in the franchise can adopt masculine traits when associated with abjection, minimizing the horror surrounding the monstrous-feminine that Creed foregrounds (p. 1). Brit also offers an alternative reading of gender roles in relation to abject displays as her assertive and penetrative yet still feminized role contrasts with Mallick's passive instability when faced with abjection, heightening the male relationship with abject displays.

Patriarchy and the Menstrual Monster

Appearing initially in *Saw*, Amanda (Shawnee Smith) displays a relationship with abjection that presents her overtly abject feminine nature as in conflict with Jigsaw's patriarchal expectations. Amanda is configured as wholly abject; she is a self-harming junkie who frequently pollutes her body with drugs and defiles its borders by penetrating her skin with needles and knives. Amanda's body is subsequently a site of uncontrollable abject displays that present her as a highly unstable being. Although she is comfortable with her own abject nature, she appears terrified when confronted with the abject displays of men. For example, in *Saw*, Amanda must retrieve a key from inside the body of a man to release a trap affixed to her mouth that, if activated, will rip her head open. She fearfully approaches the man and stands over him before frenziedly and repeatedly stabbing him with the knife, causing blood to flow. As such, the notion of border violation and gender displacement via the penetrative act are central to the scene. Amanda claws through the man's entrails searching for the key, blood dripping from her hands and arms as she unlocks the head trap and screams in horror at the sight of the mutilated and bleeding male corpse in front of her. Her bloodstained hands and capacity to murder align her abject state with masculinity, undermining the reproductive and life bearing capabilities of women that Creed positions as in conflict with the act of murder (p. 62). Amanda has confronted the abject and has survived, her rebirth and re-entry into the patriarchal symbolic marked with male blood.

Amanda's fear of male displays of abjection is similarly evident in *Saw III* (Darren Lynn Bousman, 2006, Lionsgate and Twisted Pictures, Canada and U.S.) as she, now an apprentice to Jigsaw, is unable to tolerate his abject displays. For example, Jigsaw, dying from a brain tumor, starts to convulse and vomit, blood and bile bursting uncontrollably from his mouth as abjection threatens to overwhelm his body. Amanda loses control at the sight and cannot bear to look; instead she screams, "What's happening to him?!" and runs crying from the room. Her behavior suggests that masculine displays of abjection are both alien and horrifying to her, and have surpassed the horror of the monstrous-feminine. This challenges Creed's assertion that only female abject displays are monstrous by presenting male bodily secretions as terrifying instead (pp. 12–13).

However, Amanda is highly comfortable with her own unstable displays and struggles to repress them, presenting her as an overtly feminized menstrual monster. Subsequently, her relationship with abjection is an unstable one that is in conflict with the expectations of patriarchy, suggested as Jigsaw forbids her to indulge in such displays. Amanda is depicted self-harming in both *Saw II* (Darren Lynn Bousman, 2005, Twisted Pictures, Canada and U.S.) and *Saw III*, rupturing her own borders to bring forth abjection. The frequency of this act presents her bloodletting as a ritual overtly linked to the female menstrual cycle. For instance, in *Saw III*, she lays out knives to cause her blood to flow alongside hygiene and sanitary products, emphasizing links to menstruation. The sense of ritual and repetition in Amanda's bloodletting is further heightened by a close-up to her legs as she begins to cut, displaying many scars and wounds from which abjection secretes, suggesting that this is a regular occurrence. The relaxed look that passes over her face suggests this is a release, even comforting for Amanda, an abject expulsion that is required to maintain her feminine identity despite Jigsaw's disavowal of its appearance. This suggests the taboo nature of female sexual difference in patriarchal society. Furthermore, as Amanda cuts herself her blood signifies the subjugation of females in patriarchal culture via the depiction of menstruation as unclean. For example, it is revealed in a flashback as she self-harms that Amanda captured Jigsaw's victims wearing a pig mask. Such imagery aligns with Creed's discussions of blood as dirty and ultimately positions Amanda as wholly abject in relation to menstrual displays. Creed writes that the pig symbolizes the myth of "the grotesque, disgusting body" that patriarchal culture invokes to perpetuate "negative views about women and menstruation" (p. 80). Amanda's desire to self-harm and violate her own borders to bring forth the blood that her father denies suggests that she is openly rebelling against the patriarchal subjugation of menstruation and female sexual difference.

Amanda's abject displays are also presented as a taboo expression of desire for her father figure. For example, Amanda displays incestuous feelings towards Jigsaw, and desires a return to the abject display that initially united them. This reworks Creed's discussions of the taboo nature of the abject in recalling the mother-child dyadic through the placing of Jigsaw in the role (pp. 12–13). Such a suggestion is evident as Amanda displays jealousy at an intimate moment between Jigsaw and a female doctor tending to him, before she defiantly self-harms and revels in her abject display. This forbidden act suggests both Amanda's desire to return to the phase of imaginary unity she previously enjoyed with her father figure and to rebel against his patriarchal rules. Eventually Amanda's abject nature overwhelms her. Unable to follow Jigsaw's rules, she gets shot in the neck and bleeds out before dying. This suggests the failure of Amanda's feminine identity to withstand the strain of patriarchal dominance. As such, patriarchy is depicted as overwhelming to female displays of abjection.

The Not So Monstrous Maternal

Jill Tuck (Betsy Russell) is Jigsaw's ex-wife, and highlights the mutable nature of gender roles through abject displays in the franchise. The character of Jill allows for several points of discussion that directly challenge the gender assumptions associated with abject displays in the horror film. For example, in a flashback to an attack on Jill that caused her to lose her unborn baby in

Saw IV (Darren Lynn Bousman, 2007, Twisted Pictures, Canada and U.S.), gender roles are asserted and subverted. During the flashback Jill is heavily pregnant and is coded as maternal and nurturing in a white dress, suggesting an innocent and vulnerable femininity that is heightened by her attackers' threatening and phallic knife. Creed argues that white symbolizes the milk bearing capabilities of the mother, recalling the phase of imaginary unity between mother and child. Further to this, Creed writes that the presence of blood and milk together violates the notion that the substances must be kept separate, signifying "a collapse of boundaries between self and other" and a desire to return to unity between mother and child (p. 69). Such imagery is invoked when Jill's pregnant belly is injured by her attacker and blood runs onto her white dress and shoes, symbolically merging blood with milk. Her reaction of horror points to the taboo nature of blood and milk. Creed's assertions are thus upheld as Jill's clean and proper body becomes marked with abjection, her body merging with that of her unborn child.

It is also possible to argue that Jill's abject display marks her body as unable to support life; abjection encroaches from within her body, staining her white dress with blood. Subsequently the violated and unstable borders of Jill's body become a symbol of decay, signifying the monstrous, all-consuming womb. Creed describes the womb as having a "double signifying function as both source of life and abyss [...] the all-incorporating black hole which threatens to reabsorb what it once birthed" (pp. 25–27). Whilst this can initially be seen through the loss of Jill's child, such a claim is undermined by the fact that a male was responsible for the child's death, rooting the abject display in masculine aggression. Similarly challenging Creed's assertions that woman's mothering and reproductive functions are coded as monstrous and overbearing in the horror film, Jill is presented as moving on with her life following the death of her baby (p. 13). However, it is of note that this event acts as the catalyst for Jigsaw's destructive games, as he subsequently re-enacts the threat of the all-consuming womb on his subjects. As such, Jigsaw's obsessive murderous actions and heightened relationship with abjection are presented as a product of his child's death. This is suggested in *Saw VI* (Kevin Greutert, 2009, Twisted Pictures, Canada and U.S.) as Jill visits Jigsaw and tells him to "Stop, don't do this," only to be horrified at his murderous plans.

Like Clover's "final girl," Jill must assume masculine qualities if she is to defeat the phallic and overtly threatening figure of Hoffman (1992: p. 63).[1] In *Saw 3D* (Kevin Greutert, 2009, Twisted Pictures, U.S.) for example, Jill is trapped as Hoffman approaches, and grabs a scalpel to defend herself with. She stabs him in the neck before running to hide, screaming in terror as she encounters the dead bodies Hoffman has left behind. This aligns Jill with both feminine coding as passive and vulnerable and masculine attributes of aggression and penetration akin to Clover's "final girl," suggesting gender ambiguity and fluidity (p. 63). And yet, rather than defeating Hoffman by retaining masculine and penetrative abilities, Jill is overtly feminized as Hoffman finds and viciously beats her. Her body becomes limp and passive and her face is covered in blood and tears, exposing an inner abject state that undermines Clover's discussions of the "final girl" as impenetrable and intact (p. 60). Furthermore, Hoffman kills Jill by affixing a head trap onto her, tearing her mouth open and exposing a shocking, gaping, terrifying wound. Such imagery recalls Creed's discussions of the mythic *vagina dentata*, signifying the castration threat that women pose to men. For example, Creed writes that horror films generally show "that woman is castrated or that woman is castrating" (1993: pp. 115–116). However, when it is exposed Jill is already dead, so the fulmination of female sexual difference to patriarchal society is undermined and the threat of castration is situated with the overtly masculine figure of Hoffman.

Accepting the "Monstrous-Masculine"

The character of Doctor Gordon (Cary Elwes) illustrates both a prominent displacement of abjection onto the masculine body and a confrontation with and eventual acceptance of males with their own abject displays. Gordon's appearance as a victim in *Saw* to his re-emergence as an apprentice to Jigsaw in *Saw 3D* allows for several aspects of Creed's abjection theory to be engaged with, such as gender ambiguity, the notion of penetration and border violation presented by external threats, and the role of patriarchy as the driving force behind abject displays. For instance, Gordon awakes in *Saw* to find himself chained up inside a bathroom. Blood seeps from a dead body on the floor, excremental matter covers the walls, and Gordon is bathed in sweat. Abjection is all around, a metaphorical womb that threatens to overwhelm and encroach him; it will be the source of his rebirth, or his tomb. The notion of confrontation with the abject is heightened by a dead body in the room, which Creed argues is the ultimate abjection (p. 9). And yet the body is rigid, imposing and male.ABjection is all around, a metaphorical womb that threatens to overwhelm and encroach him; it will be the source of his rebirth, or his tomb. The notion of confrontation with the abject is heightened by a dead body in the room, which Creed argues is the ultimate abjection (p. 9). And yet the body is rigid, imposing and male. Gordon recoils in horror at the sight of it, suggesting a deep-rooted fear of vulnerable and unstable masculinity. Gordon's task points to the highly mutable nature of gender in the franchise, as he must cut his own foot off to escape, becoming penetrated, castrated and feminized. However, he must then shoot dead his fellow captive, presenting masculine characteristics of aggression, penetration and murder. Gordon subsequently challenges Creed's assertion that abject displays are always grounded in femininity (p. 13).

When Gordon eventually cuts off his foot, it is an overtly masculine act that is motivated by a desire to fulfill his patriarchal role in the family as an active, dominant and protective male. This is suggested as Gordon hears his family cry and scream in terror over a telephone as they face danger. In a fit of despair he cries and pulls at his chains before frantically and maniacally sawing his foot off, screaming, "My family needs me!" As such, Gordon's confrontation with abjection is rooted in patriarchal ideals that reinforce rigid gender roles, undermining the prominence of the female to the notion of the monstrous-feminine. Furthermore, Gordon becomes crazed and feral as his blood spurts out, aligning the act of self-castration with highly aggressive and penetrative masculine characteristics. Creed's assertion that metaphorical castration renders one feminized is thus undermined by the inclusion of overtly masculine traits during the act, and through the desire of Gordon to reaffirm patriarchy (p. 149).

Following his foot severing, the rigid gender assumptions adopted by Creed to support her theory are again subverted as Gordon becomes gender ambiguous, appearing vampiric and deadly as he attempts to shoot his fellow captive dead. He shoots and penetrates his victim, causing blood to flow, yet the apparent masculinity of the act is displaced by Gordon's pale and bloodied appearance; he is bleeding heavily, his body no longer complete and intact. The instability of his body renders him feminized in abject displays despite the act of murder. Gordon crawls away, leaving a bloody trail as he bleeds heavily. He cauterizes the stump to stop the abject secretion, suggesting male stoicism that contrasts with the abundance of abjection on and from his body. That he is nursed back to health by Jigsaw, who assumes a maternal and instructive role in training Gordon to be his apprentice, emphasizes the continual displacement of both feminine and masculine attributes. The presentation of gender in relation to the abject in the franchise is therefore as mutable and unstable as the very notion of abjection itself.

Ultimately accepting his monstrous rebirth, Gordon revisits the scene of his ordeal in *Saw VII*. He is aligned with feminine "Otherness" as he is depicted wearing a pig mask to capture Hoffman. This is emphasized by his limp, which serves as reminder of his castrated state. However, he is also phallic and imposing in appearance, suggesting that his masculine and feminine attributes reside alongside each other. Gordon pauses and looks at his own rotten foot in the corner of the room before he emotionlessly walks away. Such an act suggests that he is now comfortable with his own abject state; he is no longer panicked by and fearful of abjection. Gordon's final words, "Game over!" suggest that he has adopted Jigsaw's patriarchal outlook, assuming the role of abject, punishing father. As such, despite his castrated and feminized state, masculinity and patriarchy are reinforced as central aspects of the portrayal of abjection in the franchise.

The Male as Abject Monster

The character of Detective Mark Hoffman (Costas Mandylor) directly challenges Creed's assertion that male displays of abjection are rooted in feminine qualities, due to his overtly masculine engagement with the abject (p. 70). Hoffman is a detective working to solve the Jigsaw murders in *Saw III*, yet it becomes apparent by the close of *Saw IV* that he works for Jigsaw. After Jigsaw's death, Hoffman becomes a villainous and deadly foe who abuses Jigsaw's murder trials for his own gain in *Saw 3D*. Hoffman is consistently masculine in appearance due to his stiff, phallic and imposing presence, and he appears unaffected by abject displays. Conversely, he remains calm and even fascinated when confronted with abjection, making his response to it distinctly different to the terrified reactions of males in the series. In *Saw III* for example, Hoffman appears unaffected by the various body parts of another Jigsaw victim strewn around the room in varied states of decay, and is more interested in the mechanisms of the device that killed him, emphasizing his more active and masculine nature. Furthermore, he appears cold towards the enforced disintegration of the victim's body, suggested by Hoffman's comments of the victim that "all he had to do" was rip chains out of his skin. This displays a very disaffected, even aggressive attitude towards the failed abject rebirths of others that heightens the masculine nature of his relationship with abjection.

Emphasizing the dominance of his masculinity, Hoffman is overtly voyeuristic and enjoys watching the enforced mutilation and bodily secretions of others. Such heightening of his male characteristics acts to displace the centrality of the female in Creed's abjection theory in various ways. In *Saw V* for instance, Hoffman watches through a peep hole as a male victim is forced to crush his own hands before being slowly disemboweled by a swinging pendulum blade. Creed's discussions of the "active and sadistic" role of the male voyeur are subsequently upheld, yet are also subverted by the objectification of a male body rather than that of a female (p. 7). Similarly, the camera focuses on Hoffman's eye, making the act of watching dominant and masculine. However, when his victim returns the gaze, Hoffman leaps back in shock and can no longer look. This presents Hoffman's pleasure in abject displays, both watching and causing them, as a taboo subject. He is not terrified by abjection; he enjoys it. He fears the threat of exposure for harboring abject desires, and inevitably kills to maintain this secret. Hoffman becomes a brutal and vicious murderer, who routinely kills and maims innocent victims in *Saw VI*. For instance, he swiftly slashes the throat of his boss, uses a female technician as a human shield and viciously stabs Agent Perez (Athena Karkanis) in the stomach. Further exemplifying the dominant nature of his masculinity in causing blood to flow, Hoffman displays pleasure at causing the abject displays of others. This is suggested as he repeatedly stabs Perez, smiling gleefully as he twists the knife and becomes covered in her blood. Such penetrative and aggressive behavior positions him as overtly male and aligns his masculinity with Creed's assertion that women's blood reminds man of their own capacity to murder (p. 62).

There are several instances in which Hoffman is presented as being overtly vampiric, suggested as he routinely causes the blood of others to flow in order to maintain his own life, often prominently via the throat of his victims. For example, in *Saw 3D*, Hoffman makes his way through the police precinct to capture Jill. Now a target, he kills officers to evade capture, becoming an unstoppable and overtly male monster. A coroner opens a body bag to find Hoffman alive inside, suggesting vampiric imagery. This is heightened by his aggressive and penetrative actions, as he violently kills several people by brutally stabbing them in the neck with a knife, becoming splattered with blood. More so, he appears to enjoy unrestrained murder, a masculine trait. When followed by Agent Strahm (Scott Patterson) into a trap, Hoffman willingly enters a coffin filled with crushed glass intended for Strahm. Hoffman's role of causing abject displays is emphasized as blood pours down onto the coffin as Strahm is crushed above, his blood pouring down over Hoffman's grinning face. Not only does this imagery accentuate the link between Hoffman and vampiric activity, but his actions also indicate a willingness to violate his own borders and to encounter his own abject displays for survival. Similarly, after escaping a head trap, Hoffman becomes vampiric in appearance as his cheek is torn open and ruptured, exposing his bloody mouth and teeth. He is wholly abject, his bodily surface "no longer closed, smooth and intact" (p. 58). This is evident in Hoffman's gleeful smile and flashing, phallic teeth, which recall Creed's description of the female vampire's "open mouth, sharp pointed teeth and blood covered lips" in relation to *vagina dentata* (p. 64). As such, Hoffman's abject state is rooted firmly in oppressive and destructive masculinity.

Nonetheless, Hoffman is still subject to patriarchal authority, and is frequently admonished by Jigsaw for his brutal and murderous nature. Jill can also be viewed in relation to the female role of castrator and as an extension of Jigsaw's rule. Creed argues against Freud's assertion that women are castrated, stating instead that "man's fear of castration has [...] led him to construct another monstrous phantasy — that of woman as castrator." Such a figure is evident in Jill's attempts to capture and punish Jigsaw's wayward disciple Hoffman in *Saw VI*. For example, Jill affixes him with the head trap that is intended to tear his head open, symbolically castrating him. However, she is acting on behalf of Jigsaw, and so the castration threat remains rooted in patriarchy. However, Hoffman breaks his own hand, smashing it with metal to free himself and disintegrating his own borders to live. This presents his relationship with the abject as fluid, natural and aggressive, undermining the prominence of feminine qualities to male displays of abjection in Creed's theory (p. 70).

The Monstrous-Masculine as Ultimate Abjection

Jigsaw appears as wholly abject throughout the *Saw* franchise and presents a relationship with the abject that rejects the primacy of the female in abject displays. As such, he will be discussed in relation to gender ambiguity and fluidity, presenting abject displays as grounded in both masculinity and femininity, contrary to Creed's assertions (p. 70). Jigsaw will also be discussed with regard to his function as *the* primary site of abject displays in the franchise, subverting the notion that only women's bodies can provide abject spectacle (p. 42). Finally, Jigsaw's reworking of the role of "archaic mother" will be discussed, firmly locating abjection within masculinity and patriarchy due to his positioning as dominant yet intrinsically connected to abject displays (p. 16). In *Saw* for example, Jigsaw's "dead" body is the first major site of abjection; he is a penetrated, ruptured and feminized spectacle. He remains dominant and in control however, electrocuting Gordon and his fellow captive as punishment whilst in his death facade, an all seeing father. The process can thus be viewed as a masculinized reworking of the maternal role, fully positioning abject displays with masculinity and undermining Creed's assumptions that female mothering and reproductive abilities are solely abject (p. 7). It is also of note that whilst Jigsaw dies in *Saw III*, his patriarchal reign is felt throughout the franchise. The abject nature of the central protagonist subsequently encroaches and overwhelms each film, aligning abjection firmly with the male body.

Often appearing as dually masculine and feminized, Jigsaw is presented as gender ambiguous within his abject state. For example, in *Saw*, Jigsaw is dressed in a black robe with a red interior, appearing rigid and phallic externally, whilst hinting towards his inner abject instability. Foregrounding his male attributes as dominant, he appears unthreatened by a detective's gun, talking boldly as the detective becomes increasingly agitated, and even walks away after being shot. This suggests that Jigsaw is impenetrable, initially presenting his body as "closed, smooth and intact" in line with Creed's discussions of the male body (p. 58). Jigsaw's masculinity is also made prominent through his penetrative acts. For instance, he severs the throat of the detective with a knife, a phallic and threatening object which aligns him with the masculine characteristic of aggressive penetrator. Regardless of such masculine tendencies, Jigsaw is still presented as wholly abject. This is suggested as he makes reference to his cancerous illness, stating, "Yes I'm sick, Officer, sick from the disease eating away at me inside." Jigsaw is therefore presented as dually masculine and feminine, intact and abject, making his relationship with abjection a fluid and pedagogical one that undermines Creed's restrictive gender assumptions.

Jigsaw's body is foregrounded as both horrifying spectacle and as the primary site of uncontrollable abject displays in the franchise. In *Saw III* for example, Jigsaw is sick and dying from cancer, and requires medical treatment from female doctor Lynn (Bahar Soomekh). Without warning, he starts to shake and is sick, his body convulsing, collapsing, and highly unstable. Blood explodes from his mouth, abjection literally bursting forth from inside and threatening to overwhelm his body. The notion of border violation is heightened by the depiction of abject wastes leaking uncontrollably from within Jigsaw's body. Similarly during an operation on his skull, extreme close-up shots depict spurting blood, severed skin and bone drilling in graphic detail. Jigsaw is penetrable, passive and overtly feminized as Lynn operates, penetrating him with sharp phallic tools to peel back layers of flesh and bone. Such explicitly abject scenes challenge Creed's assertion that scenes of abjection and death in males are minimized compared to those of women in the horror film (p. 149).

Gender roles are also unstable and interchangeable throughout the scene. For example, Lynn fulfils a traditional, nurturing role as mother and nurse. She is rendered feminized and vulnerable by the booby trap around her neck that threatens to penetrate her. However, Lynn also exhibits masculine attributes, appearing active, dominant and phallic as she cuts and drills into Jigsaw's skull, and is emotionless at his abject displays. Jigsaw is also overtly feminized in his passive, vulnerable and penetrated state. Such a reversal of gender roles is accentuated by the presentation of Jigsaw's head surgery as a metaphorical sex act. This is suggested as Lynn penetrates his skull with a drill, causing blood and pus to flow from a gaping wound, symbolic of the act of "deflowering" him. Jigsaw's words also support this as he deliriously tells Lynn, "I love you," and experiences memories of his ex-wife. Nevertheless, he retains his patriarchal authority. This is suggested as he aggressively commands Lynn to, "Look at me! Answer the question," and continues to control Amanda's unstable behavior. More so, if Jigsaw dies Lynn will die with him, emphasizing his overwhelming patriarchal control over both life and death. His masculine attributes thus remain central to his identity regardless of his feminized and passive bodily state, undermining Creed's assertions that male displays of abjection are overtly feminized (p. 50).

After his death, Jigsaw's body remains the primary site of abjection and continues to be exploited as abject spectacle. In *Saw IV* for instance, Jigsaw's abject state is depicted in gory, excessive detail through extreme close-up shots as a doctor performs his autopsy. His body is laid on the autopsy table, naked, exposed and vulnerable to penetration. Death has encroached into the subject; Jigsaw has become a corpse, the ultimate abjection. Undermining this initial feminization, however, Jigsaw's body is rigid, phallic and dominant. His dead flesh, gaping head wound and slashed throat are made visually prominent and overwhelm the screen, whilst the harsh and angry lines of the dissection make his abject form appear overtly masculine. The scene revels in abject excess as Jigsaw's skull is cut open and his brain removed, his skin peeled back to reveal muscle, intestines and thick black secretions. His body has been opened up, its borders eviscerated and on display for all to see. Even in death, Jigsaw's abject displays are overtly masculine. This is indicated by the very "male" appearance of his naked body as his penis is briefly visible, locating his abjection firmly with masculinity and displacing the centrality of the female body in Creed's abjection theory.

Jigsaw's role as "father" and as potentially both creator and destroyer of life subverts Creed's discussions of the "archaic mother," a matriarchal figure whose presence forms "a vast backdrop for the enactment of all the events" (p. 19). Creed argues that this figure dominates visual imagery, influences the actions of its subjects, and fundamentally causes "procreation and rebirth [to] take place without the agency of the opposite sex" (p. 17). However, Jigsaw makes this role appear masculine and dominating, emphasized further through the fact that the mother is invariably absent. For example, he forces his victims into a confrontation with the abject, theirs and/or others, and makes such confrontations necessary to enable re-entry of the victim into the symbolic. They must face abjection and loss to assume their correct role in society, should they survive the ordeal. This recalls Creed's assertion that "that which threatens to destroy life also helps to define life [...] the activity of exclusion is necessary to guarantee that the subject take up his/her proper place in relation to the symbolic" (p. 9). As such, abject displays are strongly aligned with overt masculinity and effectively foregrounds the prominence of patriarchy by abjectly reworking the subject's entry into the symbolic. This is further illustrated as Jigsaw explains that he offers his victims a "new appreciation for life," suggesting rebirth and positioning him as a wise, all knowing figure. The association of Jigsaw with rebirth is heightened by womb-like and birthing imagery evident in the *Saw* franchise. In *Saw* for instance, Adam (Leigh Whannell) awakens in a bathtub full of dirty water and falls from it, coughing and spluttering, onto the floor. Similarly in *Saw III*, Jeff (Angus Macfadyen) is encased in a small, dark and entombing box that he is violently ejected from, head first. Such imagery strongly aligns Jigsaw with the figure of the "archaic mother," presenting a masculinized reworking of the role in creation, birth, and potentially death.

Jigsaw also makes masculine the maternal role of instructing his offspring in the proper ways of the body. For example, after Amanda survives the ordeal that Jigsaw constructed for her, he tells Amanda, "Your life has just begun." This suggests both rebirth and a reworking of the mother-child dyadic in his adoption of the birthing role. He also teaches and instructs her, scolding her when she disobeys and reminding her of his rules, as a father would. The ambiguous maternal/patriarchal nature of their relationship is heightened by Jigsaw forbidding Amanda to self-harm, suggested as he tells her, "You will give everything to me, every cell in your body … the marks on your arms, they're from another life." From this, Jigsaw can be viewed as both paternal in his forbidding of unauthorized abject displays, and as maternal as he fulfils a traditional role in instructing Amanda in the ways of the "clean and proper body" (p. 11). Similarly, Jigsaw also poses a penetrative and castrating threat to Hoffman, punishing his overtly masculine nature by rendering him vulnerable and feminized. For example in *Saw V*, Hoffman awakes in a chair, restrained and threatened with a shotgun trap that will blow his head off should he try to escape. The shotgun appears intrusive and phallic, indicating a penetrative threat that presents Jigsaw as dominant and in control of his subjects" relationship with the abject. Jigsaw subsequently displaces the primacy of the mothering role as an abject one that must be disavowed upon entry into the patriarchal symbolic order by making the role overtly masculine, undermining Creed's assertions (p. 13).

Jigsaw's reworking of the "archaic mother" role continues after his death, illustrating the dominant nature of his masculine characteristics. This is evident throughout the franchise in the form of audio tapes, in which he instructs his victims' behavior, and in videos, appearing to Jill in *Saw V* to request that she carry out his games and punish Hoffman on his behalf. Jigsaw also appears in other characters' flashbacks, such as in *Saw VI*, when Jill envisions a visit he made to her clinic to prove that his torturous and punishing abject games are more effective at rehabilitating drug addicts and criminals than Jill's caring, maternal approach. Jigsaw's prominent presence is as such felt throughout the franchise, driving the continuation of abject displays from within and without the symbolic. Patriarchy and masculinity are foregrounded as the main sites and causes of abjection in the *Saw* films, made possible through the figure of Jigsaw. With this in mind, the presentation of the abject in the series challenges the centrality of the female in the monstrous-feminine, instead presenting the monstrous-masculine as indelibly linked to abjection.

Game Over?

In summary, this essay intended to outline how the *Saw* franchise allows for several pertinent aspects of Creed's theory surrounding abjection and the "monstrous-feminine" to be challenged. For instance, the female relationship with abjection is depicted as comfortable and natural rather than monstrous in the series, suggested through characters such as Brit and Amanda as they appear at ease with their own abject states and with the abject states of others. However, it is of note that male displays of abjection cause terror in Amanda, suggesting that the male body as a site of abject displays is an alien and frightening occurrence. Related to this, the franchise displaces the primacy of the female in Creed's discussions of the abject by presenting males as overtly linked to abjection. Scenes of dead, mutilated and abject men are abundant and prevalent in all of the *Saw* films, suggesting that male displays of abjection are regarded as more monstrous and horrifying than that of females, most evident in the character of Jigsaw. Finally, the franchise undermines the notion that abjection is solely rooted in femininity by presenting gender ambiguous and fluid characters such as Brit and Gordon, who both subvert rigid gender roles to present new ways of interpreting gendered relationships with the abject.

The portrayal of gender and abjection as seen in the *Saw* franchise is evident in other contemporary texts, such as *Predators* (Nimrod Antal, Twentieth Century–Fox, 2010, U.S.), *The Thing* (Matthijs van Heijningen, Jr., Morgan Creek Productions, 2011, Canada and U.S.) and *Prometheus* (Ridley Scott, Brandywine Productions and Dune Entertainment, 2012, UK and U.S.), wherein female bodies generally remain intact and stable whilst male bodies are heavily aligned with grotesque displays of abjection. In *The Thing* for instance, male bodies are torn to pieces and disintegrated into monstrous and unrecognizable forms, and in *Prometheus* males are depicted as responsible for creating abject displays whilst women are presented as capable and dominant. As such, this discussion of the *Saw* films reinforces gender representations found elsewhere, suggesting that Creed's theory is not holding up anymore in terms of interpreting gender relations within the horror film. This implies that notions of sexual difference, female "Otherness" and gender rigidity are no longer viewed as such a threat to contemporary Western patriarchal society. Instead, it presents a critique of patriarchy and masculinity that is threatened by its own reductive gender assumptions in relation to the abject by presenting the male form as unstable and monstrous.

Some critics such as Mark Kermode dismiss the series as "increasingly rotten to the core" (2011, pp. 75–76). Similarly, Marriott and Newman write that *Saw* is "as much a turn-off as any number of tied-to-a-chair-and-tortured sequences," arguing that there is "more life, more intelligence and more interest" in other contemporary horror films (2010: p. 309). Contrary to this, this analysis has attempted to illustrate how the series can indeed offer insight into gender relations in our post-millennium, post–9/11 world. Indeed, there are several critics whose opinions on the *Saw* franchise also suggest the potential for more in-depth critical analysis of the *Saw* films as reflective of the contemporary moment. For example, Cherry, Howell and Ruddell describe a "morbid fascination with death and decay" in the franchise, hinting at viewing practices on- and off-screen as increasingly tolerant of and interested in abject displays (2011: p. 2). Similarly inviting a more culturally relevant analysis, Kevin J. Wetmore Jr. writes that Jigsaw "is the centre of the films, even after his death," presenting the notion that patriarchy and abjection are intrinsically linked throughout the *Saw* franchise (2012: pp. 101–102). In the *Saw* films, the male body is presented as unstable, vulnerable and subject to extreme abject displays and bodily disintegration, presenting an attitude towards gender in the series that depicts the American male as under threat and in crisis post 9/11 and following U.S. involvement in Afghanistan and Iraq. However, Jigsaw is presented as a dominant patriarch whose strong male characteristics both cause and endure abject displays. This suggests that abjection is rooted in the patriarchal discourses through which gendered difference is interpreted. More so, abject displays are presented as a product of patriarchy, firmly positioning notions of abjection and female monstrosity as a patriarchal construct. Interpreting Creed's theory in relation to the contemporary period in this manner suggests expansive potential beyond the *Saw* films, presenting further points for research.

Notes

1. The centrality of bodily difference in the horror film has been challenged by critics such as Carol Clover (1992), who primarily discusses audience identification with regard to both the adopting of both male and female perspectives and gender ambiguity in the genre. For instance, Clover discusses the "final girl" role as displaying both feminine and masculine characteristics, the former of which aligns her "Otherness" with the role of monster, whilst the latter ensures her survival (pp. 60–63).

Bibliography

Cherry, Brigid, Peter Howell, and Caroline Ruddell. 2010. *Twenty-First-Century Gothic*. Newcastle Upon Tyne: Cambridge Scholars.
Clover, Carol. 1992. *Men, Women, and Chain Saws: Gender in the Modern Horror Film*. Princeton, NJ: Princeton University Press.
Creed, Barbara. 1993. *The Monstrous-Feminine: Film, Feminism, Psychoanalysis*. London: Routledge.
Grant, Barry Keith, ed. 1996. *The Dread of Difference: Gender and the Horror Film*. Austin: University of Texas Press.
Kermode, Mark. 2011. *The Good, the Bad and the Multiplex: What's Wrong with Modern Movies?* London: Random House.

Knee, Adam. 1996. "Gender, Genre, Argento." in Grant's (ed.) *The Dread of Difference*, pp. 213–230.
Kristeva, Julia. 1982. *Powers of Horror: An Essay on Abjection*. New York: Colombia University Press.
Marriott, James, and Kim Newman. 2010. *Horror! 333 Films to Scare You to Death*. London: Carlton.
Wetmore, Jr., Kevin J. 2012. *Post-9/11 Horror in American Cinema*. New York: Continuum.
Young, Elizabeth. 1996. "Here Comes the Bride: Wedding Gender and Race in *Bride of Frankenstein*." in Grant's (ed.) *The Dread of Difference*, pp. 309–337.

Filmography

Alien (Ridley Scott, Twentieth-Century–Fox, 1979, UK and U.S.).
Carrie (Brian De Palma, Redbank Films, 1976, U.S.).
The Exorcist (William Friedkin, Hoya Productions, 1973, U.S.).
Predators (Nimrod Antal, Twentieth Century–Fox, 2010, U.S.).
Prometheus (Ridley Scott, Brandywine Productions and Dune Entertainment, 2012, UK and U.S.).
Saw (James Wan, 2004, Twisted Pictures, U.S.).
Saw II (Darren Lynn Bousman, 2005, Twisted Pictures, Canada and U.S.).
Saw III (Darren Lynn Bousman, 2006, Lionsgate and Twisted Pictures, Canada and U.S.).
Saw IV (Darren Lynn Bousman, 2007, Twisted Pictures, Canada and U.S.).
Saw V (David Hackl, 2008, Lionsgate and Twisted Pictures, Canada and U.S.).
Saw VI (Kevin Greutert, 2009, Twisted Pictures, Canada and U.S.).
Saw 3D (Kevin Greutert, 2010, Twisted Pictures, U.S.).
The Thing (Matthijs van Heijningen, Jr., Morgan Creek Productions, 2011, Canada and U.S.).

Hearing the Game: Sound Design
Jeffrey Bullins

In the introduction to *Lowering the Boom*, a collection of essays on film sound, editors Jay Beck and Tony Grajeda reflect on the past and future of sound theory. They refer to Rick Altman's assertion that sound studies is "a field whose time has come," and Michele Hilimes comment that sound studies is an "emerging" field that has been emerging for a hundred years. In a historically visual-centric medium, it is true that film studies of sound have often been sporadic or lacking in common bonds. However, recent collections such as *Lowering the Boom*, *Sound Theory/Sound Practice* edited by Altman, and the pioneering work of Michel Chion have served to bring some unity to the analysis of film sound. Referencing *Lowering the Boom* and *Sound Design for Science Fiction*, Mark Kerins notes, "For years now, any new works dealing with film sound have been obligated to begin ... by lamenting film studies' history of marginalizing the topic. Thankfully this no longer seems necessary, not only because this complaint has been repeated so often but also because current scholarship is increasingly working to address it" (3).

Books such as William Whittington's *Sound Design for Science Fiction*, have pointed out universalities within certain genres. He claims, "in general, horror films use music and sound effects to establish emotive intensity and impact far more aggressively and conceptually than any other genre" (130). Following this, while sound is a necessary and important part of film, within the horror genre it functions as the catalyst for the desired emotional response from the audience: fear. Some critics have surmised that sound may have been a necessity for the creation of the genre. Robert Spadoni notes, "the genre's inception fell directly on the heels of the coming of sound ... sound was needed before victims could be heard screaming" (2). Similarly, Roy Kinnard notes that the horror genre "was officially born in the early sound era, on November 16, 1931 [the day *Frankenstein* was released]" (1).

Beginning in 2004, almost 75 years after the release of *Frankenstein*, the *Saw* films represent the culmination of decades of sound design evolution in the genre. Likewise, beginning with the first film, motifs and themes are determined for the entirety of the franchise. Previous genre conventions root the soundtrack of *Saw* as contemporary horror: use of "shock cuts" (a loud sound meant to cause the audience to jump), non-diegetic sound effects (non-musical effects outside of the diegesis), and highly stylized or "hyper-real" effects. Examination of these elements will show how previous genre films have influenced the sound design of the Saw franchise. Equally, the soundtracks of these films also build upon themselves, establishing their own aesthetic; an aesthetic meant to always keep the audience's hearts racing and palms sweating.

Following that an audience's reaction of fear is paramount in the horror genre, the *Saw* films appear to move towards a style that is more experiential than representational, making the viewer feel as if he is in the film world. Early horror films like *Frankenstein* and *Dracula* (1931) lacked non-diegetic underscore and featured, due in part to technological limitations, minimal sound effects. Likewise, genre films in the 1970s such as *The Texas Chainsaw Massacre* (1974) and *I Spit on Your Grave* (1978) feature "realistic" soundtracks; they have little to no non-diegetic music, lack of non-diegetic sound effects, and subtle instead of stylized sound effects. These soundtracks serve to present the onscreen action as realistic or factual, similar to a documentary, with the audience watching the events objectively unfold. Conversely, following a trend begun in the 1980s, contemporary horror films like *Saw* have a more "hyper-real" soundtrack that creates a subjective world in which the audience experiences the film. The soundtrack becomes focused on having all the elements work towards eliciting a reaction from the audience instead of realistically representing the onscreen action.

While the medium of film builds upon itself both technically and aesthetically, the horror genre appears to do so fervently. *Saw* and its six sequels stand alongside other long-running franchises such as *Friday the 13th* (11 sequels, 1 remake), *A Nightmare on Elm Street* (8 sequels, 1 remake), and *Halloween* (7 sequels, 1 remake with a sequel). Rick Altman proposes a way of looking at film that treats "cinema as event." He states that the film exists at a point of interchange between production and reception. Once a film is produced, it can be received in a number of ways. Those receptions in turn will influence subsequent productions. Such is the case with *Saw* and other genre franchises. Reception of the first films feeds the sequel, which in turn feeds the third installment, and so on. Sound design aesthetics will evolve with other filmic elements.

Conventions within the Horror Genre

SHOCK CUTS

In discussing the horror genre, Steve Neale cites that its "principle aesthetic aim [is] to horrify" (93). It is a genre that is dependant upon the emotion that it causes for the viewer. If a horror film is not scary, then it has not been successful. "The success of these genres is often measured by the degree to which the audience sensation mimics what is seen on the screen ... whether the spectator at the horror film actually shudders in fear" (Williams, 730). A practice even early in the genre, used to hopefully ensure a scare and hopefully a physical jolt, was the shock cut. Also known as "stingers" or labeled by critic Robert Baird as the "startle effect," the shock cut combines a quick visual cut with a sudden aural event in the attempt to cause the viewer to actually "jump out of their seat." The shock cut has become a staple of the horror genre and David Diffrient claims, "few textural markers distinguish a film as "horror" so explicitly and dynamically as the shock cut" (53).

Following the classic horror films with Dracula, Frankenstein, and the Mummy, the monster movies of the 1940s, and the post-bomb "creature features" of the 1950s, *Psycho* (1960), by aiming the threat inward, is considered a turning point for the genre. In regards to the film's influence on the occurrence of the shock cut, Baird marks it as a dividing point in his discussion of the original and remake of *Cat People*. The latter (1982) contains four times the number of "startle effects" than the former (1942) and is "a typical example of the hypersensationalization of the post–*Psycho* horror/thriller film" (Baird 13). *Psycho* not only popularized the serial killer as a genre villain, which would be featured numerously through the 1970s and give way to contemporary villians such as Jigsaw, but also paved the way for more extensive use of the shock cut, a la the famous shower scene.

Shock cuts have been described as "sudden violent eruptions" that serve to continue "modernity's constant assault on the senses" (Diffrient 52). If indeed modern horror's delegation is to invade our at-stasis existence and cause disruption, it logically follows that as genre films progressed, the practice of doing so would increase. Perhaps as viewers became more comfortable, savvy horror viewers, the genre has been forced to include more shock cuts in order to maintain the same level of emotional and physical response than caused previously. Shock cuts are a major part of the soundtrack for *Saw* and they continue in varying quantities throughout the franchise. Though certain installments may make heavier use of them than others, like most early twenty-first century horror films, shock cuts are more numerous than in older movies.

Halloween, released in 1979, is considered a hallmark of the genre and a pinnacle example of the "slasher" sub-genre. It included a score by director John Carpenter, which contained musical hits as shock cuts, similar to the use of screeching strings during Marion's death in *Psycho*. In regards to the number that he placed in the film, Carpenter notes, "I'm now ashamed to admit that I recorded quite so many stingers for this one picture." Certainly compared to the lack of shock cuts in early horror films such as *The Mummy* (1932) or

Bride of Frankenstein (1935), *Halloween* contained many. However, shock cuts would continue to multiply and the sounds accompanying them to branch out beyond just music.

Five years after *Halloween*, Wes Craven's *A Nightmare on Elm Street* (1984) featured shock cuts at the opening and closing of the film. In contrast to using only music, these shock cuts implemented sound effects. The opening, following a flourishing of Freddy's deadly glove against synthesized music, jumps to his knife-fingers tearing through cloth. Accompanying the tearing noise is a scream. The end of the film culminates with the loud breaking of glass and wood as Freddy's hand bursts through a window to grab protagonist Nancy's mother. Also present is a thunderous, explosive sound. The choice to not use a musical cue as two of the major shock cuts in *Nightmare* is significant in that by the '80s the commonality of the shock cut demanded new methods for an old practice.

Following this method, the contemporary *28 Days Later* (2002) features a shock cut amid music. Just as the lack of music can forego telegraphing the occurrence of a shock cut, so can constant, unchanging music. After Cillian Murphy's character Jim awakens in a hospital, music is introduced during a lengthy montage of his journey through deserted London. By the time he tries to open a car door, setting off a startling alarm, the music's consistency has made it a transparent part of the scene and the high volume of it does not matter as the viewer is still surprised by the noise of the alarm. Here the effectiveness of the shock cut is independent from specific factors such as accompaniment of music or sound effects and is more dependent upon the relationship of the aural elements within the scene.

Throughout the *Saw* franchise, shock cuts are used to punctuate startling moments using both music and sound effects. Like *28 Days*, these shocks at times occur while other sounds are at high volume in the mix. For instance, in the second scene of the first film during a crime scene investigation, amid sounds present at the investigation, there is a quick cut to the victim struggling in a barbed wire trap. This fast visual cut is accompanied by a loud, percussive sound and the introduction of up-tempo music. Other significant shock cuts occur when both Dr. Gordon and Adam are kidnapped by the Pighead figure; each features a loud, percussive sound and other dissonant effects. Using the genre staple of the shock cut, *Saw* fits stylistically with other contemporary horror films by not just displaying disturbing images to the viewer, but by also causing him to startlingly jump from his seat.

While the use of shock cuts continues throughout the franchise, their frequency is variable. It appears that within the series, there are more shock cuts in *Saw II* than in the first film, and then the usage decreases some. They are still used, of course, such as in *III* when Lynn reaches for the reverse bear trap, in *IV* when Rigg reveals victims in various traps he comes upon, and at the beginning of *V* when Strahm is kidnapped by Pighead. In *Saw VI*, there appears a significant increase in frequency. At 26:00 William Easton is grabbed by Pighead, nine minutes later a shock cut occurs when Pamela Jenkins is abducted, and then a third occurs just three minutes later when a trap is set into motion. The increase in shock cut frequency could be a product of a number of factors such as the directorial change from Darren Lynn Boseman to David Hackl (the production designer for previous franchise films) for *Saw V*, the editor of previous franchise films, and the change to Kevin Greutert who directed *Saw VI* and *VII*. Also, other genre films at the time were featuring extensive use of shock cuts.

The year 2007's *30 Days of Night* juxtaposes shock cuts back to back for constant startles. During an early scene in which a woman is attacked by a vampire, three shock cuts occur in less than a minute. Such extensive use of shock cuts could be contributed to the medium-awareness of the contemporary viewer. As the viewer is more familiar with the event, more constant sensory barrage may be necessary in order to be jolted. The use of these startling moments within the *Saw* franchise establishes the focus of the soundtrack as physically and emotionally affective for the audience. Like the thrill of a roller coaster, it can be enjoyable to experience fear while still in a safe environment, and according to Baird, "Startles prove to us, in the very maw of virtual death, how very much alive we are" (22).

Nondiegetic Sound Effects and Spaces as Characters

Near the seven-minute mark in *Saw*, a nondiegetic, low frequency impact sound occurs when Dr. Gordon pulls an envelope from his pocket. The sound is not necessarily musical or part of the underscore itself. Rather, this sound is there to let the viewer know the importance of the item that Gordon has just found. Just as percussive hits were present when the body on the floor was first revealed, the soundtrack is signaling to the audience important plot points. Clearly, this is not a neutral perspective of the action. Nor is it necessarily a subjective perspective in regards to the characters; they certainly do not hear the low frequency impacts that the audience does. The soundtrack here is constructing the viewer's perspective. Certain events are being highlighted via nondiegetic sound effects; not just events meant to scare the audience as a shock cut would, but plot points as well. Instead of the events unfolding in a neutral fashion, the soundtrack is guiding the viewer through each scene. Karen Collins comments on this stylistic trend also present in the *Hellraiser* franchise, "The use of sound and music in the *Hellraiser* films illustrates the changing attitudes towards sound design in film in general. Sound design is no longer just for 'real sounds,' or the creation of a realistic world, but is becoming more of a creative aspect of filmmaking" (210). In just this first scene of *Saw*, a style is established that will persist through the entire franchise. It does not necessarily recreate a realistic environment, but rather establishes a mood and experience for the viewer.

Nondiegetic sound effects continue through the second scene of the film where police are investigating another of Jigsaw's victims. In addition to low frequency hits during plot revelations, another commonality to the franchise is established: flashbacks during police investigations to the ordeal of the victims in their traps. Literal visual flashes to frames of white, quick edits, sped up time, and blurred focus characterize these flashbacks; these are accompanied by layers of sound effects such as high pitched screams and squeals, metal on metal "shings," whistles, groans, creaks, and sometimes laughter. This cacophony embodies the chaos and terror felt by the trapped characters. These sounds occur in varying degrees of severity throughout the franchise and become the established style for the trap flashbacks. We hear similar sounds during Amanda's bear trap ordeal. Following Jigsaw's explanation of the trap, screeches accompany a high volume score and swoosh sounds as the camera circles Amanda.

These trap flashbacks are an example of how the soundtrack is created for the audience's experience rather than mimesis of the real world. Like the characters, the audience is meant to experience the terror of the traps. The dissonance of the nondiegetic effects mirrors the desperation and terror of the victim's (our) perspective. The high frequency whistles are shrill and piercing. The "whooshing" sound effects associated with camera pans and zooms suggest panic as the victim (we) searches for a way out.

The disregard for realism and the construction of an aural environment for the audience follows Kerins ideas of the "ultrafield." Building upon Chion's concept of the "superfield," which refers to the ambient sounds that are outside of the visual frame, Kerins states, "the ultrafield seeks not to provide a *continuous* aural environment, but rather to *continuously* provide an *accurate* spatial environment where aural and visual space match" (92). Though Kerins writes specifically about sound effects, dialog, and diegetic music, this concept applies also to the nondiegetic effects in *Saw*. As horror films are tasked with frightening the audience, and the construction of an aural space aids this, the soundtrack is continuously changing to match the onscreen action and immerse the audience. The nondiegetic sounds are also part of the ultrafield, which "situates the audience *in the middle of the action*" (Kerins 106).

Going further with construction of space, in *Saw II* the house that the victims are trapped in is characterized sonically. Near the end of the film when

Amanda is fleeing from Xavier, percussive sounds and low frequency drones can be heard as she and Daniel run down the hallways. This is similar to how spaces were treated two years earlier in 2003's remake of *The Texas Chainsaw Massacre*. During a scene where the characters are in an abandoned mill, the soundtrack is thick with layers of atmospheric sounds. Sound Supervisor Trevor Jolly stated that he wanted it to appear as if "this mill could be alive" (Nispel, 2003). In addition to "ominous tones," wind/air sounds and machinery noises are included. Even though the mill is long since inactive, these sounds are part of the ambience. The objective is not creating a realistic space, but the sonic personification of the environment in order for it to appear more threatening. *Saw III* continues this characterization of the space by including metallic hits and other nondiegetic sounds as Jeff navigates the warehouse in which he is trapped.

Stylized Sound Effects

Similar to the use of nondiegetic effects, a feature also building upon itself in contemporary horror is the use of stylized, diegetic sound effects. Some critics see the stylized soundtrack as a negative trend, with one commenting of *Saw* that the "loud soundtrack is equivalent of an incessant "Boo!" goosing" (Harvey). Following this opinion, *Saw* is often basing its fright factor upon use of shock cuts and jumps (not to mention a great deal of grisly, bloody visuals). However, beyond a loud hit as a figure jumps out from the shadows, many more moments in the film, not just those assumed to be startling, are punctuated by stylized sounds. The trend of stylized effects evidenced in the 80s during the dream sequences in the *Nightmare on Elm Street* series, in the 90s with the self-aware *Scream* franchise, and through the 00s with remakes of *The Texas Chainsaw Massacre* (2003), *The Hills Have Eyes* (2006), and *Halloween* (2007), does not seem to be ending any time soon.

The opening of *Saw* takes place with a dark screen. Bubbling, watery sounds are heard, then coughing and yelling. Due to the amount of reverberation on the voices and sound effects, the viewer gets an idea of the space before it is visually revealed. Kerins claims that the advent of digital sound has allowed for spaces to be constructed sonically, thus reducing the need for establishing shots and moving perspective closer. "In fact, the ultrafield — with its robust ability not only to create *spaces* but also to convey the proper *relationships* amount the various important elements *within* those spaces — should spur an even heavier reliance on close-up shots" (104). In this case, the shot is not even close up, but too dark to see.

When the victim Adam awakes and accidently pulls the stopper from the drain, an exaggerated bubbling sound is heard as well as metallic clanking, letting the viewer know that the key briefly seen has gone down the drain. As the visuals here are dark, it is important that the audience be aware of what has happened, so the action is supported as much by a sound effect than the image of the disappearing key. This event begins a theme that progresses through the rest of the film: exaggerating sounds in order to highlight important plot points. For example, this occurs again during the flashback to Amanda's first trap. As she stands up, most of the soundtrack drops out so that we can focus on the sound of the pin in slow-mo being pulled on the timer. The visual cut happens so quickly that the action could potentially be missed if the sound effect were not heightened.

After Adam's loss of the key, once the fluorescent lights are turned on, the viewer becomes visually aware of the space. The reveal of the body at 2:48 is shown from overhead. A synthesized tone is heard and then a gun shot, assumed nondiegetic, and the camera begins to spin. A processed scream/squeal follows the spin. As the image cuts quickly from the corpse's head, to a cassette recorder in one of its hands, and to a gun in the other, loud, percussive sounds accompany each visual cut. This lets the viewer know the importance of these items, as well as suggesting a somewhat subjective perspective from the characters in the room. We are seeing these items at the same time they are.

After this first scene, the rest of *Saw* predominantly uses stylized effects during trap sequences and other impactful scenes such as those with Dr. Gordon's abducted wife and daughter. When Zep has kidnapped them, loud beeps are heard as a timer counts down Dr. Gordon's trap's time limit. The more mundane scenes of the police investigation are constructed with a realistic soundtrack: diegetic sound effects, lack of music, subtle instead of stylized effects. This follows a similar technique from the original *Texas Chainsaw Massacre* (1974). Featuring a realistic soundtrack for the majority of the film as the doomed teenagers wander searching for help, the style changes during Franklin's murder sequence. "At this point the sound design increases in density and complexity as the chainsaw snarls are combined with sounds like broken glass, rattling chains, processed voices, percussion and Sally's screams as she pushes through the undergrowth to the farmhouse" (Coyle and Hayward 128). Like *Massacre*, *Saw* contrasts expositional sequences with those involving death. This can at times happen within a single scene such as the cutting between Amanda describing to the police her ordeal and escape from the reverse bear trap and flashbacks to the event itself.

Breaking from this convention, *Saw II* features stylized sounds throughout, even during more mundane sequences. Effects that are introduced during Matthews dream sequence continue after he wakes up and during the operation to find Jigsaw. Like the opening scene of *Saw*, a subjective perspective is established here. The audience will be experiencing these events as Matthews does, thus confirming him as our protagonist. However, during scenes that happen within the trap-filled house, this subjective perspective determined by stylized effects appears to change from victim to victim depending on who is in a trap at that time. Thus, it remains the audience who is ultimately in the traps as our perspective follows each victim.

Saw III continues the style established in *Saw II* by having constant stylized effects. Part of this may be due to a narrative difference between this film and the previous installments in that the focus is not on any police investigation but on the character Jeff's moral decisions to kill/save other victims and on the relationship between John and Amanda. Consequently, there are not as many "mundane" scenes as in the previous films. However, even a sequence such as Lynn taking pills out of her locker features a "whoosh" sound when the camera pans to her, as well as a reverberant sound of a large, metal door when she closes her locker.

The rest of the films in the franchise continue to have layered, complex sound effects. In fact, more so than shock cuts, the amount of these effects increases. The soundtrack during the trap sequences is always complex and layered. Kerins has discussed the importance of digital sound and its role in the increasing complexity of film soundtracks. He references other critics in this regard saying:

> William Whittington has argued that the shift from analog to digital in the post-production realm has made soundtrack construction more complex, pointing out that in places in *Terminator 2* (1991) one hundred original sounds are playing at once. Walter Murch concurs, arguing that "the general level of complexity ... has been steadily increasing over the eight decades since film sound was invented" [Kerins 67].

It was established early in the series that scenes of victims in traps are meant to be tense and frightening for the audience. The soundtrack is constructed to amplify the fearful experience for the viewer, to emphasize moments of terror. Though the soundtrack's aesthetic is building upon previous films, it is still affective in its elicitation of horror. Similarly, Heyward notes in regards to *Halloween* (1978), "While neither the film nor score can be considered as particularly original, its efficient activation and reinvigoration of genre traditions identify the variety and potency of the genre" (Heyward 3).

Following *Saw* as part of the commonly labeled horror subgenre of "torture porn," films, which focus on graphic depictions of said act, is *Hostel* (2005). While this film does contain instances of image punctuating shock cuts, some of the most notable elements are the stylized diegetic sound effects. During character Josh's first torture scene, his antagonist uses a drill to bore a hole in his leg. The perspective at the beginning of the scene is Josh's, seen though a hood covering his head. One can hear his muffled breathing, supporting a subjective sonic perspective for the audience. As the drill is the main tool of torture, its sounds are layered with various drill sounds, stylized with emphasis on gurgling blood sounds, and predominant in the mix.

This sort of complex sound creation seems quite elaborate compared to the dull stabbing sounds of a *Black Christmas* (1974) or *Last House on the Left* (1972). Similarly in *Saw*, the sounds during Amanda's search for the key that will remove her trap are equally complex and hyperreal. The key she is searching for is located inside the stomach of a body lying nearby. The ticking of a timer adds urgency to this scene with a build up to the moment when Amanda brings down a sharp, loud, and squishy sounding stab into the (newly realized alive) body. Each subsequent stab also appears to have sharpness to it. This is similar to the treatment of knife sounds in *Scream 2* (1997), when every time the killer's knife is brandished, there is a metallic "shing." As Amanda searches through entrails for the key, sound effects appear overly liquid, with reverberant "plopping" sounds.

Following these effects, throughout the franchise, emphasis is consistently put on sounds associated with blood. This importance is also evidenced by *Saw II*'s tagline, "Oh yes. There will be blood." At the beginning of this installment when a victim triggers the door-gun trap and is shot through the eye, exaggerated liquid sounds are heard when his body drops to the floor. Likewise, the sounds of blood are prominent in the mix when John is being operated on in *Saw III*, during a trap in which the victims pull metal rods out of their bodies in *Saw IV*, as the victim is being disemboweled by the pendulum trap at the beginning of *Saw V*, and in numerous other moments throughout the franchise.

Blood and liquidity are important elements to highlight in films such as *Saw* and *Hostel*. This focus on blood and the labeling of these types of films as "torture porn" ties in closely with Linda Williams' theories regarding genre types and their similarities, notably horror and pornography. She theorizes that horror, like pornography, is preoccupied with fluids (blood and semen, respectively) and that the "ecstasy" or fulfillment of the genre (death and orgasm) is obtained when these fluids are seen/heard (Williams 737). Therefore, the increased and stylized sounds of blood are an attempt to deliver a greater amount of "horror ecstasy" to the viewer. It could follow that contemporary horror, aware of its conventions and purposes would contain greater excesses of blood as each film tries to go one step farther than the film before it. Indeed, *Hostel Part II* (2007) was promoted as "more violent, intense, and bloody than the original" (Sciretta, 2007) and contained an excessive (and sexual) use of blood in a scene where a victim's throat is cut sending a literal shower of blood on top of a naked woman below her.

Themes within the Franchise

While the Saw franchise contains generic conventions such as stylized sound effects, nondiegetic effects, and shock cuts, there are also a number of elements that are distinctive within the margins of the franchise. The music that plays during the climactic moment in the first film occurs throughout the sequels, the timbre of Jigsaw's voice is established in the first film and is consistent through the series, and the motif of camera and flash sounds are established in *Saw* and continue through the other installments.

MUSIC

Of the three generally accepted categories within the soundtrack (dialog, music, and sound effects), music is often most associated with the conveyance of emotions. "A jarring musical soundtrack has been perceived as one of the crucial ways in which the horror film achieves its psychological impact" (Heyward 187). The original music present in all of the *Saw* films is stylistically consistent, featuring sustained drones and intermittent percussive hits, with former Nine Inch Nails band member Charlie Clouser composing each score. Following the style of his former band, the scores for the *Saw* films have an industrial feel. This also follows an aesthetic established in the original *Texas Chainsaw Massacre* in which "substantial elements of [the] film soundtrack prefigure elements of the 'industrial' music genre that developed in the 1980s" (Coyle and Hayward 134).

As mentioned, the use of music in the first *Saw* is relegated predominantly to trap sequences and moments of conflict and climax; scenes involving police investigation and exposition are relatively minimal in regards to the soundtrack. However, in later installments music is featured throughout the film. For example, during interrogation sequences in *Saw II* between Matthews and John Kramer, sustained drones, by continuing without sonic resolution, serve to create tense feelings for the viewer. According to David Sonnenshien, music allows "us to be more susceptible to suggestion. In a kind of trance with music, our lowered threshold of belief is essential to watching films and being immersed inside the story" (105). It would follow that the increased use of music serves to further immerse the viewer into the film world. By including nondiegetic underscore, the soundtrack is built with focus upon the emotional reactions and involvement of the viewer.

While the style of music in the franchise is consistent, there is also a particular musical piece that is present in all seven films. Titled "Hello Zepp" and first featured in *Saw I* when Zep is revealed as one of Jigsaw's victims instead of accomplice, it has become the franchise's "theme song." In the first film, the piece continues through the twist ending when Jigsaw's identity is revealed. In *Saw II*, it begins when Xavier enters the bathroom seen in the first film. This not only telegraphs the climax of the film but also references the space and events from the previous installment. Likewise, the climactic action of *Saw III* is foreshadowed when "Hello Zepp" is heard as Jigsaw's heart rate monitor flatlines. It is also heard in *Saw IV* when Hoffman is revealed to be the villain, in *Saw V* during Strahm's death, in *Saw VI* when Jill attacks Hoffman, and in *Saw VII* when Dr. Gordon locks Hoffman in the bathroom first seen in *Saw I*.

While "Hello Zepp" is heard in all of the films' final climactic moments, it is also featured during other revealing moments, but usually as a variation of some type that is lower in the mix. It is heard during a flashback of John painting a puppet and constructing Amanda's trap in *Saw III*. In *Saw IV* it is heard near the beginning of the film when, during the autopsy, an audiotape is found in John's stomach. From these points on this musical cue is used to highlight important or revealing plot points. The music cue itself bears some similarity to the Catholic hymn "Dies Irae," which is featured during the opening credits of *The Shining* (1980) (Barham 8). Though the hymn describes events during the Day of Judgment, which is certainly in line with Jigsaw's modus operandi, it is unknown if Clouser, either consciously or subconsciously, was channeling the score from the classic Kubrick film or from Catholic liturgy.

While the actual scores of the *Saw* films are predominantly instrumentals composed by Clouser, all of the installments except for *Saw V* feature heavy metal rock songs during the closing credits. These and other songs are subsequently featured on the films' "official soundtracks." *Saw*'s CD soundtrack features the actual score from the film, but the CDs released for the sequels feature songs by metal bands such as Marilyn Manson, Slipknot, Mudvayne, Ministry, and Drowning Pool. While these songs may not have been featured in the films specifically, the hard-edged image of heavy metal music fits neatly with the gory spectacle of the *Saw* franchise. Likewise, other artists have borrowed imagery from the films themselves. The music video for Helloween's 2010 single, "Are You Metal?" features a trio of girls who wake up trapped in a house with Jigsaw-esque traps on their heads.

CAMERA AND FLASHES

Beginning in the first film, a motif is established both visually and sonically. Following the opening scene in the bathroom is a police investigation of another of Jigsaw's victims who died crawling through razor wire. Sounds of camera shutters and flashes accompany quick visual cuts to black and white stills of the crime. This is comparable to the opening of *The Texas Chainsaw Massacre* (1974) in which police photos are being taken of the titular crime scene. *Massacre* was billed as being based on true events, even though the inspiration may have come from real-life killer Ed Gein and not a family of backwoods psychopaths. John Larroquette's journalistic voiceover and the suggestion of a crime scene investigation add to the legitimacy of the story. Assumingly, audiences may be more frightened by a story if they think, "it could actually happen!"

Following this, *Saw* establishes a level of documentation even if the visual and sonic aesthetics do not follow a minimalist documentary style. When Dr. Gordon confronts Adam about his identity, Adam defends his voyeuristic occupation stating, "My camera doesn't know how to lie. It only shows you what is put right in front of it." This is not only an avowal of Dr. Gordon's lecherous guilt but also an assertion of the "real-ness" of Jigsaw's victims. Where the scenes involving traps are stylized with quick, visual cuts and nondiegetic sound effects, their cinematic spectacle is belied via the truthful eye of the camera.

During a flashback to Adam's abduction, the camera and flash play a central role in the navigation of his darkened apartment as well as building suspense. In this scene, the soundtrack is characterized only by diegetic sound effects. No music is present, nor are any low frequency drones or percussive hits that characterize the backgrounds of later installments. The stillness of the apartment is broken only by intermittent camera shutter sounds followed by the electrical crescendo of the flash warming up. These tiny builds increase the tension for the viewer as one waits for something to be found by the camera's flash. In regards to how silence can be useful as a narrative tool, Balazs stated, "The presentation of silence is one of the most specific dramatic effects of the sound film. No other art can reproduce silence" (Balazs 117). This quiet is broken suddenly with an initial jump scare of the puppet's iconic laughter. This ends up being a precursor to a bigger jump scare when Adam finds Pighead in his closet. This revelation is accompanied by screeches, growls, and loud percussive sounds that are in stark contrast to the minimal diegetic sound effects that led to it. Though the audience may initially be put into a realistic space as Adam moves about his apartment, the climactic action is ultimately experiential for the audience. When Pighead jumps out of the closet, he/she is grabbing *us* not Adam. The nondiegetic sound effects provide a shocking experience, not realistic representation.

The motif of visually flashing to still crime scene images with the accompaniment of camera sounds continues throughout the franchise. For instance, they are especially present in *Saw V* during Strahm's investigation to uncover Hoffman as Kramer's accomplice. However, these sounds are not as present in the final two films, as there are fewer flashbacks from the crime scene to the victim. With most of the crime scenes in *Saw VI* and *VII*, we have already seen the trap and a flashback is unnecessary. Camera sounds accompanying flashes to still images support the idea of Jigsaw's constant surveillance in *Saw IV* when Jigsaw tells Rigg, "there are cameras everywhere."

JIGSAW'S VOICE

Since the first scene of the first film in the series, the importance of Jigsaw's voice is established. The voice on the tape that Adam and Dr. Gordon hear is a representation of the power of their captor over them as well as a necessary narrative element. The information spoken on the tape holds the possibility of their salvation. From a technical standpoint, the voice is prominent in the mix, loud enough and clear enough (despite its processing) for the audience to hear. Like Adam and Dr. Gordon, the audience is focused on every word spoken, straining to find every clue possible.

Michel Chion noted of the presence of the voice in the soundtrack, "For real spectators, there are not all the sounds including the human voice. There are voices, and then everything else. In every audio mix, the presence of a human voice instantly sets up a hierarchy of perception" (*Voice* 5). In addition to this concept of "vococentrism," Chion also suggested the category of "semantic" listening, which separates our perception of spoken words from other sounds. Whether or not the voice can be considered to be intrinsically "more important" than other sounds in the film is an undeterminable claim. However, it remains of the utmost importance for the viewer to be able to understand the dialog in the film and thus the narrative. With this in mind, one can hear that Jigsaw's voice on the tape, and later during the puppet's video instructions, remains unprocessed in regards to space. In a medium sized, tiled bathroom, any sound would be reverberant as the sound waves bounce off the numerous reflective surfaces. However, Jigsaw's voice remains dry. Granted, it is processed in order to hide John Kramer's actual voice and to reinforce the low quality sound of a mini tape recording.

Keeping Jigsaw's voice clear and less reverberant sets it above other sound elements in the mix. It embodies the idea of vococentrism in that all other elements seem secondary to it. The magnitude of Jigsaw's voice as it is presented in the first scene of *Saw* continues through the rest of the franchise. Jigsaw's voice sounds the same in the second film when Amanda finds the first tape recorder and plays it for the group. Likewise, the tape Jeffrey hears at the beginning of *Saw III* is processed similarly, as is the voice that instructs Rigg in each of the traps he finds, and so on through the rest of the films. Chion states, summarizing a claim by Christiane Sacco, "The presence of a human voice structures the sonic space that contains it" (*Voice* 5). Having the voice hierarchically above other sounds and above realistic spatial processing establishes it in a way as nondiegetic even at the same time as it is in the diegesis.

Though the characters can hear his voice, and it is important that they do for their own sake, the voice is ultimately for the viewer. As with nondiegetic sounds that accompany camera movements and add to the excitement of the fast edits, this Oz-like voice pulls the viewer into the film world. The viewer is experiencing this event as if the tape recorder were next to his ear rather than being a fly on the wall of the bathroom.

Giving further power to Jigsaw's voice is the fact that the source of it is unseen. In his analysis of the voice in film, Chion uses the term "acousmetre" to refer to voices within a film of which the source is not known or not seen. Ross Fenimore states that "acousmatic sounds are a hallmark of horror film — the dislocation between what we hear and see creates a fundamental tension that blurs the known and the unknown" (80). Since the acousmetre is coming from everywhere and nowhere, it is inscribed with omnipresent power. However, when the source is revealed, as in the Wizard of Oz's case, the truth of the sound source divests any power it may have had. However, through the entirety of the first *Saw* film, we are unaware of Jigsaw's true identity. Zep, the assumed villain, becomes a flesh and blood man when his face is revealed. The final twist ending of the film should, in theory, humanize the voice as it is attributed to John Kramer. However, John rises from the floor as if resurrecting from the dead. Like his voice, he remains somehow superhuman. Likewise, there are a few moments in *Saw* when Jigsaw's voice is heard as a nondiegetic voiceover, such as when Adam is reading the back of the Polaroid he finds in Dr. Gordon's wallet and when Dr. Gordon is rereading the note that suggests how to kill Adam. This further gives the voice an omnipresence and omniscience.

In *Saw II*, Jigsaw is humanized as he spends almost the entire film in conversation with Detective Matthews. Although he still speaks gruffly, there is a difference between the processed voice we have heard on tapes and videos and John's "real" voice. This allows the audience to see another side of the villain, especially as his demeanor is calm. The third and fourth films extrapolate further back-story, showing more and more of John's life before and during his transformation into Jigsaw. While some of the myth and mystery of Jigsaw is explained away, the iconic voice explaining the victim's fate remains constant.

In *Saw IV*, John is seen with a reel-to-reel tape recorder constructing Jigsaw's voice. When he puts his first victim Cecil in a trap, his actual voice sounds similar to the processed voice. This is a significant moment as John's transformation into Jigsaw is illustrated with his own voice fading and being replaced both literally and figuratively. Contrasting the gruffness of his voice in conversations with Matthews and Cecil, John's voice is higher in pitch when speaking to his wife; a dichotomy is present between his two parts.

Likewise, in *Saw V*, the timbre of John's voice on his video message to his ex-wife is his own and not the rougher tone associated with Jigsaw. It is evident here that some part of John's original self was present even after he became Jigsaw.

Saw V contains another significant moment for Jigsaw's voice: it is the first time that we hear a voice other than John's on a trap tape. When Strahm discovers the class coffin trap near the end of the film, it is Hoffman's voice that is on the tape and not John's. Arguably, though, it is still the voice of "Jigsaw." John claims at the end of *Saw III* that he will live on after his death. This is evidenced in two ways: his deeds will persist through history and the voice of Jigsaw will live on in his recordings and through others like Hoffman. This is seen immediately when Jeffrey plays a tape after killing Jigsaw and later in Hoffman's recordings. Fenimore comments on film's at times unsuccessful attempt to hide the dualism of the recorded voice and the photographed body, and yet "it is exactly this unearthing of the seam and the tearing of the parts that constitutes the thrill of horror film" (82). Jigsaw's disembodied voice contains the mystery and mythos of the character in a way that seeing John Kramer or Detective Hoffman speak cannot.

In *Saw VI*, Jigsaw's voice is finally deconstructed when a technician processes a recording to reveal Hoffman's disguised voice. This is a revealing of the acousmetre, the humanizing of a powerful, disembodied force. While John revealed himself via a video, the police never decoded his voice. This action illustrates Hoffman's failure as Jigsaw's successor. The last film, *Saw: The Final Chapter* (VII), foreshadows the reality behind who is truly Jigsaw's heir when Dr. Gordon speaks gruffly from the shadows during a Jigsaw survivors support group meeting. There is a similarity here between his voice and the processed Jigsaw voice. This sound is pushed further during the climax of the film when Gordon speaks the iconic line, "Game over," as he slams a door, sealing Hoffman inside the same bathroom seen at the start of the first film.

Conclusions

The sonic environments of contemporary horror films such as *Saw* and its sequels appear designed to provide a film world that is experiential more so than representational. The nondiegetic sounds that characterize the world of *Saw* do not mimic those of the real world, but are rather a product of stylistic conventions established within the genre. Subsequently, *Saw*'s sequels build upon its style. Elements such as Jigsaw's voice and musical themes such as "Hello Zepp" are motifs representative of the series as a whole.

Donnelly states, "horror films are created as whole environments that the audience enters, equating a mental state with a sonic construct" (94). Therefore, contemporary soundtracks create a hyperreal space, a stylized simulacrum in which the viewer inhabits. Layering complex sound effects instead of mimicking real-world sounds allows the soundtrack to create an environment exclusively to manipulate the viewers' emotional responses. In more contemporary soundtracks, extensive use of shock cuts also allow for physical and not just emotional reactions. Immersion into the story occurs through the immersion of oneself into the filmic world: a fully constructed, all-encompassing, surround-sound environment.

References

Altman, Rick. *Sound Theory/Sound Practice*. New York: Routledge, 1992.
Baird, Robert. "The Startle Effect: Implications for Spectator Cognition and Media Theory." *Film Quarterly* Vol. 53, No. 3 (Spring 2003).
Balazs, Bela. "Theory of the Film: Sound." *Film Sound: Theory and Practice*. Ed. Elisabeth Weis and John Belton. New York: Columbia University Press, 1985.
Barham, Jeremy. "Incorporating Monsters: Music as Context, Character and Construction in Kubrick's *The Shining*," in *Terror Tracks*, edited by Philip Hayward, pp. 137–170. London: Equinox, 2009.
Beck, Jay, and Tony Grajeda, eds. *Lowering the Boom*. Chicago: University of Illinois Press, 2008.
Carroll, Noel. *The Philosophy of Horror or Paradox of the Heart*. New York: Routledge, 1990.
Chion, Michel. *Audio-Vision*. New York: Columbia University Press, 1994.
_____. *The Voice in Cinema*. New York: Columbia University Press, 1999.
Collins, Karen. "Like Razors Through Flesh: *Hellraiser*'s Sound Design and Music," in *Terror Tracks*. Ed. Philip Hayward, pp. 198–212. London: Equinox, 2009.
Coyle, Rebecca, and Philip Hayward. "Texas Chainsaws: Audio Effect and Iconicity," in *Terror Tracks*, edited by Philip Hayward, pp. 125–136. London: Equinox, 2009.
Diffrient, David Scott. "A Film Is Being Beaten: Notes on the Shock Cut and the Material Violence of Horror," in *Horror Film: Creating and Marketing Fear*, edited by Steffen Hantke. Jackson: University Press of Mississippi, 2004.
Donnelly, K.J. *The Spectre of Sound: Music in Film and Television*. London: BFI, 2005.
Fenimore, Ross. "Voices That Lie Within: The Heard and Unheard in *Psycho*," in *Music in the Horror Film*, edited by Neil Lerner, pp. 80–97. New York: Routledge, 2010.
Hayward, Phillip. Ed. *Terror Tracks*. London: Equinox, 2009.
Harvey, Dennis. "Saw." *Variety*. Retrieved April 23, 2006, from http://www.variety.com/review/VE1117922951.html?categoryid=31&cs=1&quer y=Saw.
Hutchings, Peter. *The Horror Film*. New York: Pearson, 2004.
Kerins, Mark. *Beyond Dolby (Stereo): Cinema in the Digital Sound Age*. Indianapolis: Indiana University Press, 2011.
Kinnard, Roy. *Horror in Silent Films*. Jefferson, NC: McFarland, 1995.
Neale, Steve. *Genre and Hollywood*. London: Routledge, 2000.
Nispel, Marcus, director. "Audio Commentary." *The Texas Chainsaw Massacre*. [Motion picture]. New Line, 2003.
Sciretta, Peter. "Movie Review: *Hostel: Part II*." May, 31, 2007. Retrieved April 24, 2008, from http://www.slashfilm.com/2007/05/31/movie-review-hostel-part-ii/.
Sonnenschein, David. *Sound Design*. Studio City, CA: Michael Wiese, 2001.

Spadoni, Robert. *Uncanny Bodies: The Coming of Sound Film and the Origins of the Horror Genre.* Berkeley: University of California Press, 2007.
Wiater, Stanley. *Dark Visions.* New York: Avon, 1992.
Wittington, William. *Sound Design in Science Fiction Films.* Austin: University of Texas Press, 2007.

About the Contributors

James **Aston** is director of studies for film at the University of Hull, and his principal research interests focus on the field of cinematic representations of the past, especially in Hollywood during the 1960s and 1970s and post–9/11. He has co-edited the books *Television, Sex and Society: Analyzing Contemporary Representations* and *Screen Revelations: Apocalypse on the Small Screen* as well as being published on pre-and-post millennium apocalyptic cinema and the films of Michael Haneke.

Jeffrey **Bullins** is an independent scholar and sound designer. He has taught courses in sound design and audio postproduction. His research centers on genre studies, specifically in horror and science fiction. He will have an essay discussing mental illness in horror films in the upcoming book *Evil in American Pop Culture*.

Brian **Collins** holds the Drs. Ram and Sushila Gawande Chair in Indian Religion and Philosophy at the Department of Classics and World Religions at Ohio University in Athens. He received his Ph.D. in history of Religions from the University of Chicago Divinity School, where he wrote a dissertation on the Sanskrit epic poem the *Mahabharata*. He is finishing a monograph, "Yajnantara, the End of Sacrifice: Mimetic Theory and Hindu Myth."

Amy M. **Davis** is a lecturer at the University of Hull and her research focuses on American animation history (especially the Disney studio), representations of gender roles in U.S. animation and popular culture, and issues connected with Hollywood cinema and American cultural history. She is writing a book on representations of masculinity in Disney's feature animation and a longer-term project on the Disney theme parks.

Jacob **Huntley** is a tutor in literature and creative writing at the University of East Anglia. He has written on various aspects of the Gothic, as well as on J. G. Ballard, William Hope Hodgson, Clive Barker and the *Saw* films. His research interests, covering literature and film, are principally concerned with genre or non-mimetic fiction. This material is frequently addressed from a post-structuralist perspective or employing continental philosophy and much of the focus of this involves the work of Gilles Deleuze and Felix Guattari or Deleuze's individual philosophical writings.

Steve **Jones** is a senior lecturer in media at Northumbria University, UK. He has published numerous articles on horror film, pornography, ethics, feminism, and the philosophy of self. His first book will be *Torture Porn: Popular Horror After Saw*.

Dean **Lockwood** is a senior lecturer in media theory in the School of Media at the University of Lincoln. He has researched and published in a number of areas, including cinema, music and sound studies, and digital culture. His research focuses on affective politics in the contemporary media ecology. With Rob Coley, he is author of *Cloud Time*, a critical discussion of the cultural and political implications of cloud computing.

Ben **McCann** is senior lecturer in French studies at the University of Adelaide. He is the co-editor of *The Cinema of Michael Haneke* (2011) and the author of *Le Jour se lève* (2013). He is writing a book about French director Julien Duvivier. Other research interests include French horror cinema, the actor Raimu, and contemporary film adaptation practices.

Fernando G. **Pagnoni Berns** is a graduate teaching assistant at the Universidad de Buenos Aires — Facultad de Filosofía y Letras (Argentina). He has published articles on Argentinian and international cinema and drama in *magofagia, Cinedocumental, Telondefondo.org, Stichomythia, Ol3media, Anagnórisis-Theatrical Research Magazine, Lindes* and *UpStage*, as well as chapters in edited collections such as *Undead in the West* and *Horrofilmico: Aproximaciones al Cine de Terror en Latinoamerica y el Caribe*.

Madeleine **Smith** is a post-graduate film studies student at the University of Hull. She is researching the portrayal of vigilantism in American film and television and has an essay in *Television, Sex and Society: Analyzing Contemporary Representations*.

Evangelos **Tziallas** is an SSHRC doctoral fellow and Ph.D. Candidate at the Mel Hoppenheim School of Cinema at Concordia University in Montreal. He has published articles on the torture porn horror sub-genre and on the queer Greek-Australian film *Head On* in *Jump Cut*. His dissertation explores the intersections between cinema, surveillance, pornography and queer sexuality.

John **Walliss** is senior lecturer in criminology at Liverpool Hope University. He has published widely in several areas, such as the sociology of religion, new religious movements and violence, religion and popular culture, and fan cultures. His research interests are in representations of crime and punishment in the nineteenth-century press.

Index

À l'intèrieur/Inside 35, 36, 37
The Abominable Dr. Phibes 6, 79–82, 83–84
Abu Ghraib 23, 34
acousmêtre 7, 86; definition of 95, 96–99, 190, 191
Agamben, Giorgio 140–142, 154
Alien 3, 157
Alien 3 65
Altman, Rick 176, 177
Artaud, Antonin 145
The Assassination of Jesse James by the Coward Robert Ford 22

Bell, Tobin 15
Bendle, Mervyn 15
Bentham, Jeremy 47, 84n2
The Blair Witch Project 1
body horror 34–37, 56, 63, 159
Bogard, William 61, 69n75, 148–149
Bousman, Darren Lynn 14, 180
Buchanan, Ian 126, 135
Buckland, Warren 52–53, 54, 56, 68n39
Bush, George W. 25, 34, 41–42, 49, 140; and Dick Cheney 14, 23, 30

The Cabinet of Doctor Caligari 33
Cannibal Holocaust 32
Captivity 13, 41
Caputo, John 92, 93
Carrie (1976) 157
Carroll, Noël 39, 40, 68n41
Cat People (1942/1982) 178
Cheney, Dick 14, 23, 30, 105–106
Cherry, Brigid 140, 174
Children of Men 22
Chion, Michael 7, 86, 97–98, 176, 181, 189–190
Chun, Wendy 57
cinéma du corps 35–36, 42
Clover, Carol 67n21; final girl 87, 164–165, 174n1
Cloverfield 1, 22
Clute, John 144–145

Crane, Jonathan 140
Creed, Barbara 9–10; on abjection 157–174
Cronenberg, David 31, 35, 99
Cube 62

Dawn of the Dead (2005) 32
Death Wish series (1974–1994) 18
Debord, Guy 51
Deleuze, Gilles 51, 66n14, 126, 127, 129, 140, 148–149; assemblage 8, 129–138, 142; and Felix Guattari 8–9, 123, 127; Societies of Control 9, 47–48, 140, 149, 154
Deliverance 41
The Devil's Rejects 2, 34
Dirty Harry 18, 26; series 18
Discipline and Punish 47, 67n17, 77
Dr. Mabuse the Gambler 33
Dolar, Mladen 7, 86, 98–100
Douglas, Mary 5; body 24–25, 30–31; boundaries 37–40
Dracula (1931) 177
Dyer, Richard 64, 69nn87,88

Ebert, Roger 2
Edelstein, David 2, 13, 34
Eden Lake 34
Elsaesser, Thomas 52–53, 54, 56, 59, 68n39, 152–154
Elwes, Cary 14–15
Enzensberger, Hans 105, 116
The Evil Dead (1981) 32
Existenz 31, 58
The Exorcist 157
The Exterminating Angel 62

Fight Club 58–59, 69n81
Final destination series 86
Fitting, Peter 64, 69n83
Foucault, Michel 51, 61, 67n17, 77, 134, 143, 148; *Discipline and Punish* 47, 67n17, 77; *The History of Sexuality* vol. 1 47
Frankenstein (1931) 176, 177, 178
Friday the 13th 87, 177
Friedman, Ted 60

197

From Caligari to Hitler 33
Frontière(s)/Frontiers 35, 36, 37
Funny Games (1997) 43n3

Galloway, Alexander 52, 57–61
The Game 58–59
Gamification 6, 45–46, 50; and cinema 52–62, 65, 151, 154
Girard, René 40, 24
Gleiberman, Owen 2
Goldberg, Elizabeth, Swanson 20
Gottschalk, Simon 53
Guantanamo Bay 23, 25, 33, 41
Guinness Book of Records 13

Hale, Mike 1, 13
Halloween (1978) 39, 87, 103n28, 177, 178, 179, 184
Halloween (2007) 177, 182
The Happening 42
Hardt, Michael 141, 154
Hartlaub, Peter 2
Hegel, Georg Wilhelm Friedrich 120, 126–127
Hellraiser 180–181
Hills, Matt 9, 41–42, 140, 142, 150
The Hills Have Eyes (2006) 32, 182
Hiltbrand, David 13
The History of Sexuality, vol. 1 47
Hoffman, Mark 5, 18–20, 26, 48, 53, 76–78, 81, 82, 83, 84n1, 94, 96, 99, 101, 106, 108, 110, 118–119, 120, 121n4, 125–126, 130, 134–137, 164–168, 172, 187, 188, 191
Hollywood 1, 3, 51, 55
Homeland Security 20
Hostel 13, 20, 21, 27n2, 32, 34, 41, 184, 185
Hostel II 185
House of a 1000 Corpses 32
The Human Centipede 62–63
The Human Centipede 2: Full Sequence 3
The Hunchback of Notre Dame 33
Huntley, Jake 19
Hurley, Kelly 31

I Know What You Did Last Summer 32
I Spit on Your Grave (1978) 177
Identity 58
Ils/Them 35, 36, 37
Insidious 100
Invasion of the Body Snatchers 33
Irreversible 35

Jameson, Frederic 58
Jay, Martin 51
Jigsaw 4–10, 14, 16, 25, 34, 45–46, 48, 54–55, 65, 67n16, 80–82, 83–84, 123, 138n2, 139–140, 141, 142, 146, 147, 150, 151, 153, 154, 157, 158, 159, 162, 163, 165, 166, 174, 178, 181, 183, 186, 187–189; as abject 169–172; as death 95–100, 148–149; ethics 17–23; and Kierkegaard 91–95; as monster 39–40, 41, 167–169; morality 105–121; as omnipotent 73–78; surveillance 48–50; traps/games 86–90, 124–132, 134–138, 143, 164; voice 189–191
Jones, Steve 17, 19

Kane, Robert 75–76
Kellner, Douglas 14, 15, 20, 23, 106
Kerins, Mark 176, 181, 182, 184
Kermode, Mark 173
Kierkegaard, Søren 7, 86, 91–95, 100
The Killing Fields 20
King, Stephen 32
Knee, Adam 157
Kracauer, Siegfried 33
Kramer, John *see* Jigsaw
Kristeva, Julia 39–40, 157–158

The Last House on the Left (1972) 34, 185
Lazzarato, Maurizio 143
Lecercle, Jean Jacques 123, 130, 131–132
Lee, Nathan 1
Lockwood, Dean 19, 64, 66n13
Luppa, Nicholas 54

M 95
Manovich, Lev 61, 68n61
Martyrs 35
Massumi, Brian 151
McGrath, Patrick 145
Memento 58
The Merchant of Venice (play) 25
La Meute/The Pack 35
Middleton, Jason 20
Millington, Brad 59–60
The Mist 42
Moylan, Tom 63
The Mummy (1932) 178
Muscle 32
Mutants 35

Naked Blood 32
Neale, Steve 177
Negri, Antonio 141, 154
New French Extremity 35–36
The New York Times 1, 2, 13
Nietzsche, Friedrich 7, 105–108, 109–110, 116, 120–121, 121n2
A Nightmare on Elm Street 39, 103n28, 177, 179; Freddy Kreuger 124
9/11 4, 5, 9, 10, 15; post-9/11 cultural pessimism 18–26, 27, 34, 41–42, 49, 140, 160, 173, 174

Index

Nineteen Eighty Four (book) 63
Nosferatu 33

O'Hehir, Andrew 1
The Others 1

Palmer, Tim 35
Paranormal Activity 1
The Passion of the Christ 2, 13
Penley, Constance 63–64
Perron, Bernard 56, 68nn44,49
Phantasmagoria (video game) 52
The Phantom of the Opera (film) 33
Phillips, Michael 14
Pinkerton, Nick 13
Polan, Dana B. 39, 69n88
Predators 173
Prometheus 173
Psycho 98, 100, 178

Rand, Ayn 87
Rouse, Richard 55–56
Ruppert, Peter 64

Salon 1
Salvador 20
Salvos, Mark 2
Sartre, Jean-Paul 7, 86, 87–90, 91, 100, 101
Saw: abjection 167–172; box office gross 1; control and correction 45–52, 55, 57, 59, 61–64, 65–66, 67nn16,24, 68n52, 69n77, 84n1, 140–141, 147, 189; critical reception 1–3; 13–14, 30, 173–174; dystopia 6, 15, 62–65; 69nn81,83; free will 74–78; gamification 52–62; monstrous feminine 160–161; monstrous masculine 165–166; morality 18–26, 27, 31, 32, 33, 34, 106–109; nihilism 109–119; patriarchy 161–163; post-9/11 41–42, 43, 53, 54, 65, 67n15, 86–87, 88, 89, 90, 96–100, 102n16, 105–106; revenge 79–82; *Saw* (video game) 13; *Saw: Flesh and Blood* (video game) 13; *Saw: Rebirth* (comic) 13; *Saw: The Ride* 13; sound 186–191; surveillance 6, 9, 20, 34, 42; transgression of boundaries 38–40
Scarry, Elaine 41, 133–134, 136
Scary Movie 32
Schaeffer, Pierre 95–98
Sconce, Jeffrey 3
Scream 32, 99, 103n28, 182
Scream 2 185
Se7en 86–87
Sharrett, Christopher 14, 17, 19
Shaviro, Steven 142
Sheitan 31
The Shining 3, 187

Shuck, Glenn 15
The Silence of the Lambs 86, 87
Simons, Jan 154
Skal, David J. 33
Slotkin, Richard 21
Society 32
South Park: Humancentipad 62–63
Straw Dogs (2011)
Strong, Benjamin 1
Stroup, John 15

The Terminator 63–64, 65
Tetsuo: The Iron Man 32
Texas Chainsaw Massacre (1974) 3, 34, 41, 177, 186–188
Texas Chainsaw Massacre (2003) 27n2, 32, 182
Them! 33
There Will be Blood 22
The Thing (2011) 1, 173
The Thing from Another World 33
torture porn 2, 6, 13, 20, 34, 45, 46, 63, 64, 66n13, 84, 124, 134, 138n1, 140, 184, 185
Tudor, Andrew 33, 37, 43n2
28 Days Later 179
Tziallas, Evangelos 34, 42

The Usual Suspects 58

Vanishing on 7th Street 42
Videodrome 31, 99
La Vie nouvelle/A New Life 35

War on Terror 4, 5, 6, 20, 21, 25, 26, 106, 140
Wetmore, Kevin 4, 42, 174
Whannell, Leigh 32–33
When a Stranger Calls 39, 99
Whittington, William 176, 184
Wii console 59–60
Williams, Linda 32, 56, 64, 185
Williams, Tony 22
The Wizard of Oz 95, 98, 190
Wolf Creek 2, 34
Wood, Robin 1, 33–34, 42

Young, Amanda 5, 16, 18, 19, 20, 26, 48, 53, 76, 81, 83, 91, 94, 96, 98, 101, 102n16, 106, 108, 109, 112, 113, 116, 118, 119, 121n6, 126, 130, 135, 136, 137, 139, 147, 150, 161, 162, 163, 170, 172, 173, 181, 182, 183, 184, 185, 187, 189
Young, Elizabeth 157

Zimmer, Catherine 45, 70n93, 140–141, 150
Žižek, Slavoj 101

www.ingramcontent.com/pod-product-compliance
Ingram Content Group UK Ltd.
Pitfield, Milton Keynes, MK11 3LW, UK
UKHW042008140426
5217IPUK00015B/1053